GOLDEN ROCK C

by Mark Rolofso

A complete guide to North Table Mountain (incluc
sport climbs of Golden Gate State Park r

ISBN: 978-0-9829574-0-0

COVER PHOTO: Mark Rolofson leading **Mrs. Hen Places A Peck** (**** 5.12a) on the Overhang Wall. at the Golden Cliffs. Photo by Mike Dallin

BACK COVER: Sharon Kloepfer leading **Old Roof Route** (A.k.a.: **Lemons, Limes & Tangerines**) (**** 5.8) on the Brown Cloud Crags - Right Side. Photo by Mark Rolofson

Thanks to Alan Nelson, Richard Wright, Tod Anderson, Ken Trout, Marsha Trout, Kirk Miller, Lindie Brink, Dan Hare, Rick Leitner, Keith Ainsworth, Mary Riedmiller, Dennis McCarron, Dave Field, Martin Birch, Ernie Moschovics, Brian Hansen, Ralph Bidwell, Leon Henkleman, Charles Tabor, Mark Felty, Moe Hershoff, Claire Mearns, Mark Tarrant, Mike Freischlag, Curt Fry, Paul Gagner, Dan Neber, Henry Lester, Stacy Carrera, Jimmy Menendez, Stuart Ritchie, Brad White, Mark Milligan, John Flunker, Rick Thompson, Pat Thompson, Hank Caylor, Alvino Pon, Anna Brandonburg Schroeder, Ben Schneider, Guy Lords, Jason Haas, Ray Barrow, Jeanette Barrow, Dianne Dallin, Mike Dallin, Kaelen Williams, Bob Horan, Kevin Gallagher, Wayne Crill, Vaino Kodas, Mary Zuvela, Dave Turner, Tally O'Donnell, Mike Cichon, Tim Slater, Jeroen Van Wolferen, Josh Gross, Madoline Gross, Sharon Kloepfer and anyone else who has contributed either by information, developing new routes or as a great climbing partner at these areas.

Special thanks to Chris Archer, Rick Thompson, Jim Ghiselli & the Access Fund for their hard work that made the Golden Cliffs, its trail and parking lot possible.

The utmost of gratitude & special thanks to Mayford Peery, who donated the Golden Cliffs to the Access Fund for public use. This property includes most of the Golden Cliffs, land on the hillside around the cliffs and the parking lot. This is one of the most generous donations a land owner has ever made to climbers and the public.

The effort to replace old bolts and worn top anchors at the Golden Cliffs is ongoing. Since 1996, I have been involved in this effort, donating both time and money for fixed hardware. A special thanks to Ken Trout for replacing bolts & anchors in 2007 & 2008 and to Richard Wright for replacing top anchors in 2002. Thanks to everyone who has helped this effort as a belayer & ground support, or through their monetary donation.

A very special thanks to: Sharon Kloepfer for proofreading. Kirk Miller for photo finish. Dianne Dallin for helping me with previous editions & this edition. Mike Dallin for climbing photos & the cover design.

WARNING: This book is not designed as an instructional manual to teach climbing. It is no substitute for experience, and is not 100% accurate. If something doesn't appear correct, such as the rating, number of bolts, route location, it probably isn't. This is a guidebook designed to be used by experienced climbers, and in no way can replace good judgment and discretion.

This guidebook and past editions are published by:

MARK ROLOFSON
FREE WEST ROCK GUIDES
P.O. BOX 732
BOULDER, COLORADO 80306-0732

First edition - **1993 BOULDER SPORT CLIMBER'S GUIDE** - Copyright July 1993

2nd edition - **1995 BOULDER SPORT CLIMBER'S GUIDE** - Copyright 1995

IN MEMORY OF ALAN NELSON, WHO DIED DECEMBER 23, 2008 FROM GASTROINTESTINAL CANCER AT THE AGE OF 48. ALAN LED BY EXAMPLE. THE GIFT HE GAVE TO SO MANY OF US LIVES ON.

Alan Nelson did not live to be an old man, but he lived a full life filled with great accomplishments. He touched the lives of hundreds of people and had many good friends. Alan's climbing career began in California, where he became highly skilled at both free and aid climbing. He climbed El Capitan numerous times, including a solo of **Tangerine Trip**. He made ascents of bold run-out routes such as **Bachar-Yerian** and **You Asked For It**. He established many first ascents in Joshua Tree & Tuolumne Meadows.

He was not a sponsored climber or a climbing bum. He worked full time as an architect, until 2000, when he became a computer programmer. Climbing had no monetary value in his life, but he was very driven to explore the great untapped potential.

In 1989, Alan moved to Colorado. He was one of the first climbers to establish sport climbs in Clear Creek Canyon. He became the driving force of new route activity in Clear Creek from 1990 through 2000. Many of the best lines in the canyon are the work of Alan, including **Sonic Youth**, **Anarchitect**, **Finger Prince** & **Ten Digit Dialing**. He established the brilliant arete, **Genius Loci**, in Eldorado Canyon and dozens of routes in Boulder Canyon and at the Golden Cliffs. Most notably at the Golden Cliffs are **Pumcat**, **Chick Filet** and **Bimbo In Limbo**.

Alan had the vision to pioneer new terrain that most climbers would have ignored and not seen for its great potential. It is one thing to repeat difficult climbs; it is another to find them and turn untouched cliffs into a great playground.

Alan had no children of his own. He leaves behind a stepson from his ex-wife, his sisters and a long list of friends. In his younger days, he was known to party and indulge in drink and smoke. After he married in 1996, Alan started attending church and took up a Christian faith. Alan was not known to bestow his religious beliefs on others. His faith was personal and in the end it gave him strength knowing that his death would not be the final chapter. After exiting this world, I hope he has found eternal life and happiness in the vast universe.

Alan's spirit lives on as an inspiration of what hard work, honesty and perseverance can accomplish. Alan was humble and soft spoken. He was always considerate of others. He could relate to many people, and did not have an elitist attitude. I will miss the great times I spent with him. He was a great climbing partner, a great friend and a great guy.

Alan Nelson at age 40 leading **PEER REVIEW** (**** 5.12b) on Highlander Crag in Clear Creek Canyon.

Many climbers, especially those new to the sport, probably don't know me from Adam. I live in Boulder and I have been climbing for 38 years on Colorado's Front Range. I have written several editions of guidebooks to Boulder Canyon, Clear Creek Canyon & Garden Of the Gods. I wrote my first guidebook **Soft Touch - A Climbers Guide to the Garden Of The Gods** in 1979 at the age of 20. I grew up in Colorado Springs and started climbing at age 13 on nearby granite & the soft sandstone of the Garden Of The Gods.

I can't say I miss Colorado Springs or the Garden. The amount of climbing within 40 miles of my home in Boulder has been more than enough to keep me busy. I've established hundreds of new routes (both trad & sport) in Boulder Canyon, Eldorado Canyon, Clear Creek Canyon, South St. Vrain Canyon, Golden Gate State Park and North Table Mountain. I have climbed most of the routes in Boulder Canyon, Clear Creek and North Table, so I know these areas like the back of my hand. I've spent a lot of time documenting the details. I've gone without much sleep to finish many guidebooks. Much like climbing 5.13 guidebook writing is often a struggle. I have self published most of my books. I operate on a shoe string budget and the wing of a prayer.

In 1993, I wrote & published **1993 Boulder Sport Climber's Guide**, which was the first guidebook to the climbs on North Table Mountain (now known as the Golden Cliffs). This guide covered 7 areas on the Front Range of Colorado, including Clear Creek Canyon, Boulder Canyon, Mickey Maus Wall, the West Bank, Button Rock Reservoir and South St. Vrain Canyon. Chapter Two was the guide to North Table Mountain. Prior to my guidebook, "Table Mountain Mini Guide" by Ken Trout was published in Rock & Ice #47 (January / February 1992). This magazine article was the first written information to the area.

Six months after I published my 1993 guide, Chockstone Press published **Front Range Crags** by Peter Hubble. This guide covered many climbing areas on the northern Front Range including some of the same areas the **1993 Boulder Sport Climber's Guide** had covered including North Table Mountain, Clear Creek Canyon, South St. Vrain Canyon & Button Rock Reservoir. In 1995, I published a new edition to my guide, the **1995 Boulder Sport Climber's Guide**. This outdated **Front Range Crags**.

In 1997, Chockstone Press published the first guidebook exclusively covering just North Table Mountain titled **Golden Cliffs** & written by Peter Hubble with the help of Deaun Schovajsa. This book was a blatant act of copyright infringement. After I hired a copyright attorney, Chockstone Press paid me & my attorney an out of court settlement. Over the years, I have seen many people lost at the Golden Cliffs with Hubble's guidebook. The complex computerized drawings & the often dark photos have proven not to work very well.

Since 1999, I have managed to publish a few editions of my guides to Boulder Canyon & Clear Creek Canyon, but I have not released another guidebook to North Table Mountain. I have spent much time climbing at the Golden Cliffs in the winter months. I also devoted much time since 1996 to replacing bolts and worn out top anchors. In 2002, I raised some cash donations from a jar at Bent Gate Mountaineering, in Golden, to help pay for new hardware. In 2002, many of the coldshut top anchors had become dangerously worn. Immediate action was independently taken by both Richard Wright and myself. Thanks to the Access Fund I received a pile of stainless bolts & hangers from the American Safe Climbing Association. On pages 14-17 of this book I have included information with photos about bolts and top anchors to help educate climbers.

In Winter & Spring of 2008, I spent a great amount of time at the Golden Cliffs and almost released this book in Fall 2008. I decided to hold off and not compete with the new color guidebook **North Table Mountain - Rock Climbs at the Golden Cliffs** (by Ben Schneider and Jason Haas) published in Fall 2008. Their beautiful guide is very seductive and major step up from Hubble's work. What I soon came to realize was that the adventure on North Table Mountain was just getting exciting. In 2009 & 2010, I climbed what are by far the best cracks and sport climbs on North Table at the South & East Quarry Walls. There are also new climbs at the Sea Cliffs & Crater Crag (the north quarries). North Table Mountain now has much exciting new climbing to offer.

Finally, I have included the sport climbs near Dude's Fishing Hole in Golden Gate State Park, that I helped to establish beginning in 2003. These areas have never been documented in any guide. For years information about them has only been spread by word of mouth. Unlike the slick basalt crags of North Table located in the foothills near Golden, the granite crags of Golden Gate State park are in the secluded mountain pine forests above 9,000 feet. This guide offers climbing for every season, on two rock types from 5.6 to 5.13. Enjoy!

INTRODUCTION

Atop a grassy, treeless hillside, above the north end city of Golden, Colorado sits a long reddish brown basalt cliffband. The cliffband is 30 to 120 feet tall and curves for miles around the top of most of the hillside known as North Table Mountain. Above the cliff is a large mesa. The southwest section of North Table Mountain has some of the tallest and most prominent cliffs that are known as the Golden Cliffs. The Golden Cliffs offers over 200 rock climbs, most of which are safely bolted sport climbs ranging in difficulty from 5.6 to 5.12.

This area offers year round climbing opportunities, even though summer is too hot to climb the harder routes. The best months for climbing here are from late October to early April. From May through September it is possible to climb on the west face in the morning and on the south face in the evening. Watch out for rattlesnakes from April through October. The area is perfect on a sunny winter day. This is the time of year when the slick basalt rock will offer its best friction unlike hot days when the holds will feel greasy & very slippery. Since the Golden Cliffs are at lower elevation in the foothills, the snow melts off the cliffs & hillside much sooner than in the nearby Clear Creek Canyon & other mountain areas at higher elevation.

This area has many good climbs for novice & intermediate climbers. There are several good 5.6 & 5.7 climbs. Having at least one member of your climbing party who can lead the climbs is recommended. There are a few climbs that can safely be accessed from above to set up a top rope, but many climbs present a real danger to descend to the top anchors. Setting up a top rope can cause rockfall on the loose hillside above the cliff that is especially dangerous to people below at the base of the wall, who often don't know someone is above them. Leading the climb is the recommended approach.

Most of the climbs can be done with a 50 meter (165 ft.) rope & a dozen quickdraws or less. There is numerous 5.8 & 5.9 routes & an abundance of 5.10a to 5.11 climbs. The area has a limited but notable selection of 5.12s, usually with short bouldery cruxes. There are a few power endurance routes for a pump, don't expect to it to offer the great long overhung climbs you'll find in Clear Creek, Boulder Canyon, the Flatirons or Rifle. There are currently no 5.13s at the Golden Cliffs. Most climbers who can climb 5.12 or harder climb here only when its too cold to go elsewhere or because it is a convenient place to go after work (if they climb here at all).

While the Golden Cliffs are known mostly as a sport climbing area, there are good crack climbs. Nut & cam placements are generally reliable in the hard stone. Like the sport routes, the best crack climbs usually have a two bolt anchor at the top to descend from. There are also a few mixed gear & bolt routes, that require a small rack of small to medium sized nuts or cams.

The area can get crowded especially on a warm weekend from late fall to early spring. Thankfully there are two large parking lots to accommodate. Thankfully this long cliffband has lots of routes. It is the 5.6 to 5.9 routes that see that most traffic. The area gets used throughout the week, but it generally not crowded, except on the weekends. It is a fun area with many puzzling moves & cruxes, bullet hard stone & good protection.

It does have an urban feel being right above the city of Golden with its houses & the large Coors beer brewery. The grassy hillside and the rocks presents a beauty found in nature that the city can not completely detract from. The area is a great place to spend a relaxing afternoon. There is a great trail system and the area is also popular with hikers and local dog walkers. The uphill approach provides 15 to 30 minutes of aerobic exercise before climbing.

Most of the Golden Cliffs are owned by the Access Fund. This is thanks to Mayford Peery, a local developer, who donated 28 acres of his land to the Access Fund in 1996. Some of the north end of the west face is owned by Jefferson County Open Space. The climbing community is very fortunate that their organization, the Access Fund, made this important land acquisition. The Access Fund has done much to preserve the area, while providing convenient access to climbers and hikers, including building the trail up the south side of the mountain, the construction of the large parking lot with a toilet & an access road.

The Golden Cliffs provides many climbers in the Denver metro region with a convenient climbing area with a year round season. Its a great place to spend the day climbing or get out for just a few hours. The basalt adds diversity to Front Range rock, that is mainly composed various types of granite & sandstone.

ROAD MAP TO THE GOLDEN CLIFFS

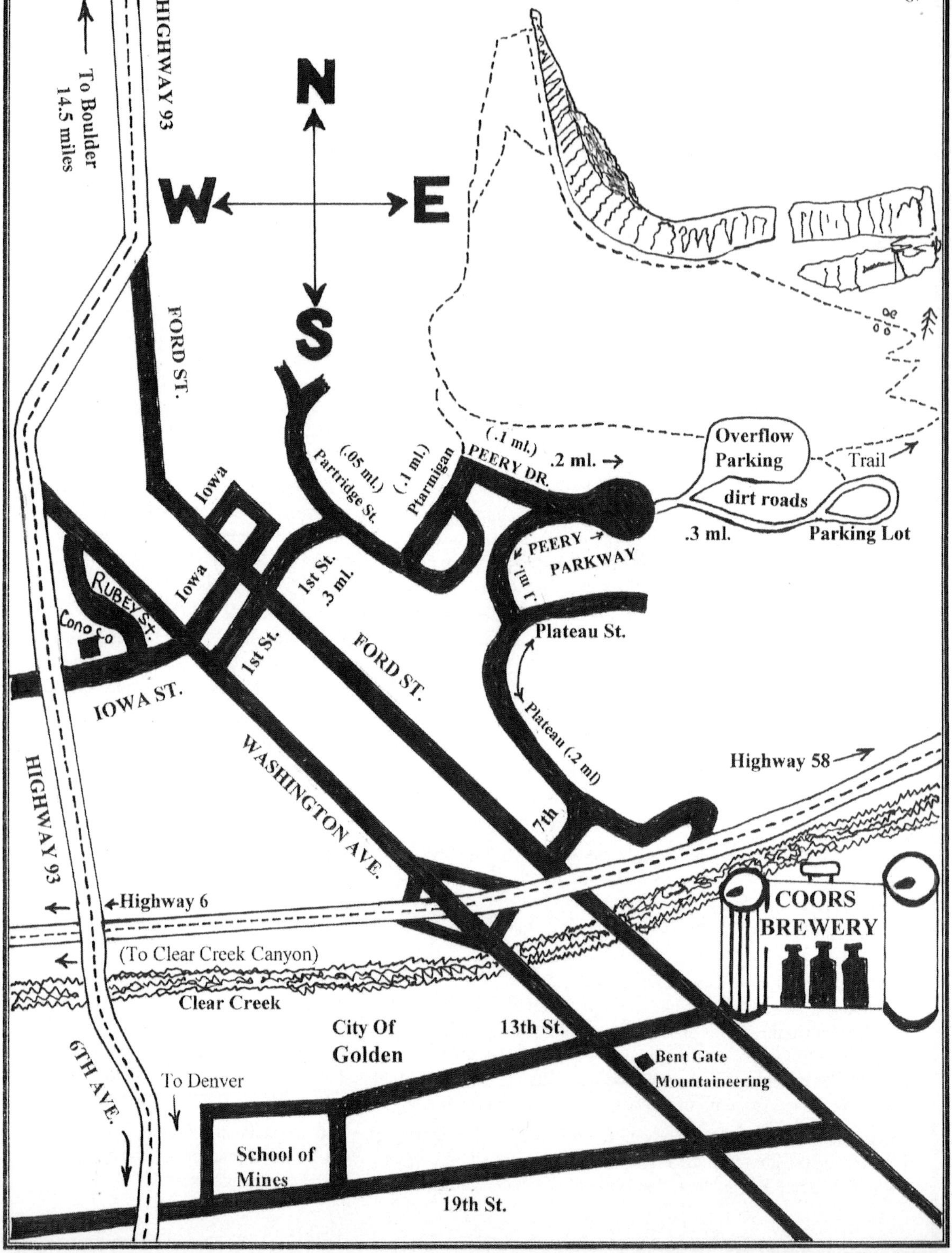

MAP OF THE GOLDEN CLIFFS ON NORTH TABLE MOUNTAIN

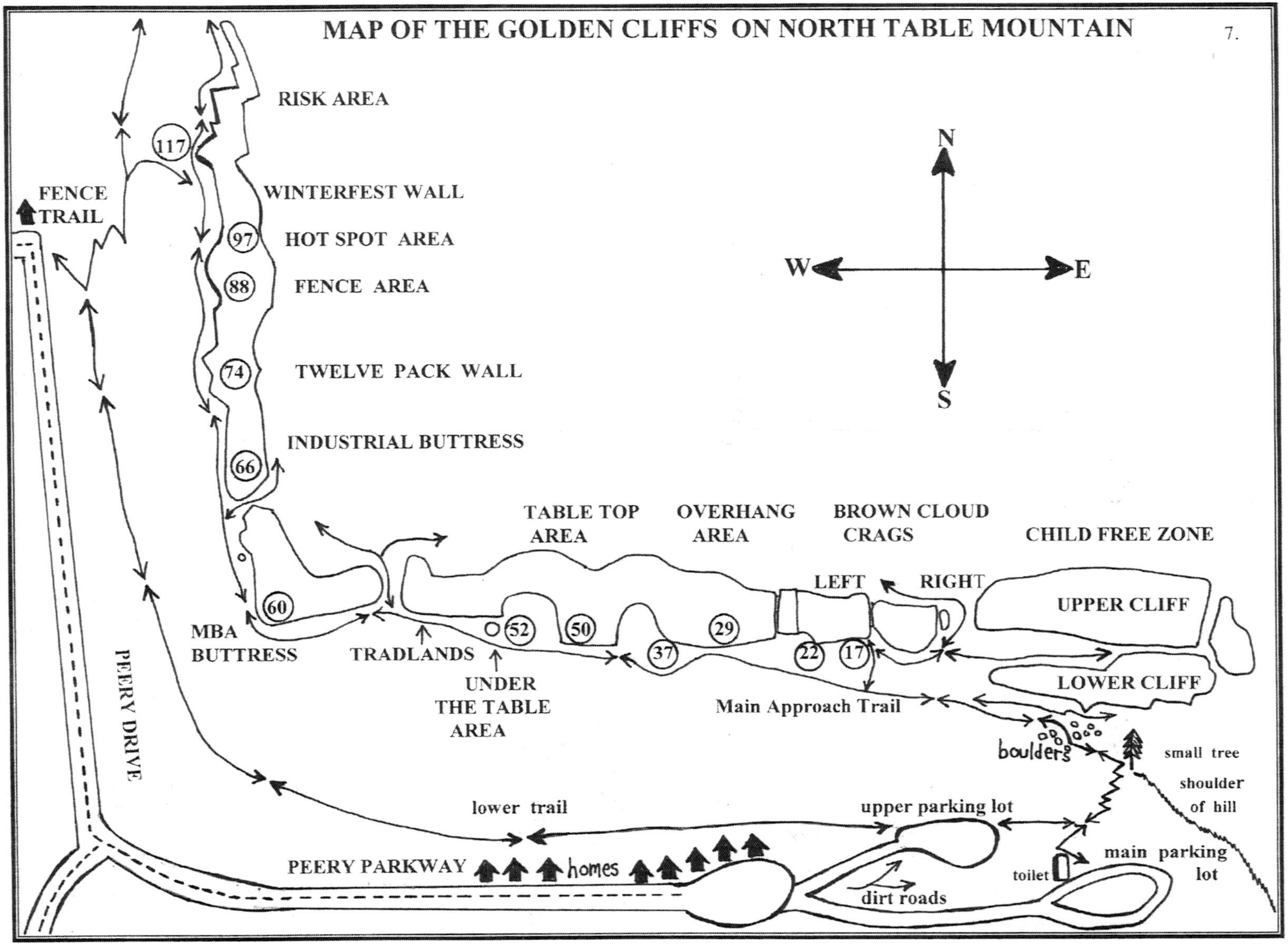

GOLDEN ROCK CLIMBS GUIDE * TABLE OF CONTENTS

GOLDEN ROCK CLIMBS GUIDE * TABLE OF CONTENTS

Kaelen Williams on the first redpoint of **STIMULUS** (**** 5.12d) at South Quarry Wall - Right Side.
See pages 111 & 114-115. The South Quarry is one of four quarries on North Table Mountain

SAFETY, ETHICS & ENVIRONMENTAL CONSIDERATIONS

1. **Park in lower dirt parking lot**, unless it is full and then park in the upper overflow parking lot. **Park thoughtfully in one space**. Avoid parking on the residential streets that lead into the area.
2. **Drive slowly** (15 to 20 miles per hour) through the residential neighborhood & on the narrow dirt road leading into the parking lot. Watch out for pedestrians, children & pets. Be prepared to stop.
3. Please **use the approach trail** to preserve vegetation and minimize erosion. Avoid short cutting up the hillside and leaving the trail. There is a good trail starting at the two parking lots and leading up to the cliffs and along the cliff's base. The trail does get muddy & slippery after rain and snow storms.
4. **TRASH** - Trash is not a real problem at the Golden Cliffs. Most climbers are careful to pick up after themselves before leaving the cliff. Most climbers are very conscientious about not leaving any trash. This may be because most of them love and appreciate the areas that they climb at and wish to preserve the beauty of the crags. **Always pick up your trash, tape, cigarette butts, Powerbar wrappers, etc..** Please try to lend a helping hand picking up any trash that other climbers have carelessly forgotten or intentionally left behind. If you catch anyone littering please inform them that such behavior is not appreciated. Check the base of the wall & your rope up spot before leaving, to avoid leaving anything (trash, clothes, gear, etc.)
5. **DOGS** can be a real nuisance and a big problem. Keep your dog on a leash. The Golden Cliffs is a busy area and lots of people bring their dogs including hikers. A dog or two at the cliff may not bother anybody, but if almost everyone shows up at the cliff with a dog it can become a **Real Big Problem**. It can be the cause of dog fights and human fights. If you bring a dog, be prepared to clean up after it, if it takes a dump on the trail or at the base of the climbs. If your dog isn't well behaved it won't be welcome. Responsible dog owners aren't the problem, it's arrogant, irresponsible dog owners who think everyone should put up with their noisy, messy or vicious pet. Any area with limited space or dangerous rock fall potential is a place not to bring your dog.
6. **Human Waste** There is a toilet in the parking lot. If you have to relieve yourself up on the hill, don't do it near the base of the climbs. If you have to urinate, get far enough away from the base, so the area doesn't end up smelling like a gorilla cage. If you have to take a dump, go well below the trail into the brush & boulders and bury it. Avoid using toilet paper, which is litter. Use a stick or rock. If you use toilet paper, burn it, unless it is a fire hazard and pack it out.
7. **Avoid leaving bright webbing** if you have to bail before the top anchors. Use black, gray, or brown rust colored slings, if you must leave one. Most anchors don't have webbing which rots with time. Webbing is an eyesore. Never lower directly through a sling, as although it is strong, the rope will easily burn and cut through it. Leave a carbiner or a quick link.
8. Please **do not retro bolt without permission from the first ascentionists** or place bolts on climbs that were originally led using removable protection. You will find plenty of closely bolted 5.9 to 5.13 routes in the area. Several routes have been retro-bolted by the first ascent party. On some routes, retro-bolting makes the route safe and enjoyable, but in other cases it can take away the thrill and add unneeded clips.
9. **Never chisel or manufacture holds** on any existing climb or on a wall with many established routes. Manufacturing holds is discouraged and frowned upon as a method to develop new routes.
10. **Always double check your knot** before leaving the ground and after threading the anchor (to lower off). The belayer should always pay attention to the climber and watch for the end of the rope when lowering the climber back to the ground. **Tie a big knot in the end of the rope** to avoid a lowering accident on a long pitch. The knot will keep the rope from shooting through the belay device. Avoid using the wide hole of a figure-eight descender for belaying since a big knot can fit through it. On long rappels tie the ends of the rope together with a secure knot to prevent rapping off the rope's end.
11. Avoid top-roping directly through the anchors and use your own quickdraws, or slings and locking carbiners. Repeated top-roping slowly wears through the metal, especially on coldshuts, which are made of a soft metal. Lower through the anchors only to clean your quickdraws and gear off the climb.
12. Don't steal gear (quickdraws, ropes, etc.) left on a climb. Someone is equipping or working on a route.

LOOSE ROCK, OBJECTIVE DANGERS, & WEARING A HELMET

It is important to mention a helmet as recommended equipment at the Golden Cliffs. Where many people may climb without them here, more climbers are convinced that at least the belayer should have a helmet. There is some loose rock at the Golden Cliffs, & people walking around near the top of the cliff, setting up a top rope often send rock down. Always remember to try to position the belayer out of the line of rockfall. Be careful what you grab. Most routes have been carefully cleaned of loose rock, but occasionally a chunk gets missed or if a climber should stray enough off the line, he or she may be entering blocky terrain. Use your best judgment; carefully pull on the holds to test them before fully weighting them if they look questionable.

Lead climbing also presents some situations where a fall can result in a head injury. If you are new to the sharp end, it is especially dangerous. Even though this area provides many well bolted climbs, there are some runouts and even a few potential ledge falls to avoid. Rope skills are very important and require much practice to develop the proper efficiency, for both the belayer and leader. It is possible to get flipped upside down in a leader fall if the rope gets wrapped around the leader's leg. This can result in the leader's head hitting the wall. For these reasons beginning leaders should wear a helmet.

EQUIPPING ROUTES: The Glorious Task Of The First Ascent (Hard Work, No Pay!)

There is still unclimbed rock to explore and North Table Mountain is not climbed out. Hopefully, whoever decides to put up new bolted routes will have both the proper experience and use adequate hardware. It takes skill to on-sight, flash or redpoint a hard route. It takes these skills and many more to establish fine new routes. Avoid establishing dangerously run-out bolted routes. If you are going to bolt it, make it safe.

Use 3/8" or 1/2" diameter by 3 to 4" length bolts (preferably Rawl 1/2" diameter sleeve bolts, Hilti or Fixe 3/8" diameter stainless steel wedge bolts) to establish new routes. **Use only reliable modern bolt hangers** such as Fixe, Trango, Metolius, or Petzl. **Use Fixe rap ring hangers or 3/8" diameter chains** at the anchors, instead of welded coldshuts. Coldshuts are made of a soft metal which ropes wear a deep groove into after seasons of use on popular climbs. Welded coldshuts and the commercial brand **Goldshuts** have been commonplace in the area. Many of them have been replaced. Goldshuts were professionally welded, making them more reliable than home welded coldshuts. Home welded coldshuts may vary significantly in their actual strength and reliability.

Bolting is best performed on rappel after top-roping the moves to determine the best bolt placements for clipping and falling on. The exception is when the climb is too overhanging to top-rope. On such routes placing the bolts top-down or ground-up on aid is the first step. Once the bolts are in and the rock has been cleaned, a climber can then try the route. The method (top down or ground up) of bolting is not important, while the end result is. Most routes don't need a bolt every four feet the entire way up, nor do I advise creating an extremely run-out route after much top-rope rehearsal. These decisions are left up to the equipper. Personal freedom is thankfully still what motivates new routes and not a tightly governed, snobby hierarchy. Hopefully if you set up new routes, you'll think of the climbers who will follow by designing safe, enjoyable, challenging routes.

Cleaning of loose rock is important for the safety of everyone who will repeat the route or sit at the base. Cleaning of lichen or dirt allows the holds be used. This step is often done in conjunction with rappelling down to place bolts. At least the big, loose blocks must be removed. Find lines that have natural holds. Manufacturing holds with a drill is strongly discouraged and frowned upon, since most of the Golden Cliff's beautiful stone has plenty of holds.

Camouflage all bolts, hangers and chains. Paint shiny hangers at home with red brown rust, black or gray primer. Touch up shiny bolt heads and washers on the cliff with a small paint brush and a high viscosity acrylic paint in a small tube.

The successful free ascent is called a redpoint. Routes that have not been redpointed are listed as Project. **Please respect an equipper's hard work and stay off their project.** Please give them a grace period of at least a year or until they've abandoned their project, before attempting to redpoint it and make the first free ascent. Stay off any route with **a red tag (sling or tape) marker** on the first bolt. The tag may be there to warn people of loose rock, bolts in the wrong place, bad bolts, or holds that need reinforcing with epoxy glue. The climb is not ready yet and you could get hurt on it. Find out what the situation is first. Get permission from the equipper before stealing his/her project. Be careful taking over an abandoned project.

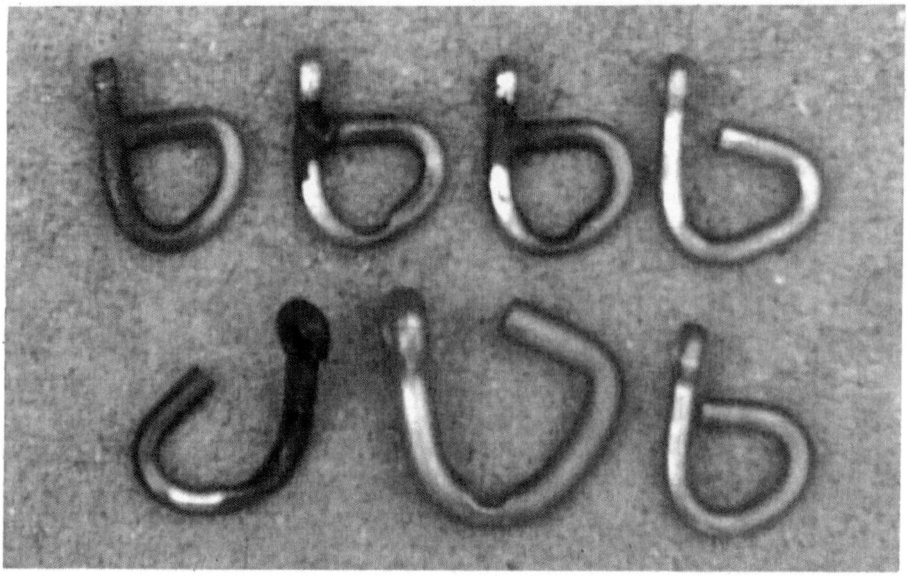

Old coldshuts that have been removed from anchors. **Upper row going left to right:** A poorly home-welded coldshut. Two coldshuts that are worn from years of repeated lowering & top-roping. An open 3/8" diameter coldshut. It is not recommended & very dangerous to use this diameter coldshut open. **Lower row going left to right:** An unwelded coldshut that was possibly bent open during use. An open 1/2" diameter coldshut that shows signs of rope wear. 1/2" diameter open coldshuts have been commonly used in pairs & can be safe if the climber doesn't climb above them while top-roping. An unwelded coldshut.

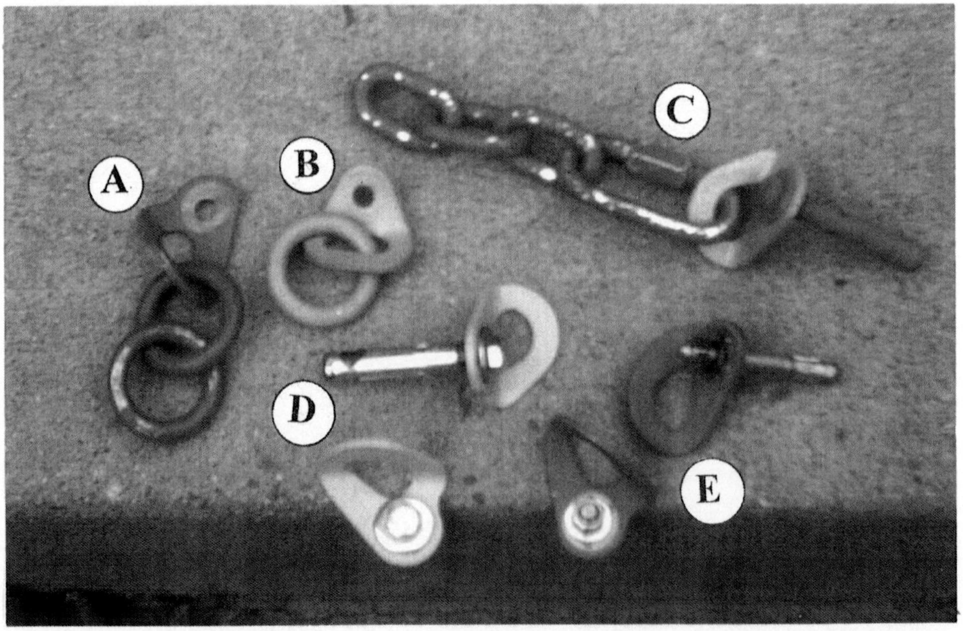

A. Fixe double ring anchor. **B.** Fixe ring anchor. **C.** 3/8" diameter chain attached with a quick link to a Fixe hanger on a painted Rawl 5-piece bolt (1/2" diameter x 2-3/4"). **D.** The Rawl 5-piece bolt (1/2" diameter x 2-3/4"). The bolt's end is a hex head. **E.** The Hilti wedge bolt (3/8" x 3"). The threaded end has a nut on it.

BOLTS AND TOP ANCHORS

Most beginning and intermediate climbers known very little about the bolt anchors that they so often use. In fact, even a significant, growing number of 5.11 to 5.13, have a minimal knowledge of bolting, because the majority of them have never placed bolts & established new routes. They have only repeated existing lines.

An understanding of what you are clipping into will increase your safety. Most bolts at sport climbing crags are reliable & very strong, but the hangers used often vary in quality & strength. For example, the standard 3/8" diameter bolt may have a modern bolt hanger (such as Fixe, Trango or Metolius brands) or have a home welded coldshut. The gear at the top anchors, to thread your rope through, varies significantly in both strength & reliability. Top anchors are usually reliable, until they become very worn from repeated use.

BOLTS placed on new routes or to replace old bolts should be the Rawl 5-piece (1/2"x 2-3/4" or longer), Fixe stainless steel 3/8" to 12 mm diameter wedge bolt, The Fixe 12 mm triplex bolt or Hilti 3/8" diameter wedge bolt. Never buy wedge bolts from a bin at the hardware store, since many brands look identical, but vary in strength dramatically. Glue-in eyebolts are an excellent bolt to use for bolt replacement. Avoid using the smaller 3/8" diameter Rawl 5-piece, which is a 5/16" diameter bolt inside a 3/8" sleeve and cone. These bolts are everywhere and they seem to be reliable once placed. It is common to break them while tightening them with a small 8-9" wrench during placement. The 3/8" diameter Rawl 5-piece has a recommended torque of 35 foot pounds versus the 1/2" diameter Rawl 5-piece has a recommended of 60 foot pounds. The 1/2" diameter Rawl 5-piece is a 3/8" diameter bolt in a 1/2" diameter sleeve & cone; therefore it will fit any standard bolt hanger with a 3/8" or 10 mm diameter hole.

It is easy to tell which size the bolt is because the smaller 5/16" bolt (on the 3/8" diameter Rawl 5-piece) takes a 1/2" diameter wrench, while all 3/8" bolts (wedge bolts with a nut or the 1/2" diameter Rawl 5-piece) require a 9/16" wrench. It is easy to recognize the Rawl 5-piece because the end of the bolt sticking out of the hole is a hex head. A wedge bolt & the Fixe triplex have a hex nut on the threaded end of the bolt that sticks out of the hole. All Fixe bolts were designed specifically for climbing, while other bolts were designed for building construction. The Fixe bolts have a nut on the end that requires a 17 mm wrench.

Most bolts holes on sport climbs were drilled with a power drill (a cordless battery powered hammer drill). Early routes were drilled with a hand drill & hammer. This is quite slow and often flares the hole. Drilling in hard rock is very difficult, therefore smaller & shorter bolts were commonly used. 1/4" diameter by 1" to 1.5" long bolts were placed from the 1950s to the early 1980s. In the 1980s, when climbers started bolting on rappel, 3/8" bolts were finally used, but they were usually short with 2" or less in the hole. Power drills are recommended because is it fast & easy to drill a longer tighter hole, thus placing a stronger bolt that is imbedded deeper in the rock.

If you find a wedge bolt with a loose nut, don't worry, just finger tighten it snug. If you use a wrench, avoid aggressively tightening the nut that could potentially break the bolt. The best way to keep the nut from loosening is to use red or blue loctite on the threads. Covering the threads and nut with liquid nails also works.

If the hanger on the Rawl 5-piece is a spinner, it is probably not because the bolt is loose, but the rock has worn away behind the hanger. Tightening it won't be possible & attempting to do so could weaken or break the bolt. Don't worry unless the bolt sticks way out. If it is easy to tighten then it has become loose, which is very rare with this type of bolt. **I strongly recommend letting the experts deal with bolt maintenance**.

BOLT HANGERS on protection bolts are often a sign of their era. Modern bolt hangers such as Fixe, can hold 5,000 to 10,000 pounds. This hanger came from Spain and was first used in the USA in 1994. Today this 4 mm thick hanger is the best one available. Other modern hangers that are 3 mm thick, such as Trango, Petzl & Metolius, are plenty strong & perfectly reliable. SMC hangers, that no longer commercially available, were commonly used on the 3/8" diameter bolts in 1980s & early 1990s. They work great on vertical walls, but bend on overhanging walls unlike modern hangers that are meant to be placed in a ceiling. The earlier SMC hangers used on 1/4" diameter bolts are weak. Leeper hangers were recalled by their manufacturer in 1997, due to being prone to stress fractures, especially when used with stronger bolts that are tightened during placement.

The **coldshut hanger** started to appear on sport climbs in the early 1990s. In 1992, the commercially available **Goldshut** showed up on the market. Coldshuts can be purchased at the hardware store without the weld. In this form, they are very weak & hold under 1,000 pounds. They were often used as top anchors, because they are made of a round shaped metal rod without a sharp edge, making them suitable to thread a rope through for lowering or rappelling. Weld the gap at the end and they become much stronger. Many were unprofessionally welded and their quality varies substantially. The Goldshut was the only professionally welded & anodized coldshut, being much more reliable than home welds. The design is flawed and tests have demonstrated that coldshuts & Goldshuts break at varying loads & don't work as well in overhangs as they do on faces that are vertical or less. Goldshuts have not been commercially available since 1994, since they were inferior to modern bolt hangers. The stubborn few climbers who have continued to use their home welded coldshuts are doing us all a great disservice, especially as these hangers age and weather.

TOP ANCHORS vary greatly from coldshuts to chains to Fixe rap ring hangers. The **coldshut or Goldshut** is the most dangerous top anchor when they become very worn, because there is no easy way to back them up. Efforts to replace worn out coldshut anchors at the Golden Cliffs started in 1996 & accelerated again in 2002. Most coldshut top anchors at the Golden Cliffs have been replaced. The larger 1/2" diameter open coldshuts were used to avoid untying & threading the anchor. Merely drop the rope in & lower off. These outlast the normal coldshuts that are made of 3/8" diameter metal rod, but also become very dangerous when worn. If you should encounter a pair of dangerously worn coldshuts, rappelling is recommended over lowering to avoid more wear.

3/8" to 1/2" high test chain is wide enough to allow the rope to be threaded through it. 5/16" diameter high test chain is too thin to easily thread a 10 mm rope, so a quicklink must be attached to the end. When the bottom link of the chain becomes dangerously worn, it is easy to add a quicklink or carbiner to the next link above it.

Fixe Ring Anchors are the best commercially available anchor hangers. Since the ring can spin, they normally don't wear out & will last for a very long time. The exception is if the weld, that joins the ends of the ring, has a dent in it. The dent will sit on the hanger. In this case, the ring won't spin as easily & a groove will eventually be worn in one spot by repeated rope wear. If a ring becomes dangerously worn, it is easy to back it up, since there is room in the hanger to add a carbiner or quicklink. A long quicklink will hang down far enough to avoid threading the ring.

Mussy hooks (commercially known as **winch hooks**) are the ultimate in convenience, and also very strong, with thick metal. Efforts were started in December 2007 by Ken Trout to equip many top anchors with mussy hooks. The mussy hook works like a carbiner at the anchor. Simply clip into it & lower off. Unlike a carbiner it isn't so easy to remove, can not be flipped around and they will not wear out as fast. The mussy hook is attached to the bolt hanger or chain at the anchor with a 5/16" or 3/8" diameter quicklink. On popular routes, mussy hooks will dramatically speed things up. The cost of installing two mussy hooks & two quick links at each anchor is very expensive compared to Fixe rings or chains. Mussy hooks will usually wear out faster than Fixe ring anchors.

Lowering off vs. rappelling from the top anchors has caused some debate. I recommend lowering off one pitch climbs in most circumstances. Threading the anchor is faster & also safer. More accidents have happened rappelling. Never say "off" or "off belay" at the anchor if you intend to lower. This miscommunication can prove fatal. Stay clipped into the anchor with slings or quickdraws attached to your harness while checking your knot & making sure your belayer is ready to lower you. Never take the climber off belay unless you are absolutely sure they are not going lower off and intend to rappel. Under normal circumstances the climber is only taken off belay after safely returning back the ground.

It is very difficult & sometimes impossible to clean a severely overhung route via rappel. Lowering allows the climber to run a carbiner over the rope that is running through the quickdraws. This allows the climber to pull into the wall to clean off the quickdraws.

Rappelling is the way to descend multi-pitch routes; it also it recommended when the top anchor is becoming dangerously worn. If the anchor is over the top or back from the edge, where lowering will cause notable wear & tear on the rope, rappelling is recommended. Setting up a rappel takes more time than threading the rope to lower. If it is raining, if you're cold from the wind, tired or in the dark, saving time is everything. At a busy crag with other climbers waiting to climb the route you are occupying, a mussy hook anchor is great. Lowering even when it requires threading the anchor is much faster than rappelling.

A pair of Fixe ring anchor hangers with the rope threaded for lowering or rappelling.

A pair of mussy (or winch) hooks with the rope clipped in for lowering & top-roping.

ROUTE NAMES. OUALITY AND DIFFICULTY RATINGS

ROUTE NAMES

Route names are usually given to a climb by the first ascentionists. Climbs are usually given humorous, imaginative, poetic, musical or dramatic names that may somehow pertain to the nature and characteristics of the climb. In some cases, it is just someone's favorite tune, movie or book. In other cases the climb is named after a particular event or to honor some individual, holiday, etc. A few of the names are explicit, rude or obscene. It is one way each first ascentionist gets to exercise his or her First Amendment rights. When a climb is not named, it may appear in this book as **UNKNOWN, UNNAMED** or a name such as **ARETE** or **CRACK** that describes the rock feature the route ascends.

FIVE STAR QUALITY RATING SYSTEM

Each climb is given a quality rating with 0 to 5 stars (*****). Quality is judged by several factors: length, position of the line, uniqueness, quality of the moves, soundness and quality of the rock, public opinion, and the author's opinion. It is very subjective and not any one person will agree with all of it. The general idea is to suggest the merit of a certain climb in relation to other climbs in a particular area, as well as throughout the Northern Front Range. A climb with no stars is probably not worth doing. A climb with one star deserves a little merit or attention. A climb with two to three stars is considered quite good and well worth doing. A climb with four to five stars is considered to be brilliant, classic, and outrageously good. At the Golden Cliffs, I give 5 stars to only two climbs.

In my guidebooks, I go one step further than other guidebook authors, by including a question mark (?) after the suggested star rating, for every route that I have not personally climbed or attempted. This way you the readers can know when I'm guessing by using the opinion of the first ascent party or another second hand source. I challenge any guidebook author to do the same. I am convinced most guidebook authors never will, because they want to be able to fool the public into thinking they've done almost everything. They wish to sell their reputation of providing meticulously researched work. These authors must remember that "you can't fool all of the people, all of the time."

DIFFICULTY RATINGS

YOSEMITE DECIMAL SYSTEM (YDS)

The Yosemite Decimal System that has always been used to rate climbs in America is used in this book. Most climbs in this guide are free climbs of fifth class difficulty of 5.9-5.12a. There are a few climbs as hard as 5.12c/d that have been redpointed in the area. Fifth class routes are defined as free climbs of the difficulty and length to require a rope and protection placements for safety. Free climbing means the rock is ascended by your body (hands, feet, etc.) using the natural holds and cracks found on the rock surface. Equipment and ropes are used for safety and can not be weighted to progress or rest; otherwise the climb is considered to have aid.

On most hard sport routes (5.12-5.14) several aid (hang-dog) ascents must be made to rehearse the moves and sequences, before a successful free ascent can be made from the ground to top. The successful ascent is called a redpoint. Routes that have not been redpointed are listed as PROJECT. The YDS rating on each route is determined by the local consensus if the route has seen numerous ascents. If the route has seen no repeat ascents the rating given by the first ascentionist is used. The opinions of the repeat ascents and the author's opinion are factors that determine the rating on new routes.

Ratings are not absolutely factual, even when they are based on a consensus. Ratings have always been debated and disagreed upon. Depending on the climber's skills and body size, a particular climb may either seem harder or easier than the given rating. A tall person may have the advantage on many climbs, but in some cases, the opposite is true. Smaller or larger fingers or hands make some jam cracks vary in difficulty.

The ratings on real rock climbs will most likely feel quite different from plastic gym climbs. For climbers used to only sport climbs on real rock, be prepared for trad climbs of the same grade to feel more difficult, because stopping to place protection takes time and energy spent on your arms or legs that is not spent while clipping a bolt on a sport route.

The climbs at the Golden Cliffs are all of 5th class difficulty, from 5.5 to 5.12c/d. There are currently no 5.13 or harder climbs, unlike nearby Clear Creek Canyon, The Flatirons, Eldorado or Boulder Canyon.

SERIOUSNESS RATINGS	Most climbs in this book are safely bolted and get no seriousness rating. Exceptions do exist including some of the traditional routes listed and runout sport climbs with long or dangerous falls. The PG-13 and the R rating applies to sport climbs with fall potential of more than 25 feet or where potentially serious falls exist. Potentially serious falls include high second bolts often with hard clips or where the possibility of hitting lower angle rock or a ledge exists. Don't think just because a climb does not have a seriousness rating it is impossible to get hurt. Climbing is a dangerous sport and even safe sport routes have not completely changed that. Inexperience, bad judgment and improper safety techniques are responsible for almost all accidents. The majority of climbs at the **Golden Cliffs** require bringing only 8-12 quickdraws (carbiners with slings), a 50 to 60 meter (165 - 200 foot) rope and personal climbing gear (harness, belay device, rock shoes and a chalk bag). In spite of the fact that most of these climbs are safe, potentially injurious fall situations may exist at some place on many climbs and that is not always documented. If the leader should fall with slack out while attempting to clip a low bolt (on most routes), a groundfall is possible unless the belayer is very attentive and skilled. A very short fall onto a ramp, ledge or protruding edge or flake could result in a minor or serious injury.
PG-13 RATING	The PG-13 rating means the potential for a serious or long fall is present and beware, especially if you are getting in over your head in difficulty. Examples may include potential short ledge out falls, a notable runout, or a dangerous runout on very easy climbing where a fall is unlikely. PG-13 is a very mild version of the R rating.
R RATING	In this guide, The R rating is split into three sub-grades R-, R and R/X. R- is generally not so serious for the experienced hardcore, who should beware of anything rated R/X. For those who are new to the sport or at an intermediate level, anything in the R category could easily be extremely dangerous or fatal. Proper experience and judgment along with a good belayer can serve to make a serious climb possible and often safe. The R rating rarely applies to sport climbs. Occasionally the R- rating is given to a sport route with long runouts of 10 to 20 feet where the leader could easily fall 30 feet or more. It is not just the length of a fall that makes falling so dangerous, but rather the nature of the fall, the position of the climber and obstacles he or she could hit or land on during the fall. Sport climbs are not meant to be R rated experiences such as traditional climbs often are. Certainly an R rated sport climb will not be popular in today's scene. Please do not retro-bolt without the permission of the first ascentionist or the agreement of other climbers who have climbed the route. The R rating is used on traditional routes with tricky, poor or strenuous to place protection. Long runouts off good or fair protection with fall potential of more than 20 feet, also receive the R rating. The R/X rating applies to very seriousness leads with poor pro and runouts that are best to never fall on. Avoid these routes unless it is the sort of haired out adventure that you crave through years of experience on serious climbs.
R/X RATING	**The X rating is almost never found on a sport route**! Some folks consider **Paris Girls** (5.13a X) in Eldorado Canyon to be sport route, because bolts are the only form of protection found on the route. The bolts protect the hardest moves, but a 25 feet fall can be taken off of 5.12 moves and there is 5.9 climbing so run-out there is potential for a 70 foot groundfall. Most climbers practice the climb on top-rope a number of times before finally leading it. Sport routes are set up to eliminate potentially injurious or fatal falls and allow many leaders the opportunity to lead the climb without prior top-rope rehearsal. The **X rating** is used when a climb has serious or fatal fall potential. Trad climbs with bad ground fall potential and bad protection on moves at or near the difficulty of that climb's YDS grade receive the X rating. For example a long 5.7 runout on a 5.11 or 5.12 route would not always be given a serious rating, but the same 5.7 runout on a 5.8 or 5.9 route would be given a seriousness rating of R or X.

Description Of the Fixed Protection, Anchors & a list of any Gear Needed	At the end of each route listing is a description of the protection. For the **sport climbs**, this is the number of bolts and the anchor. The definition of the term **sport climb** refers a safely bolted climb where there is no need to bring gear such as nuts and camming devices. All the protection is fixed being reliable 3/8" or 1/2" diameter bolts with modern, high strength bolt hangers and a 2 bolt lowering / rappel anchor at the top of the climb or the pitch, that allows for convenient descent with a 50 to 70 meter rope. For the few sport routes where a nut can be used, this gear is listed. Most such routes are called **Mixed gear and bolt routes**, where gear is needed to supplement the run-outs between the bolts. If the gear is optionally placed for safety and commonly not used, meaning that the climb is usually done using just the fixed protection, it would be considered a sport route and perhaps even boost the PG-13 rating. On **traditional routes**, a brief to detailed list of the gear (nuts, Friends, etc.) needed is displayed. The definition of a **traditional** or **trad route** is generally that most of the protection is not fixed and usually ascend a natural weakness such as a crack that allows a properly skilled leader to place the proper size and type of gear (nuts, Friends, Aliens, Camalots, etc.) for protection. **Mixed gear and bolt routes** generally have a fair number of bolts but still require bringing some gear. In some cases, a very light rack of nuts or camming devices is needed and this information is listed to save you the weight of carrying most of your rack. **Most of the climbs in this book are sport climbs** where a rack of 10-12 quickdraws is usually enough. A couple of long sport routes, at the Fence Area (on the west face), are 100 to 120 ft. in length. These routes require 14 to 17 quickdraws & a 60 meter (200 feet) to 70 meter (235 feet) rope. On most climbs, a 50 meter (165 feet) rope will be plenty long enough to descend. Information regarding the length of a climb is generally listed on the topo and in the description if it is longer than 75 feet.
EXAMPLES OF ROUTE LISTINGS.	**A sport climb = MRS. HEN PLACE A PECK.** **** 5.12a 6 bolts / 2 Fixe rings. **POWER AND LIES** ** 5.10d PG-13 8 bolts / 2 bolt anchor. **A mixed route = THE CRACK & FACE ROUTE.** **** 5.10d PG-13. **(bolts & gear)** 5 bolts / 2 Fixe rings. A small rack is useful. #.3 Alien to a #2.5 Friend. **POLITICIANS, PRIESTS & BODY BAGS.** *** 5.10a A few stoppers or small-medium cams (#.5, .75 Aliens - green, yellow) to 4 bolts / 2 chains. **A trad climb = SHADOW OF A HANGDOG.** *** 5.10b Small-medium stoppers to a # 2 Friend / 2 chains anchor.
FIRST ASCENT Information	First ascent information is listed in this guide, at the end of each route description. Included are important details of the history of a route, including who equipped the route, who made the first ascent, and if this ascent was not a redpoint, who made the first redpoint (or first free ascent). Usually, equipping a route is the biggest work chore involved in establishing most climbs. Sometimes, cleaning of loose rock and lichen often proves to be a bigger chore. Both bolting and cleaning are the important, accepted tasks of the equipper. In most cases the person who equipped the route, also was the first to climb and redpoint the route. This is not always the case, especially on many 5.13 and 5.14 routes. The equipper may not even climb all or any of the moves free, but rather prepare the climb for lead ascents. When the equipper and the first ascentionist are the same individual(s) as the first free ascentionist, this guide lists them as first ascent, that is abbreviated F.A. to save space on the page When the first free ascent (F.F.A.), the first ascent (A0) and /or the equipper are different individuals; my guidebooks lists each individual and their accomplishment.

Two Ratings Per Climb: The Direct Line Versus The Line Of Least Resistance

Many of the routes at the Golden Cliffs can be climbed via different variations to the same bolt line. The most direct line along the bolts is often the more difficult way to ascend a route & can often be avoided by climbing off to the side in a crack corner system. For example; the start of the climb **Smear Me A Beer** can be climbed straight up its beer barrel prow along the bolts at 5.11b. It is also possible to climb the corner to the right & still reach back left to clip the 2nd bolt. Before the 3rd bolt, it is possible to step back left & join the bolt line. This variation of the route makes the climb 5.10 & thus avoids the difficult 5.11b crux climbing directly past the 2nd bolt. For other routes, the direct line is also the line of least resistance, being the only path that is obvious & normally ascended. Examples of this are **Basalt & Battery** and **Mrs. Hen Places A Peck**.

The nature of this area & other basalt cliffs is to have faces & aretes between corners & crack systems. The width of the face or arete between crack corners & ledges determine how separate or squeezed in a bolted line will be. On some sport routes it will be easy to step off the face & into the nearby corner, crack or chimney or ledge. This climb may seem contrived. If a route is very contrived it will not receive 3 to 5 stars. On many other climbs, it will be possible to step off the route at one point. If it is nearly impossible or very difficult to leave the holds along the bolted line, then the route is not contrived & squeezed in. Such routes are often the area's classics with 4 stars.

This doesn't mean that routes where it is possible to deviate from the bolt line & climb more than one variation are not worth doing. It is an opportunity to pick your poison & the difficulty you can handle. Taking the direct line is more challenging & usually offers more aesthetic movement than finding easier ground off to the side. Sport climbs can be thought of as roped bouldering where the goal is to succeed without falling, hanging or climbing around the intended line versus just getting to the top as is often the goal in mountaineering or big wall climbing.

Climbing in the gym on plastic holds, where a route is designated by colored tape marking the holds you can use is by comparison far more contrived than any outdoor climbing experience. This area has some face & arete climbs that are close to neighboring crack corners or chimney. Some climbers have little imagination and insist if they can somehow reach every bolt on the route that they are climbing that route. They are missing out on some fine climbing and good training.

If the direct line provides a sequence of moves that requires power, discipline & perseverance, then it is good training & a learning experience. Climbing around the direct line means you can't cut the mustard & are opting out for a more relaxing path. The choice is yours.

Beware Of Top Ropers: The Dangers Of Approaching From Above The Cliff

For many years I have visited the Golden Cliffs and until around 2001, it was one of the safer places to climb. There have always been a good difficulty range of safely bolted climbs, and the rock is generally solid. Most of the crack climbs can be protected with bomber stopper nuts, Friends, Camalots, Aliens, etc. The hillside & low-angle rock above the top of the climbs is not always so solid, but this was rarely a concern because few climbers ever set foot in these zones. Climbs were almost always led by at least one member of a climbing party and once the leader would reach the anchor, he or she would lower back to the ground. Less experienced members of the climbing party would then top-rope the climb.

Today, a growing number of beginning climbers go to the Golden Cliffs with no leading skills & set up top-ropes by approaching from above to get down to the top anchors. Armed with a rope, a long sling, a few carbiners, harness & a copy of the guide **Front Range Topropes**, these folks are showing up in greater numbers. This has become the single greatest objective danger to anyone standing at the base of the cliff. I have personally been hit with pebbles and luckily been missed by bigger rocks. Thankfully, my partners have thus far been very lucky as well. In fact, I recommend wearing a helmet at the base, especially on busy days.

There are a few sections of the Golden Cliffs where the top can be safely accessed. Other parts off the cliff should be off limits to people approaching from above, because it is very hard not to send rock down. People at the base will not be able to see the person on top and they will be unaware of their presence until its too late & the rocks come flying down. To anyone accessing the cliff top, please remember you could be responsible for seriously injuring or killing someone if you send rocks down. There are growing numbers of people, kids, babies and dogs hanging out at the base, especially on warm days.

Approaching from above is also often dangerous to the person doing it. Getting a belay or rappelling down to the top of the climb is often the only safe way. However this does not prevent a rockfall accident happening to someone below. This also requires people in your party to warn people & keep them out of this zone and this isn't often possible since people may already be there belaying, climbing, hiking the trail, etc. Therefore, if you must set up top-ropes, I recommend the following list of routes. Otherwise find a more experienced partner or guide that can lead the climbs and safely set-up that top-rope for you.

Areas Not Suited for Top-ropers

Child Free Zone - Lower The anchors are difficult to descend to and the trail is directly below this area.

Overhang Area The exception of **Fabulous Flying Carr's Route**, which if you know the way to the top has a solid top above it. This is one of the most popular areas on the Golden Cliffs & most parties lead their ascent to the top anchors. The mesa above here has some loose gravel & rock.

Fence Area This is the tallest section of the Golden Cliffs and most of the routes do not actually summit.

Winterfest Wall (with the exception of the some of the routes on the **Left Side**). The hillside above this wall is covered in gravel & loose rock. Getting to the anchors is dangerous & not knocking down rock is very difficult. I have seen several people attempting to set up a top rope knock down large rock here. The anchors for **Pumcat, Twinkletoes, Cat's Meow & Nouveau Reach** are just below the flat top & are the easiest to access on this section of cliff. All the same, be very careful to anyone who may be at the base or climbing the routes.

Areas Best Suited for Top-ropers

Brown Cloud Crags - Right Side Accessing the top of the **Old Roof Route (Lemons, Limes and Tangerines)** is especially easy with a solid rock summit. The climbs at this area are short & the top of the cliff is relatively stable.

Tradlands It is especially easy to walk onto the ledge above these climbs & right to the top anchor for **Resident Bush.** Tie off to a large boulder to safely get down to the anchor for **X It**.

Risk Area The routes from **Hand Crack** to the left. This area is short & the top of the cliff is generally solid.

GOLDEN CLIFFS * RECOMMENDED SPORT ROUTES * 5.6 - 5.10b/c

5.6	**KEVIN SPIES THE LINE** *** at the Table Top Area - Left Side. Steep slab to vertical face. Pg. 52
	UNKNOWN CRACK *** at the Under The Table Area. Thin crack & steep face. Pg. 57
	LITTLE GREEN APPLES * at the Risk Area - Left Side. Short right-facing corner. Pg. 101
5.7	**HONEY, I SHRUNK THE HEMORRHOIDS** *** at Twelve Pack Wall. Slab to vertical prow crux. Pg. 71
	IVORY TOWER ** 5.7 at Overhang Area. Face & arete. Pg. 41
	SLOPING FOREHEAD ** 5.7 at Overhang Area. Face with overhang start. Pg. 41
	THELMA * at Brown Cloud Crag - Right Side. Arete & face. Pg. 35
5.8	**OLD ROOF ROUTE** **** at Brown Cloud Crags - Right Side. Steep prow with roof. Pg. 35
	INTERFACE ** at Brown Cloud Crags - Left Side. Steep face. Pg. 39
	LOUISE * at Brown Cloud Crags - Right Side. Face & arete. Pg. 35
5.9	**BOW OF THE TITANIC** *** at the Brown Cloud Crags - Left Side. Vertical face to narrow prow. Pg. 39
	THIS AIN'T NATURITA, PILGRIM. *** at Overhang Area. Vertical face up prow. Pg. 41
	RESIDENT BUSH ** 5.9+ at the Tradlands. Steep face & arete. Pg. 59
	BRAIN CLOUD **** 5.9+ at the Major Bolt Achievement Buttress. Vertical arete. Pg. 61 & 65
	CLIFF HANGER ** 5.9- at the Major Bolt Achievement Buttress - West Side. Face & arete. Pg. 65
	CHUNKY MONKEY ** at Twelve Pack Wall. Face & thin crack start to steep face. Pg. 71
	NINE TO FIVE *** at Hot Spot Area. Steep to vertical face with short thin crack. Pg. 83
	CAT'S MEOW *** at Winterfest Wall - Left Side. Bulging face crux to small corner. Pg. 93
	THIS BONE'S FOR YOU *** 5.9- at the Risk Area - Left Side. Short arete crux to juggy vertical face. Pg. 101
5.10a	**OFF GUARD** *** at Child Free Zone - Lower Cliff. Vertical face & arete. Pg. 29
	FABULOUS FLYING CARR'S ROUTE *** at the Overhang Area. Slab to vertical face crux. Pg. 41
	ALAN'S SEAM *** at the Under The Table Area. Vertical face and crack. Pg. 57
	SPIKE *** at the Major Bolt Achievement Buttress - West Side. Steep face and arete. Pg. 65
	POLITICIANS, PRIESTS AND BODY BAGS *** at Industrial Buttress. Crack corner to vertical face crux. Pg. 67
	THE CRUX OF THE BISCUIT IS THE APOSTROPHE *** at Twelve Pack Wall. Slab to roof to face. Pg. 71
	F.A.T.A.L. (FEMURS & TIBIAS ALTERNATING LATERALLY) *** at Fence Area. Jamming up flared dihedral. Pg. 77
	STICKIN' IT TO THE MAN ***** .10a/b at the Fence Area - Left Side. Crack corner to crux bulge to long slab to vertical face with bulge. Pg. 77 & 79
	DECK CHAIRS ON THE TITANIC **** .10a/b at Brown Cloud Crags - Left Side. Bulging start to continuous steep face. Pg. 39
	D'S DRY DREAM *** .10a/b at Table Top Area - Right Side. Bulging face to slab. Pg. 51
	HENRY SPIES THE LINE *** .10a/b at Table Top Area - Center & Right Side. Vertical to bulging face. Pg. 51 & 52
5.10b	**BROWN CLOUD ARETE** *** at Brown Cloud Crags - Left Side. Arete & face. Pg. 39
	BIMBO IN LIMBO *** at the Winterfest Wall - Center. Varied vertical face & crack. Pg. 89
	GOOD MAN DAN *** .10b/c at the MBA Buttress - South Side. Vertical face & arete. Pg. 61
	UGLY STICK *** at the Fence Area - Left Side. Crack to vertical face with bulges. Longest climb on the mountain. Pg. 77 & 79
	SILVER BULLET *** .10b/c at the Winterfest Wall - Center. Flake crack to vertical face & short corner. Pg. 89

GOLDEN CLIFFS * RECOMMENDED SPORT ROUTES * 5.10c - 5.11c

5.10c	**PROTECTION FROM THE VIRUS** ** at Brown Cloud Crags - Right side. Small roof to face. Pg. 35
	SMEAR ME A BEER *** at the Overhang Area. Vertical to bulging arete. Pg. 41
	F.A.T.A.L. (FEMURS & TIBIAS ALTERNATING LATERALLY) *** at the Fence Area. Stemming dihedral. Pg. 77
	LEANING PILLAR *** at the Winterfest Wall - Right Side. Vertical face with seam crack. Pg. 87 & 89
	BABY BEEPER *** at Risk Area - Right Side. Face & blunt arete. Pg. 99
	THE GROUND DOESN'T LIE *** .10c/d at the Table Top Area - Right Side. Arete to vertical face crux. Pg. 47
5.10d	**THE CRUX OF THE BISCUIT IS THE APOSTROPHE** *** at Twelve Pack Wall. Slab to roof to face. Pg. 71
	WINTER WARMER **** at the Fence Area - Left Side. Long, varied vertical face. Pg. 77 & 79
	CRACK & FACE ROUTE **** at the Hot Spot Area. A mixed bolts & gear route. Mostly bolts. A very light rack is recommended. Vertical face with small edges to crack finish. Pg. 83
	PASS THE TANNING BUTTER *** at the Winterfest Wall - Center. Bulging face to crack corner to face. Pg. 89
	BASALT & BATTERY **** .10d/11a at the Fence Area. Thin crack to shallow corner. Pg. 77
5.11a	**COOL THING** *** at the Child Free Zone - Lower Cliff. Crackless corner & face with sloping shelf crux with tiny holds. Pg. 29
	FABULOUS FLYING CARR'S ROUTE *** at Overhang Area. Direct variation. Slab to Vertical face crux. Pg. 41
	INTERSTELLAR OVERDRIVE **** at Winterfest Wall - Center. Stemming dihedral crux to vertical face. Pg. 89
	FIVE TO ONE *** at the Hot Spot Area. Vertical to bulging face with dyno crux finish. Pg. 83
	WHOLE LOTTA DRUNK *** on Winterfest Wall - Right Side. Bulging crux to steep face. Pg. 87
	ROPE TRICK *** at Risk Area - Right Side. Strenuous vertical to overhung face & corner. Pg. 99
5.11a/b	**FLIGHT 67** **** at the Industrial Buttress. Vertical to bulging face with reachy crux. Pg. 67
	SUNSET ARETE **** at Winterfest Wall - Left Side. Technical arete. Pg. 93
	TORA, TORA, TORA *** at the Overhang Area. Moderate crack to technical vertical face. Pg. 41
	MAJOR BOLT ACHIEVEMENT *** at MBA buttress - West Side. Face to roof. Pg. 65
5.11b	**SMEAR ME A BEER** *** at the Overhang Area. Rounded prow. Short intricate face crux. Pg. 41
	CHICK FILET *** at the Table Top Area - Center. Thin crack & arete. Pg. 51
	UNNAMED ARETE *** at the Industrial Buttress. Arete & face. Pg. 67
	REBEL YELL *** at Winterfest Wall - Left Side. Steep face & arete. Pg. 93
	NOUVEAU REACH *** at Winterfest Wall - Left Side. Stemming & thin crack crux to arete. Pg. 93
	PUMCAT *** on Winterfest Wall - Left Side. Vertical face with seam. Edges & sidepulls. Pg. 93
	CRAWLING UP ROSEANNE'S BELLY *** .11b/c at Winterfest Wall - Center. Blunt prow & vertical face with tiny roof. Pg. 89
5.11c	**INDUSTRIAL DISEASE** **** at Industrial Buttress. Thin crack to overhung face. Pg. 67
	PARENTAL ABUSE *** at Child Free Zone - Upper Cliff. Bulging face & arete. Pg. 31
	BULLET THE BROWN CLOUD *** at the Brown Cloud Crag - Left Side. Arete & vertical face. Pg. 39
	THE RESOLUTION *** at Winterfest Wall - Right Side. Technical bulging face to arete. Pg. 87
	DRIVING OVER STELLA *** at the Winterfest Wall - Center & Left Side. Strenuous bulging face crux to slab finish. Pg. 89 & 93.
	MOHARE ECLAIRE *** .11c/d at the Child Free Zone - Upper Cliff. Arete crux to bulging face. Pg. 31

5.11d	**MR. SQUIRREL PLACES A NUT** **** at Overhang Area. Steep intricate face crux to roof. Pg. 41 & 43 **CHICK FILET** *** at the Table Top Area - Right Side. Thin crack & arete. Pg. 51 **FORGOTTEN NAMES** *** at the Industrial Buttress. Technical arete with small sidepull holds. Pg. 67 **FEEDING FRENZY** *** at the MBA Buttress - West Side. Arete to stemming corner crux. Pg. 65 **KLIMBINK IS FORBOLTEN** *** at Fence Area. Technical bulging face crux. Pg. 77 **KILIAN'S RED** *** at the Winterfest Wall - Center. Face with small seam corner crux. Pg. 89 **LYING ON THE GROUND** *** .11d/12a at Table Top Area - Center. Blunt arete to overhung face. Pg. 51 **THE DISSOLUTION** **** .11d/12a at Winterfest Wall - Right Side. Sustained vertical face. Tiny edges to deadpoint crux. Pg. 87
5.12a	**MRS. HEN PLACES A PECK** **** at Overhang Area. Sustained overhung face with varied holds & moves. Crimpers & deadpoint crux finish. Pg. 41 **PSEUDO BULLET** *** at Winterfest Wall - Center. Small corner & arete crux. Face to arete finish. Pg. 89 **HANDLE THIS HARD ONE** *** at the Overhang Area. Technical, rounded arete with vertical seam. Pg. 41
5.12a/b	**MR. ROOSTER Struts His Stuff** *** at Overhang Area. Sustained, pumpy, bulging face & seam. Two cruxes: A shallow crack & a high step with tiny crimpers. Pg. 41 **ELECTROCUTICLES** *** at Fence Wall. Lieback seam to face & arete with small edges. Pg. 77
5.12b	**WIDESPREAD SHELFISHNESS** *** at Hot Spot Area. Bulging face & blunt arete with sidepulls. Pg. 83 **PUMCAT** *** (direct) on Winterfest Wall - Left Side. Smooth vertical face with hairline seam. Edges & sidepulls. Pg. 93 **MOHARE EDGE** **** .12b/c at Child Free Zone - Upper Cliff. Sustained sharp arete & vertical face. Pg. 31
5.12c	**MONKEY PUZZLE** *** at the Child Free Zone - Lower Cliff. Powerful, technical 6 foot roof crux. Pg. 29
5.12c/d	**RAFIKI** *** at the Child Free Zone - Lower Cliff. Sustained overhung face. Wide crack lieback to traverse to wild dyno crux. Pg. 29 **SOLAR PANEL** *** at Fence Area. Bulging gymnastic face with tiny roof. Technical crux. Small edges & high step to dyno for jugs. Pg. 77

RECOMMENDED CRACK CLIMBS

SHADOW OF A HANGDOG **** 5.10b on the Major Bolt Achievement Buttress - South Face. Thin crack with 1-1/4" Splitter crux finish. Pg. 61

BIG DIHEDRAL *** 5.8 on Brown Cloud Crags - Right Side. Stem & jam a v-shaped dihedral. Pg. 35

KILIAN'S DEAD ** 5.6 at Brown Cloud Crags - Left Side. Hand crack to chimney. Pg. 39

BUSH LOVES DETROIT *** 5.8 at the Winterfest Wall - Center. Lieback & jam up a dihedral. Thin hand and hands. Pg. 89.

Best selection of cracks can be found at the **Industrial Buttress** on Pg. 67 and some are listed below.

FAST BOAT TO CHINA *** 5.8 Large crack corner with varied double cracks. Stemming & jamming.

HIEDI HI *** 5.8 Double crack start to straight-in thin hand crack to corner finish.

NOODLE FACTORY ** 5.9- Crack corner. Lieback & jam.

POLYVINYL CHLORIDE ** 5.10a/b Right-facing dihedral. Stemming up thin seam to fist crack crux.

GOLDEN CLIFFS * CHILD FREE ZONE * LOWER CLIFF

2. **MONKEY PUZZLE.** *** 5.12c
4. **POWER AND LIES.** ** 5.10d or 5.9 PG-13
5. **OFF GUARD.** *** 5.10a
6. **COOL THING.** *** 5.11a

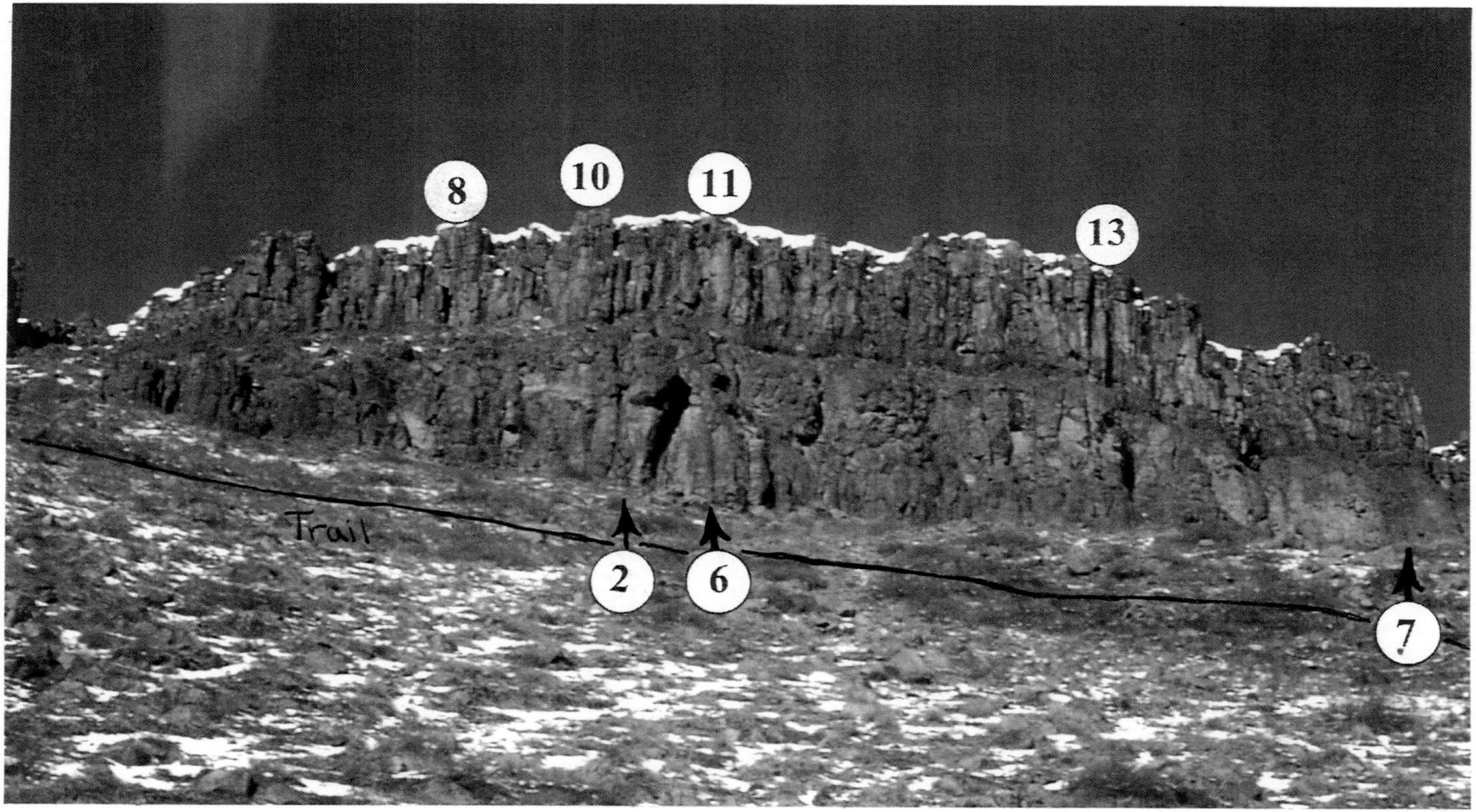

LOWER CLIFF

2. MONKEY PUZZLE. *** 5.12c
6. COOL THING. *** 5.11a
7. SKIN DEEP. * 5.10a

UPPER CLIFF

8. BIG LOOSE GOOSE. * 5.10a
10. THE RODENT. ** 5.10
11. PARENTAL ABUSE. *** 5.11c
13. MOHARE EDGE. **** 5.12b/c

GOLDEN CLIFFS * CHILD FREE ZONE * LOWER CLIFF

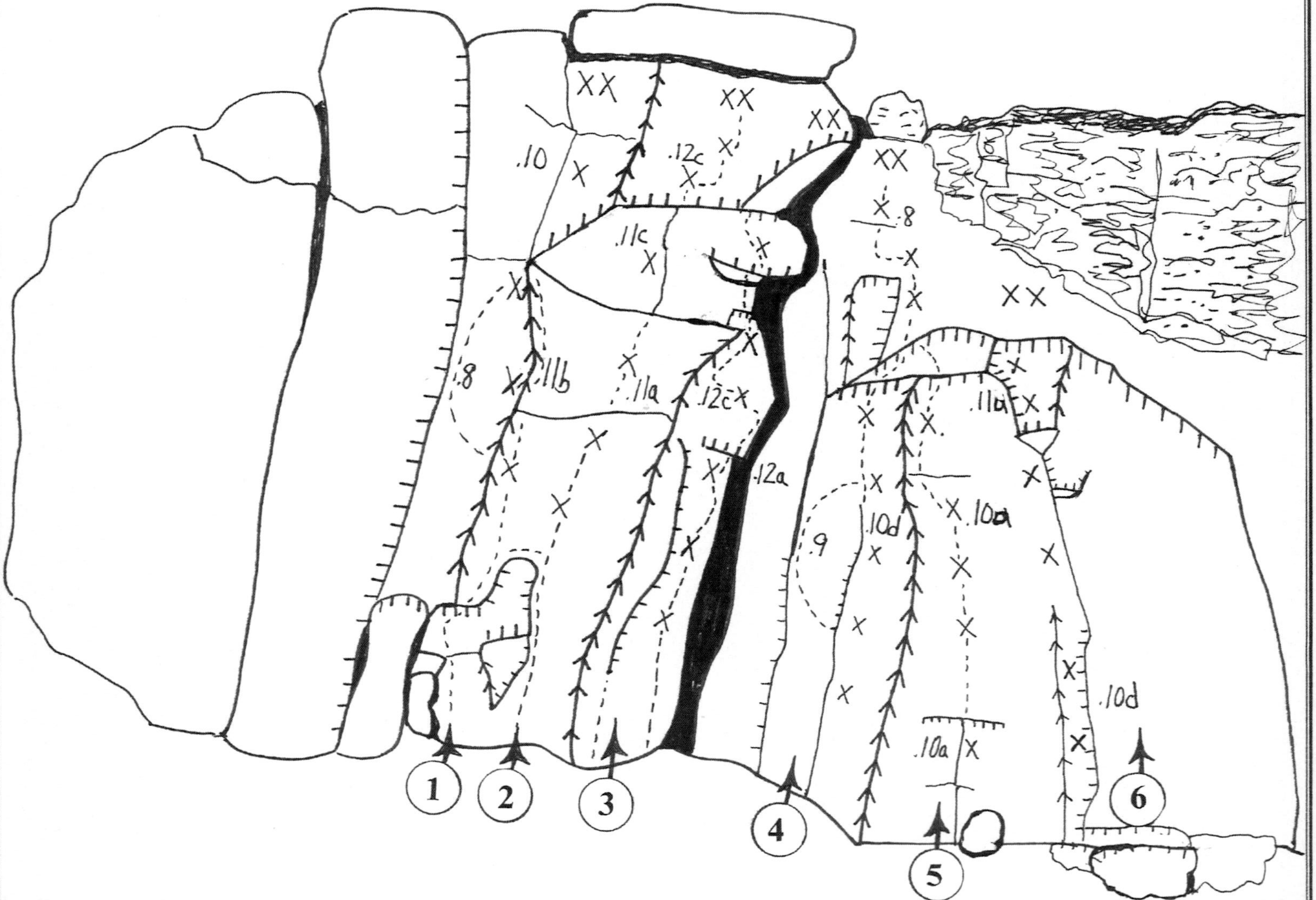

GOLDEN CLIFFS * CHILD FREE ZONE * LOWER CLIFF

This two-tiered cliff is the eastmost developed crag of the Golden Cliffs. The **Lower Cliff** is the first cliff encountered on the approach trial. Follow the approach trail to directly below the **Lower Cliff** & 50 feet downhill. Continue up the approach trail to the left side of the **Lower Cliff** & walk right (east) on a small trail for 50 feet to the base of the climbs.

The two tiers of the **Child Free Zone** are cut by a sloping ledge system. The ledge system starts out as a wide grassy hillside and then narrows to a dangerous dirt ledge above the void. The routes on the **Upper Cliff** are above this ledge system. See the following pages for topo drawing & route descriptions of the **Child Free Zone - Upper Cliff**.

1. **PUZZLING MONKEY.** ** 5.10 or 5.11b 4 bolts / 2 bolt anchor. Stay on the arete past the first 3 bolts for a 5.11 or avoid this crux by stepping left into the gully to reach the 3rd bolt. 5.10 climbing leads to the anchor. F.A.: Tod Anderson & Richard Wright on Feb. 15, 1998.
2. **MONKEY PUZZLE.** *** 5.12c 6 bolts / 2 bolt anchor. Climb a steep face past 3 bolts to a six-foot roof. Reach out the roof to clip 5th bolt, just above the lip. A wild crux is encountered at the lip of the roof. Finish with strenuous jug moves to reach the anchor.
   First ascent by Hank Caylor and Alvino Pon in 1992?
3. **RAFIKI.** *** 5.12c 6 bolts / 2 bolt anchor. This route ascends the overhanging east face. Start in the middle of the narrow face. Lieback off the right arete that forms the left edge of a wide crack. At the 3rd bolt, move left, then up & back right to good holds & clip 4th bolt. Traverse left onto the left arete & throw a big dyno to a jug. Continue with much greater ease, finishing over a small roof.
   F.A.: Mark Tarrant, Greg Purnell & Richard Wright in 2003.
4. **POWER AND LIES.** ** 5.10d or 5.9 PG-13 8 bolts / 2 bolt anchor. The obvious direct line (.10d) follows a tiny right-facing seam corner just left of the bolts. There is a committing run-out to the 3rd bolt. The bolts on this route are more spaced than the two routes to the right. As a result, most people choose the indirect line of least resistance (5.9) by moving left at the 2nd bolt & climbing the obvious crack system, then moving back right onto the face at 4th bolt. Reach a sloping ledge past 5th bolt. Move up & left past 3 bolts, on the broken, softer cap rock. The cap rock is still pretty solid & has been well cleaned. F.A.: Richard Wright, Mark Tarrant & Lisa Veraldi in 2003.
5. **OFF GUARD.** *** 5.10a 5-8 bolts / 2 bolt anchor. Begin in the middle of the face, right of the arete. A vertical start past 1st bolt leads to goods jugs & a stance to clip 2nd bolt. Climb a well protected, devious face & move left onto the arete. Gain the large sloping shelf.
   Finish with the upper 3 bolts of **Power & Lies** or move right & end the climb on a ledge at a 2 bolt anchor with Fixe rings.
   F.A.: Richard Wright. Lisa Veraldi & Ann Brandonburg Schroeder in December 2003
6. **COOL THING.** *** 5.11a 6-9 bolts / 2 bolt anchor. Start off a pile of boulders, clip 1st bolt & climb a shallow groove to a left-facing corner. The crux climbs the corner, past 5th & 6th bolt to gain a smooth sloping shelf. Finish with the upper 3 bolts of **Power & Lies** or move up right to a ledge & end the climb at the 2 bolt anchor with Fixe rings. F.A.: Richard Wright, Mark Tarrant & Lisa Veraldi in 2003.
7. **SKIN DEEP.** * 5.10a 6 bolts / 2 bolt anchor. Located on the lower tier, this is the furthest route to the east at the Golden Cliffs. From **Cool Thing**, walk 300 feet right to the base of the climb. Climb up solid red rock past 3 bolts. Continue up softer, rotten chocolate colored rock to the top of the first tier. Possibilities for a second pitch exist.
   First ascent by Richard Wright and Anna Brandonburg Schroeder on April 19, 1997.

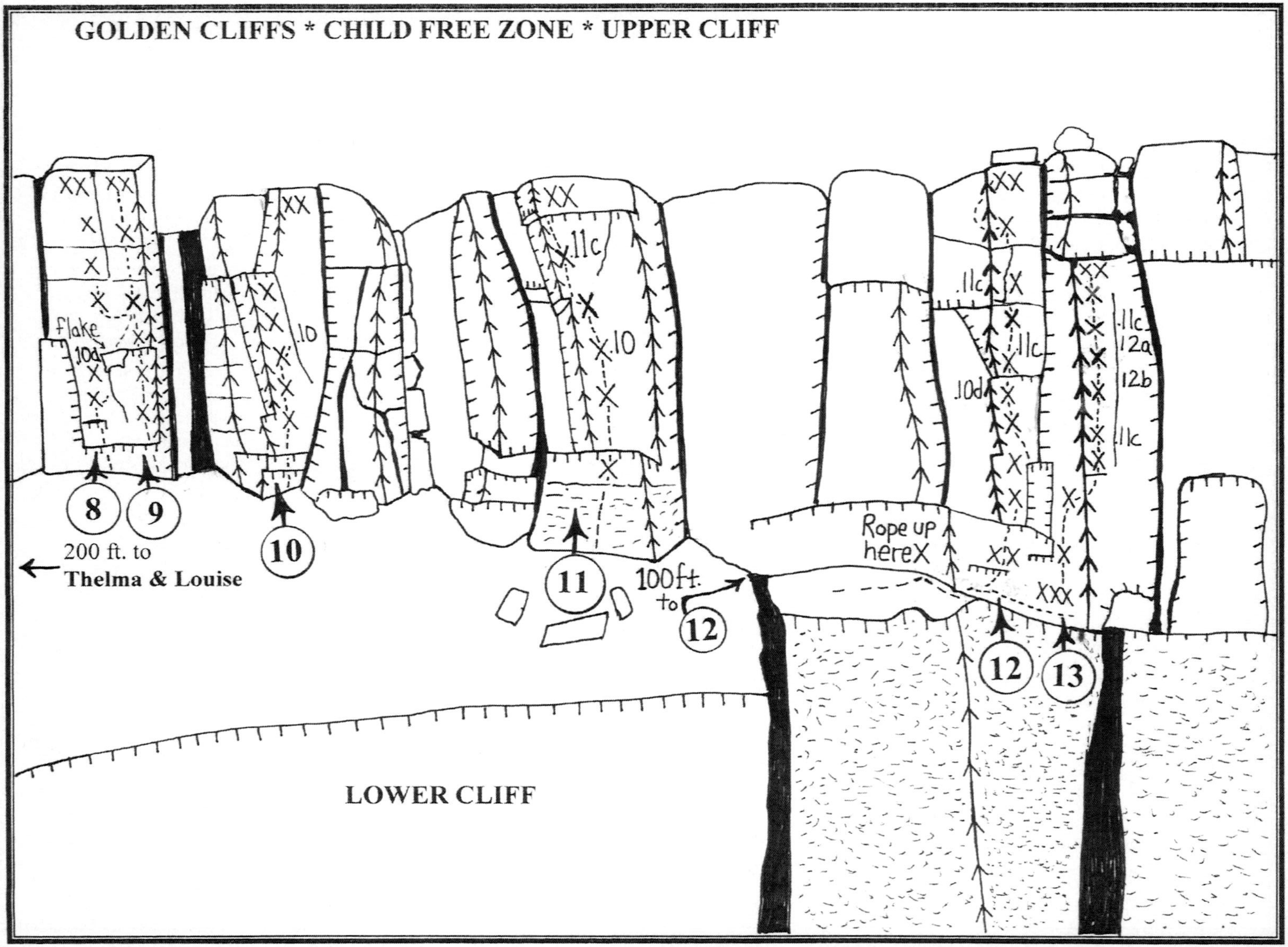
GOLDEN CLIFFS * CHILD FREE ZONE * UPPER CLIFF
flake
.10d
8
9
200 ft. to
Thelma & Louise
.10
10
.11c
.10
11
100 ft. to
12
.11c
.11c
.10d
.11c
12a
12b
.11c
Rope up here X
12
13
LOWER CLIFF

GOLDEN CLIFFS * CHILD FREE ZONE * UPPER CLIFF

This two-tiered cliff is the east-most developed crag of the Golden Cliffs. The **Lower Cliff** is the first cliff encountered on the approach trial. The two tiers are cut by a sloping ledge system. The ledge system starts out as a wide grassy hillside and then narrows to a dangerous dirt ledge above the void. The routes on the **Upper Cliff** are above this ledge system. Approach the upper tier from the **Brown Cloud Crags - Right Side**. Continue walking east (right) on a trail for 200 ft. to the base of **Big Loose Goose**. Easy walking leads 100 feet right to **Parental Abuse**. Walking any further right becomes more dangerous. The rightmost two routes (**MoHare Eclaire** & **MoHare Edge**) require roping up at a belay bolt to traverse the narrow sloping ledge to reach a 3 bolt anchor at the start of the climbs. The **Child Free Zone** is not user friendly for kids or dogs, because of the drop-off over a steep cliff.

8. **BIG LOOSE GOOSE.** * 5.10a 5-6 bolts / 2 bolt anchor. Walk 200 feet east of **Thelma & Louise**, the rightmost two routes on the **Brown Cloud Crags**, to the base of this climb. Start from a flat ledge 7 feet above the hillside. Climb onto a tiny ledge & clip the 1st bolt. Move slightly right & climb up past the left side of a scary-looking, 3 foot high guillotine flake to big holds on its top. Clip 2nd bolt & either run it out straight up to 3rd bolt or move right to a shelf & clip 4th bolt on **Unknown**. Put a long sling on this bolt & move back left & up. Climb a vertical face past 2 more bolts to the anchor. F.A.: Dennis McCarron in 1994.

9. **UNKNOWN.** *? 5.10a 5 bolts / 2 bolt anchor. Hangers missing on 3rd bolt and anchor bolts.

10. **THE RODENT.** ** 5.10 5 bolts / 2 Fixe rings. Start from a small ledge a few feet above the hillside. Clip the 1st bolt & move up onto a sloping ledge on the left side of the arete. Use holds on the sharp arete & move up to 3rd bolt. Step onto the face on the right side of the arete & reach right to jugs. Climb a thin crack to 4th bolt. Continue up easy climbing to the anchor. F.A.: Dan Hare & Noel Childs in 2004.

11. **PARENTAL ABUSE.** *** 5.11c 6 bolts / 2 chains. Begin up dark chocolate-colored rock & climb a short face, past 1st bolt, to a big ledge. Climb up the face & eventually move left onto the arete. The arete overhangs for the crux near the top.
F.A.: Mark Rolofson & Dianne Dallin in June 1993.

12. **MOHARE ECLAIRE.** *** 5.11c/d 2-3 bolt anchor / 8-9 bolts / 2 Fixe rings. This climb ascends the left of two aretes & the blunter of the pair. From the base of **Parental Abuse**, walk right (east) 100 feet. After the first 50 feet, there are a few moves of easy, exposed scrambling above a chimney. Continue right on the narrowing, sloping dirt & grass ledge. After 100 feet, there is a belay bolt, where the ledge bends to the north, becoming very narrow & sloping. Rope up at the bolt. After 12 feet there is a 2 bolt anchor, above the ledge at the base of **Mohare Eclaire**. It is easy to not see this anchor, since the path across is 5 feet lower. That's okay because 12 feet away is another 3 bolt-anchor, with a better stance. Start the lead by clipping the left 2 bolt anchor as the 1st protection. It is also possible to begin with the 1st bolt on the **Mohare Edge** & then traverse left on a sloping ledge to **Mohare Eclaire**. Climb past 2nd bolt, moving up & right into a short left-facing corner that ends on a shelf. Move left & climb the arete with a tricky crux, past 5th bolt, to reach a jug in a horizontal break. Continue up sloping holds & then up a vertical flake to the last bolt. Finish up jugs. F.A.: Dan Hare, Moe Hershoff & Claire Mearns in January 2000.

13. **MOHARE EDGE.** **** 5.12b/c 3 bolt anchor / 8 bolts / 2 Fixe rings. This is one of the best climbs at the Golden Cliffs. The dangerous approach & lack of a flat, relaxing belay zone limit its popularity. There is no easier way to climb around the difficulties on this sustained, technical arete. Follow the same approach as **Mohare Eclaire,** to reach the 3 bolt anchor. This climb ascends the right of two aretes. This is the sharper arete & stands out as a very obvious feature from the trail. From the anchor, clip the 1st bolt a few feet above. Move up past poor rock onto a shelf. Climb a short right-facing corner past 2nd bolt & then move right onto the arete's right side. Ascend the arete. Use holds on the right wall & on the arete, past three cruxes, protected by 6 closely spaced bolts. F.A.: Dan Hare & Moe Hershoff in January 1999.

GOLDEN CLIFFS * CHILD FREE ZONE * UPPER CLIFF

8. **BIG LOOSE GOOSE.** * 5.10a
9. **UNKNOWN.** *? 5.10a
10. **THE RODENT.** ** 5.10

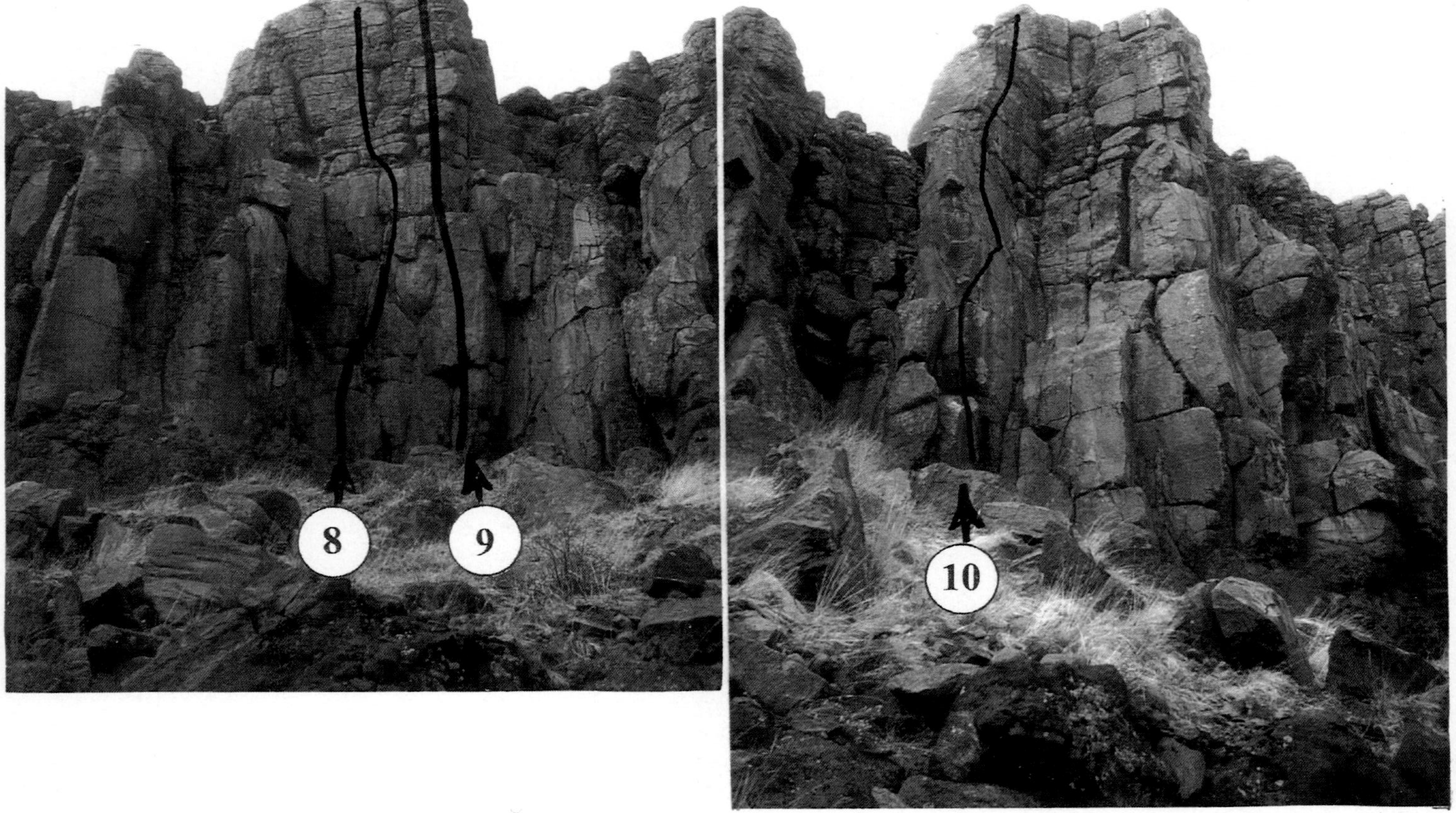

11. **PARENTAL ABUSE.** *** 5.11c

GOLDEN CLIFFS * BROWN CLOUD CRAGS * Right Side

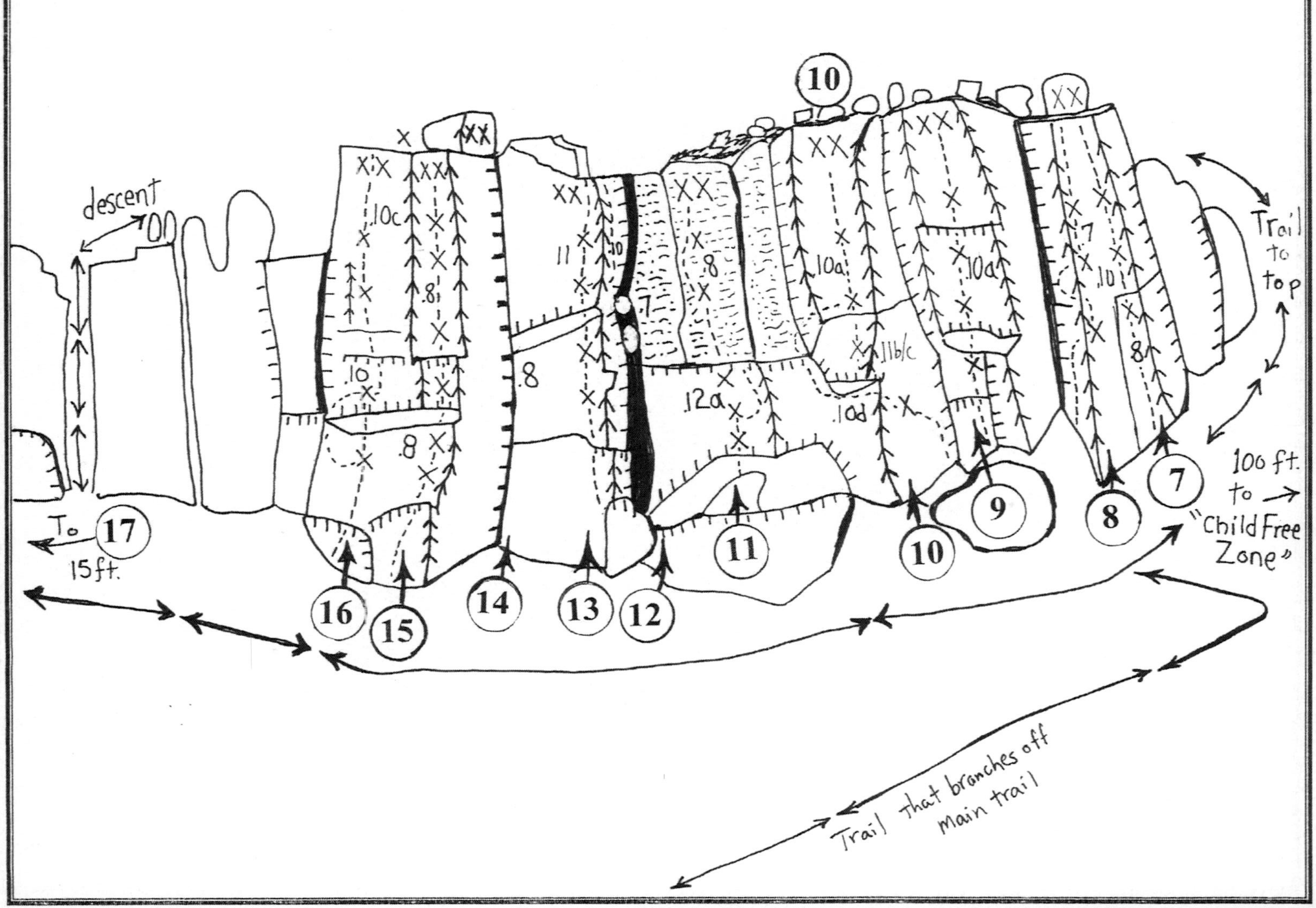

GOLDEN CLIFFS * BROWN CLOUD CRAGS * Right Side

To access these climbs, follow the main approach trail to 100 ft. directly below the climb **Interface**. A good trail branches off to the right and leads uphill for 250 ft. to below **Thelma** on the right end of the **Brown Cloud Crags**. Here, the trail branches in three directions. It heads horizontally left (west) to the base of the climbs on the **Brown Cloud Crags**. The trail also switch-backs uphill to the mesa above the **Brown Cloud Crags**. The third branch of the trail heads right (east) to the **Child Free Zone - Upper Cliff**. It is also possible to access these climbs by following the main approach trail to the base of **This Ain't Naturita Pilgrim** at the **Overhang Area** & then walking right (east) along the base for 200 to 300 feet.

Many of the climbs in this area are quite popular with top-ropers since the top can be easily accessed. These climbs are 30 to 50 feet in length.

7. **LOUISE.** * 5.8 3 bolts / Fixe rings anchor. This climb is 5.10 if you stay on the face and avoid the right arete. This climb has reasonably safe and easy access to the top anchor for top-ropers. First ascent by Charles Tabor and friends in 1993.

8. **THELMA.** * 5.7 3 bolts / Fixe rings anchor. Climb up the left arete, staying mainly to the left of it. Move back onto the right side of the arete to finish. This climb has reasonably safe and easy access to the top anchor for top-ropers. F.A.: Charles Tabor and friends in 1993.

9. **KID'S CLIMB.** ** 5.10b 4 bolts / 2 mussy hooks. Climb up to a small roof & the 1st bolt. Move up & slightly right to pass the roof. A tricky crux past 3rd bolt ends with a mantle onto a ledge. Finish up a short slab. F.A.: Geoff Slater, Tim Slater & Dillion Leitner in 1991.

10. **NEW RIVER GORGE HOMESICK BLUES.** ** 5.10d or 5.11c 4 bolts / 2 Fixe rings. Start in a corner and traverse left across a face to a blunt arete and a small roof. Clip the 2nd bolt. The easier way (.10d) continues left under the roof to a rest stance on the left above the roof. Step back right to finish. The direct 5.11 variation climbs straight up to the 3rd bolt.
First ascent: Johnathan Houck & Jim Thibodeau in 1990.

11. **THE VIRUS.** * 5.12a 5 bolts / 2 Fixe rings. Start with a wild roof crux, past the first 2 bolts, using the arete to the right. Once above the roof, easier climbing leads to the anchor below the top. First ascent by Dennis McCarron in 1994.

12. **THICK CRUST.** 5.7? Bring gear. Ascend the unattractive, blocky chimney up a right-facing corner, just left of **The Virus**.

13. **RISING PASSION.** ** 5.10c to 5.11b 4 bolts / 2 Fixe rings. A small-medium cam may be useful before 1st bolt. Climb up moderate terrain to the 1st bolt, 20 ft above the ground. Ascend the arete that becomes increasingly more difficult with the crux at the last bolt. It is easier to stay on the overhung, narrow prow of the arete's right side & much harder to climb the vertical face on the arete's left side.
F.A.: Dan Hare & Moe Hershoff 2004

14. **BIG DIHEDRAL.** *** 5.8 Small-medium to 2.5" gear (mostly #1-2.5 friends) / 2 Fixe rings. Stem & jam up the clean, v-shaped dihedral.
F.A.: Scott & Rick Berk in 1988.

15. **OLD ROOF ROUTE.** (A.k.a: **LEMONS, LIMES & TANGERINES.**) **** 5.8 6 bolts / 2 bolts & mussy hooks. This climb follows an obvious prow. Pull past an interesting roof at 3rd bolt and continue up the prow to the top. This climb has reasonably easy access to the top anchor for top-ropers. F.A.: Dave Hart & T. Howard in 1988.

16. **PROTECTION FROM THE VIRUS.** ** 5.10c 4 bolts / 2 bolt chains anchor. A tricky crux past the 2nd bolt pulls over a small roof. Reach a good stance. Continue up a tricky face to the anchor. This climb has reasonably easy access to the top anchor for top-ropers.
F.A.: Dennis McCarron - 1994.

17. **INTERFACE.** ** 5.8 4 bolts / 2 bolt anchor. See the following page **Brown Cloud Crags - Left Side** for topo drawing of the route. Start from the ground below & left of a ledge. Climb a short, enjoyable face. F.A.: Rick Leitner - 1990. Retro-bolted in December 2007.

10. **NEW RIVER GORGE HOMESICK BLUES.** ** 5.10d or 5.11c

11. **THE VIRUS.** * 5.12a

13. **RISING PASSION.** ** 5.10c to 5.11b

14. **BIG DIHEDRAL.** *** 5.8

15. **OLD ROOF ROUTE.** (A.k.a: **Lemons, Limes & Tangerines.**) **** 5.8

16. **PROTECTION FROM THE VIRUS.** ** 5.10c

BROWN CLOUD CRAGS * Left Side

17. **INTERFACE.** ** 5.8
19. **JOLOBEE.** ** 5.10d/11a
20. **BULLET THE BROWN CLOUD.** *** 5.11c
21. **KILLIAN'S DEAD** ** 5.6
22. **DECK CHAIRS ON THE TITANIC.** **** 5.10a/b
22B **LIFE RAFT** * 5.11a (top rope)
25. **BROWN CLOUD ARETE.** *** 5.10b PG-13

GOLDEN CLIFFS * BROWN CLOUD CRAGS * Left Side

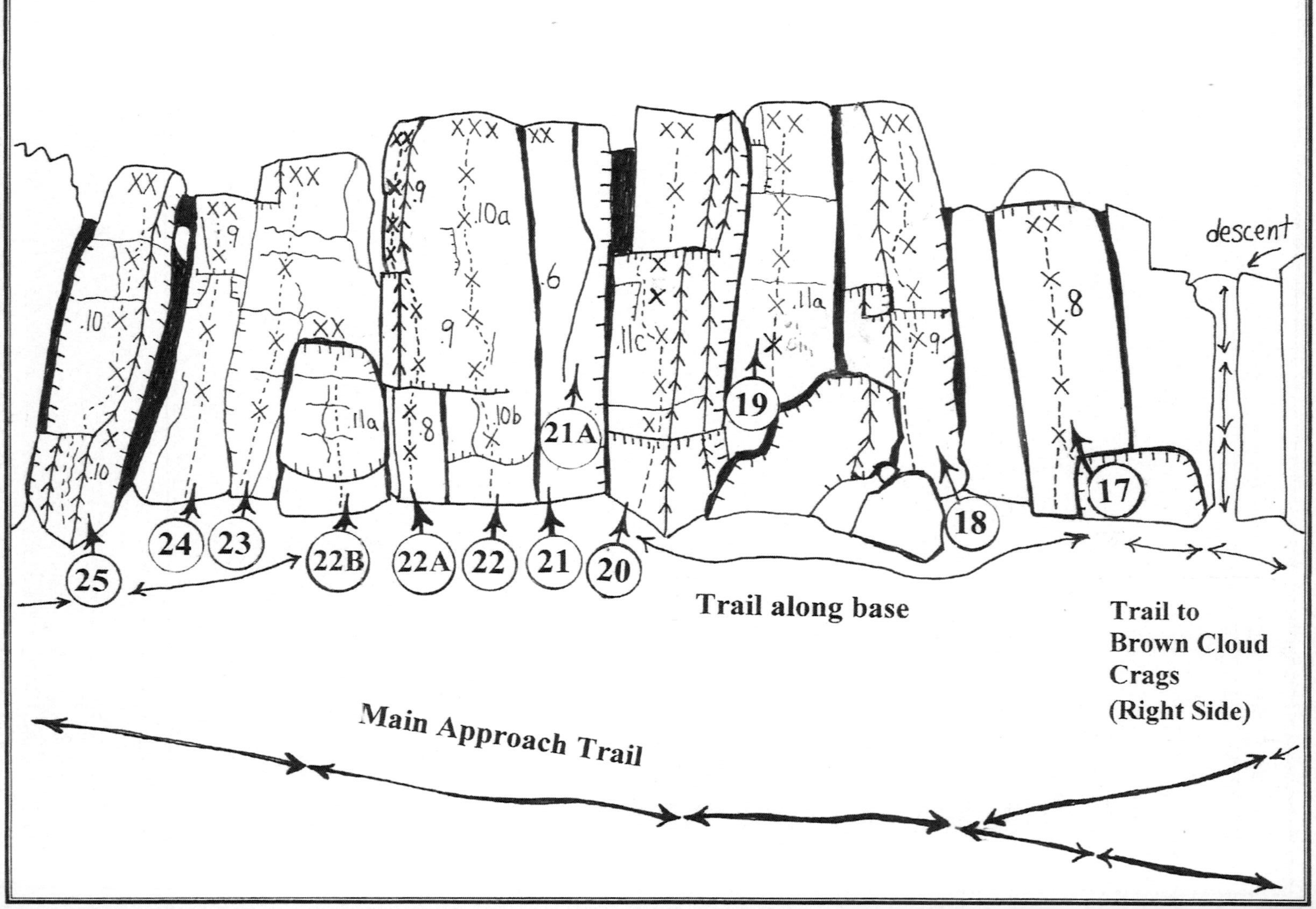

GOLDEN CLIFFS * BROWN CLOUD CRAGS * Left Side

To access these climbs, follow the main approach trail to the base of **This Ain't Naturita Pilgrim** at the **Overhang Area** (see following page 41). Walk right (east) along the base for 50 feet to **Brown Cloud Arete**. Continue right to the climb of your choice. It is possible to follow the approach trail to the **Brown Cloud Crags - Right Side** (see page 35) and walk left (west) to **Interface** (the rightmost route on this page).

17. **INTERFACE.** ** 5.8 4 bolts / 2 bolt anchor. Start from a ledge & clip the 1st bolt. It is possible to start below & left on the ledge & climb up the face to 1st bolt. Climb a short, enjoyable face. F.A.: Rick Leitner - 1990. Retro-bolted in December 2007.

18. **TENACIOUS.** * 5.9 4 bolts / 2 Goldshuts. This route ascends a short east-facing wall starting along a prow or arete. The crux is past the 1st bolt. Gain a small ledge & move right onto the face leading to the anchor below the top. First ascent by Charles Tabor and friends in 1993.

19. **JOLOBEE.** ** 5.10d/11a 5 bolts / 2 bolts & chains. Start from a ledge & ascend a narrow face via small holds. Use a thin seam in a small left-facing corner, past the last bolt, or stay right on the face for greater difficulty. F.A.: Mark Rolofson & Dianne Barrow in Spring 1994.

20. **BULLET THE BROWN CLOUD.** *** 5.11c 6 bolts / 2 mussy hooks. This route ascends a vertical west face using the arete. Climb past a horizontal break to 1st bolt. Follow the arete, past 2nd bolt, moving up the right side & back onto the left side at 3rd bolt. A desperate crux leads up the arete & then left onto the face. Gain a big ledge. Finish up a short face. F.A.: Ken Trout, Rick Leitner & Brian Kelligan - 1990.

21A. **JOHN ADAM'S ADAMS APPLE.** **? 5.7 Medium nuts & cams to #4 Friend / 2 Fixe rings. Climb a crack that leans to the right.

21. **KILLIAN'S DEAD.** ** 5.6 Medium to large nuts & cams / 2 Fixe rings. Ascend a jam crack. The crack becomes wide & turns into a chimney. F.A.: Rick Berk & Dave Hart in 1987.

22. **DECK CHAIRS ON THE TITANIC.** **** 5.10a/b 6 bolts / 3 bolts & mussy hooks. This spectacular route ascends a 60 foot high block that is detached from the rim. Start with a small bulge protected by the 1st bolt to reach a horizontal break & the 2nd bolt. An easier start climbs the crack to the left to reach the horizontal break. Continue up a near vertical face via sustained moves with small holds to reach the anchor just below the top of the large block. First ascent by Ken Trout and Rick Leitner in 1990.

22A **BOW OF THE TITANIC** (A.k.a.: **Punkin Puss & Mushmouse**) *** 5.9 7 bolts / 2 mussy hooks. Start left of **Deck Chairs On The Titanic** & just left of a crack. Climb a juggy face, past 2 bolts to a horizontal break. Continue up to the face, past 2 more bolts, to a ledge & a narrow west-facing prow. Ascend the prow (a narrow face with an arete on each side) to the anchor below the top. F.A.: Mike Cichon led it without bolts, with very marginal protection, in Fall 2006. Bolted by Ken Trout & Marsha Trout on February 1, 2008.

22B. **LIFE RAFT.** * 5.11a Top-rope / 2 bolts without lowering rings. Climb the face up a 25 ft. high block. Scramble up the block's back (north) side to access the 2 bolt anchor or top-rope off the anchor of **Bow Of The Titanic** & clip into the bolts on top of **Life Raft** as a directional.

23. **WINDY.** * 5.8 PG-13 3 bolts, plus small-medium nuts & cams / 2 Fixe rings. Start with a thin right-leaning crack past the 1st bolt to a stance in shallow right-facing corner. Continue up the 2nd bolt & climb a face to a small ledge & the anchor just below the top.

24. **PEE ON D.** * 5.9 3 bolts / 2 mussy hooks. A small-medium cam may be useful before 2nd bolt. Start from the left and climb up right to 1st bolt. Ascend a face or use the crack on the right to below a small roof. Reach the last bolt above the roof. Climb directly over the roof for a crux finish or avoid it by climbing the crack to the right.

25. **BROWN CLOUD ARETE.** *** 5.10b PG-13 4 bolts / 2 Fixe rings. Stick clip is useful for the 1st bolt. A bulging start with two aretes gains a small ledge. Ascend a vertical face up the left side of the arete with committing run-outs. Expect to get your feet above the bolts. F.A.: Dennis McCarron in 1994.

GOLDEN CLIFFS * OVERHANG AREA

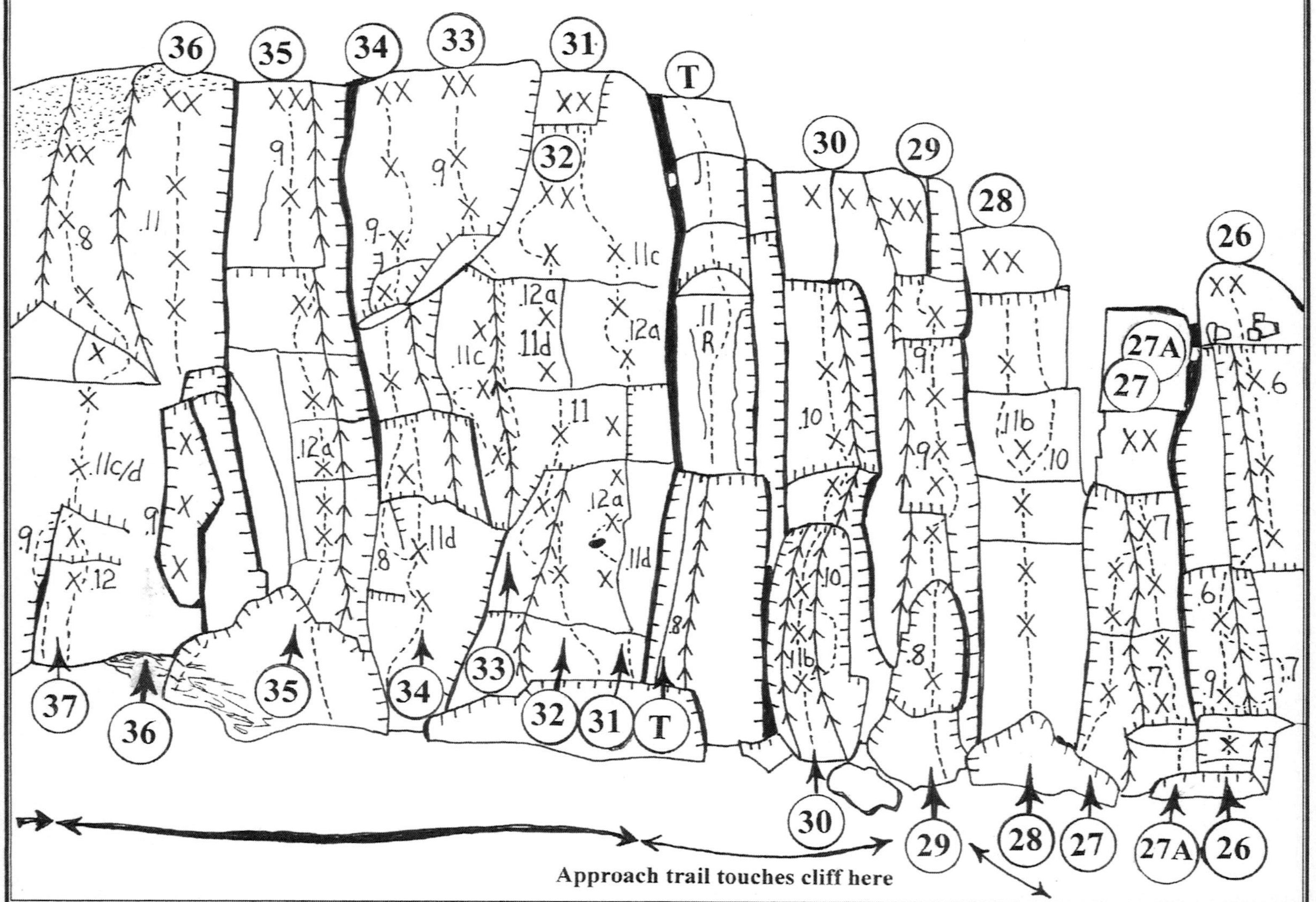

GOLDEN CLIFFS * OVERHANG AREA

The first spot where the approach trail almost touches the base of the cliff is below **This Ain't Naturita, Pilgrim** on the **Overhang Wall**. From the base of this climb it is possible to walk back right along the base to access the routes on the **Brown Cloud Crags - Left Side** (see previous page 39).

26. **WHOLLY HOLEY.** * 5.9 or 5.7 6 bolts / 2 hooks. Pull over a small crux roof at 2nd bolt or avoid it on the right. Continue up moderate climbing & move slightly right onto the arete. Finish up the arete to gain a ledge with a block & the anchor. F.A.: Alan Nelson in 2002.

27A. **IVORY TOWER.** ** 5.7 4 bolts / 2 mussy hooks. Medium gear (a #1.5- 2 Friend) is useful above 1st bolt. Pull over a small crux bulge along a left-facing crack corner. Move left & climb the face with a second crux past last bolt. F.A.: Charles Tabor & friends in 1993.

27. **SLOPING FOREHEAD.** ** 5.7 4 bolts / 2 mussy hooks. Climb a face just left of a blunt arete, past 3 bolts. Turn the arete & share the last bolt & crux on **Ivory Tower**. F.A.: Charles Tabor & friends in 1993.

28. **FABULOUS FLYING CARR'S ROUTE.** ** 5.10a or 5.11 5 bolts / 2 chains anchor. This climb is 5.11 if you stay close to and slightly left of the 4th bolt. It is only 5.10a if you climb this section off right of the bolts. F.A.: Mike and Tom Carr in 1990?

29. **THIS AIN'T NATURITA, PILGRIM.** *** 5.9+ 6 bolts / 2 mussy hooks. A short prow leads to a good ledge. Balance up a face, left of the arete, using several thin horizontal breaks. Gain a shelf & last bolt. Finish up an easy crack. F.A.: Ken Trout in 1990.

30. **SMEAR ME A BEER.** *** 5.10c or 5.11b 6 bolts / 2 chains. The start is 5.11b by climbing directly up the rounded prow. It is 5.10 by starting to the right to reach 2nd bolt & then move left onto the prow. Climb the arete's left side to finish. F.A.: Dennis McCarron - 1994.

T. **SERIOUS PLAY.** **? 5.11 R RPs to medium gear. Climb a thin crack just right of the left-facing corner, that is the easier start for **Mr. Rooster ...**, to a ledge. Ascend a crux face with a thin seam. Pull over a small roof & continue up the face. F.A. : Mike Cichon - Fall 2006.

31. **MR. ROOSTER STRUTS HIS STUFF.** *** 5.12a/b 8 bolts / 2 hooks. A sustained & technical climb. A thin seam leads past 1st bolt. Reach left to a pothole. At 2nd bolt, step back right & climb the seam to a small shelf. A crux, at 5th bolt, high steps onto the shelf using tiny crimpers. Pumpy bulging moves ease off below the top. The start was originally avoided by climbing an easy left-facing corner to the right. F.A.: Dan Hare & Moe Hershoff - Feb. 1999. F.A. with direct start & finish: Mark Rolofson, Keith Ainsworth & Ken Trout - March 6, 2002.

32. **MRS. HEN PLACES A PECK.** **** 5.12a 6 bolts / 2 rings. A moderate start gradually becomes more difficult as the wall overhangs above 2nd bolt. Ascend a fingery seam past 4th bolt. The crux at 5th bolt, involves crimpers & deadpoints. F.A. Ken Trout in 1990.

33. **MR. PEERY TAKES A BOW.** ** 5.11c 7 bolts / 2 mussy hooks. Clip the first 2 bolts on **Mrs. Hen Places A Peck** & then climb the hand crack past 3rd bolt. Move onto the overhung crux arete at 4th bolt, just before gaining the ledge above the hand crack. It is also possible to move onto the ledge & then traverse right off the ledge to gain the crux moves up the arete. This variation is less sustained & not as exciting. Climb the arete to a ledge. Move left over a tiny roof. Finish up a slab. F.A: Richard Wright & Anna Brandonburg Schroeder - Sept. 1996.

34. **HERE TODAY, GONE TOMORROW.** * 5.9- or 5.11d? 7 bolts / 2 chains. #.5-.75 cam provides additional pro past 2nd bolt. The harder variation ascends a bulging face past 2nd bolt. The easier variation steps left & climbs a right-facing corner past 3rd bolt. At 4th bolt, step right onto the face. Pull over a tricky small roof at 5th & 6th bolt. Finish up an steep slab. F.A.: Dennis McCarron - 1994.

35. **HANDLE THIS HARD ONE.** *** 5.12a 6 bolts / Fixe rings. Climb the rounded arete using the shallow, rounded seam to the left. Gain a ledge above 5th bolt & finish up easier terrain. This climb offers an unusual sequence of technical moves. F.A: Dennis McCarron - 1994.

36. **TORA, TORA, TORA.** ** 5.11a/b 6 bolts / 2 bolt anchor. Climb a crack to a large ledge. Ascend an intricate vertical face with the crux past the 5th bolt. First ascent by Tod Anderson in 1993.

37. **MR. SQUIRREL PLACES A NUT.** **** 5.11d 7 bolts / 2 mussy hooks. See the following page 43 for a detailed route description.

26. **WHOLLY HOLEY.** * 5.9 or 5.7

27A. **IVORY TOWER.** ** 5.7

28. **FABULOUS FLYING CARR'S ROUTE.** ** 5.10a or 5.11

29. **THIS AIN'T NATURITA, PILGRIM.** *** 5.9+

30. **SMEAR ME A BEER.** *** 5.10c or 5.11b

31. **MR. ROOSTER STRUTS HIS STUFF.** (A.k.a.: **Chicken Heart**) *** 5.12a/b

32. **MRS. HEN PLACES A PECK.** **** 5.12a

36. **TORA, TORA, TORA.** ** 5.11a/b

37. **MR. SQUIRREL PLACES A NUT.** **** 5.11d 7 bolts / 2 hooks. The direct start on the face right of 1st bolt is 5.12. A tricky crux at 3rd bolt, pulls past a small bulge & up a face to jugs below the 5 foot roof. Pull the roof by hand traversing left along the lip from its right end. Clip 6th bolt & pull over the lip. Finish up easier run-out terrain. F.A.: Ken Trout, Guy Lords & Mike Carr - 1990.

38. **OFF LINE.** * 5.8 PG-13 4 bolts / 2 bolt anchor. Nuts & cams provide additional protection. Start up the arete or in the corner. Pull past a small roof & climb double cracks.

39. **IN BETWEEN THE LINES.** ** 5.9- PG-13 4 bolts / 2 bolt anchor. Climb a steep face with a crux above 2nd bolt. It is easier if you use the crack to the right. F.A.: Dennis McCarron in 1994.

40. **SIDELINES.** ** 5.9+ 4 bolts / 2 bolt anchor. Small-medium gear provides additional pro before 2nd bolt. Clip the 1st bolt on **In Between the Lines** & move left & up. Climb short right-facing corner to a ledge. Ascend a steep face with a crux at the 3rd bolt.

Dianne Dallin leading **DECK CHAIRS ON THE TITANIC** (**** 5.10a/b) on the Brown Cloud Crags - Left Side. Photo by Mike Dallin.

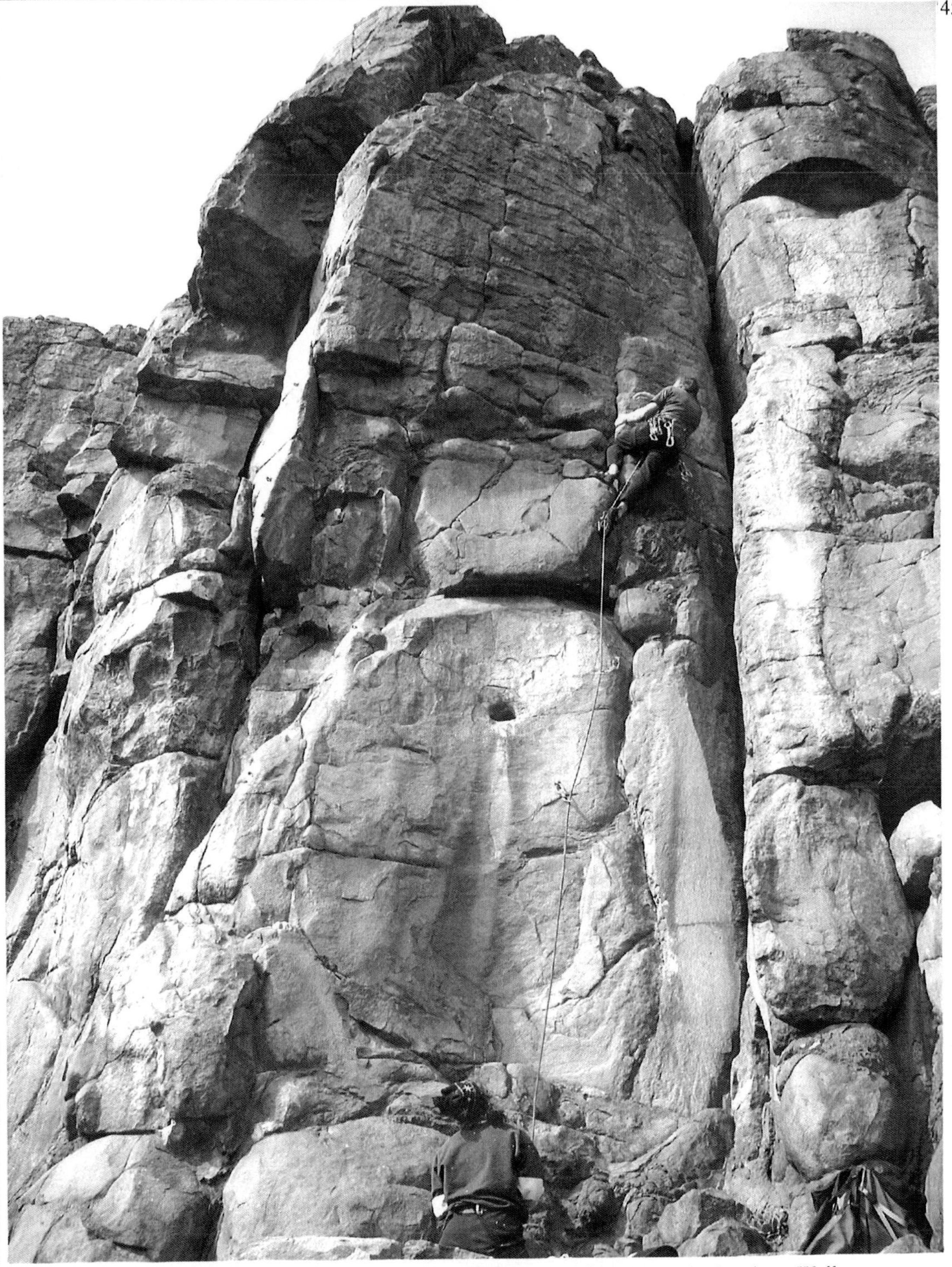

The author leading **MR. ROOSTER STRUTS HIS STUFF** (*** 5.12a/b) on the Overhang Wall.
MRS. HEN PLACES A PECK (**** 5.12a) is immediately left. See cover photo. Photo by Mike Dallin.

GOLDEN CLIFFS * TABLE TOP AREA * RIGHT SIDE

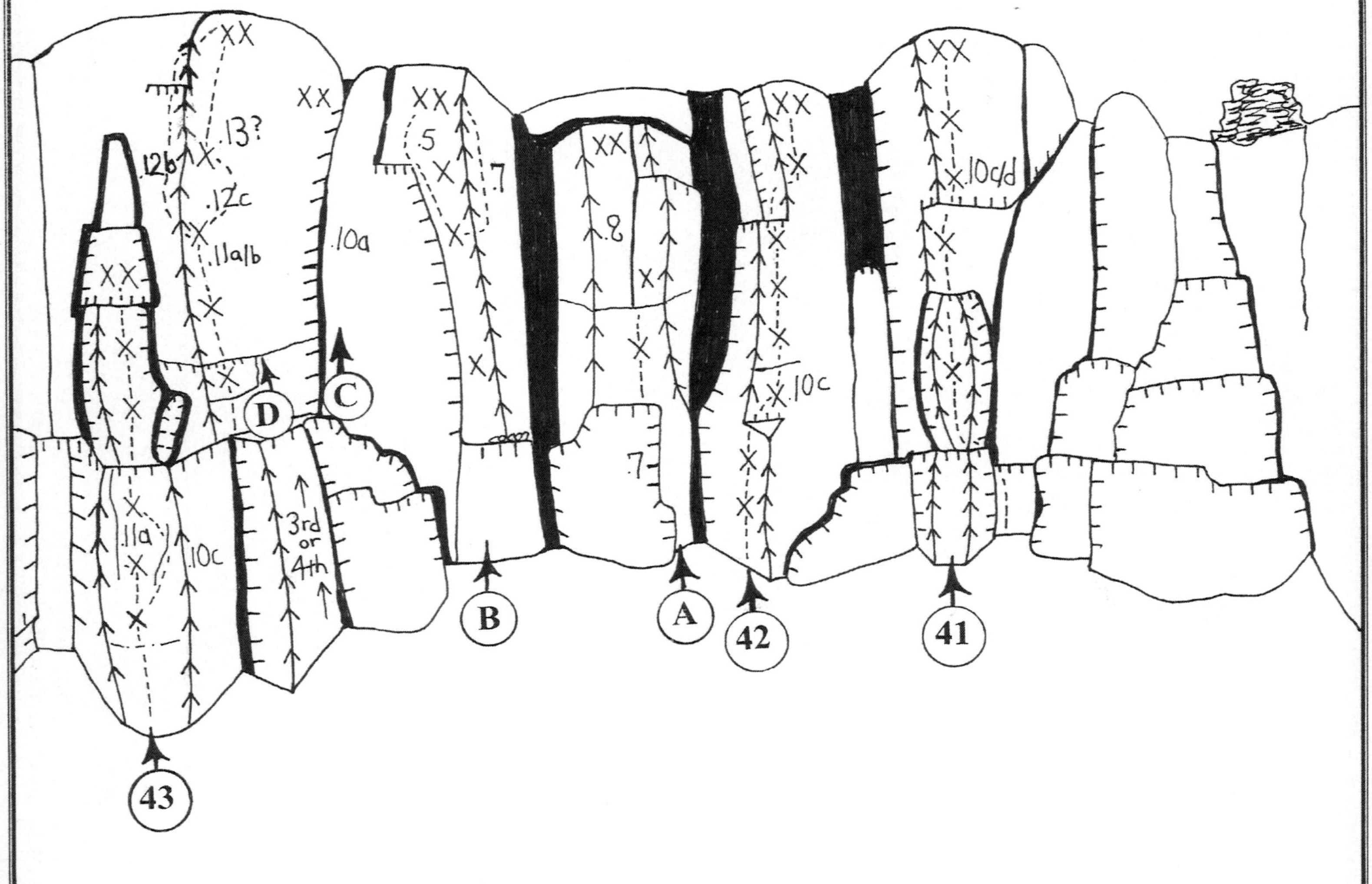

GOLDEN CLIFFS * TABLE TOP AREA * RIGHT SIDE

This south-facing section of the cliff is just left of the **Overhang Area - Left Side** & stretches for 300 feet to the west (left). The **Table Top Area** has numerous 5.10 routes, some notable 5.11 to 5.12a routes & two of the easier climbs on the mountain.

41. **BEER BARREL BUTTRESS.** * 5.10c/d PG-13 4 bolts / 2 rings. This is 30 feet left (west) of **Left Of The Lines** at the **Overhang Area**. Scramble 10 ft. up to a ledge. Climb up a blunt prow to the top of a pillar. Climb a bulging face right of the arete. Clipping the 3rd bolt is committing, with ledge fall potential. The crux is past the 3rd bolt. F.A: Dave Hart & Ernie Moskovics in 1990.

42. **THE GROUND DOESN'T LIE.** *** 5.10c/d 7 bolts / 2 mussy hooks. Start up the arete on the left past the first 2 bolts. Move right onto the face at 3rd bolt. Ascend the vertical face moving slightly left. Gain a stance at 6th bolt. Move up & right to finish up an easy face on the right side of an arete. F.A.: Ken Trout, Mike Carr & Rick Leitner in 1990. Retro-bolted & finish added by Ken Trout in December 2007.

A. **TOAST AND JAM.** * 5.8 2 bolts, a few small-medium stoppers or cams, #2- 3 Friends / 2 rings. This routes climbs a narrow buttress that is separated from the cliff-band by a wide chimney on each side. Begin 8 feet left of **The Ground Doesn't Lie**. Stem up a short right-facing thin crack corner to a ledge & 1st bolt. Face moves leads to 2nd bolt. Ascend the bulging crack to the anchor.
F.A.: Dan Hare & Tom Kohlmann in March 2008.

B. **INTUITION.** * 5.5 to 5.7 3 bolts, a few stoppers (#6-10) or cams / 2 rings. Ascend cracks to a ledge strewn with loose rock & reach the 1st bolt. A thin crack leads to a face with 2 bolts. Finish up the corner on left (5.5) or up the arete on right (5.7) for more excitement.
F.A.: Pete Davis & Dan Hare in February 2008.

C. **THE PLUMBERS CRACK.** ** 5.10a #3 steel nut to a #3. A #4 Friend or larger is optional / 2 Fixe rings. Scramble 20 ft. up to the same ledge as **Pschyasthenia**. Stem & jam up the large dihedral with a crux finish. F.A.: Dan Hare, Cary Griner & Roland Fortin on March 8, 2008.

D. **PSCHYASTHENIA.** ** 5.12b PG-13 4 bolts / 2 Fixe rings. Scramble 20 ft. up a ledge. Ascend the blunt arete up the left side of an overhanging east face. Take caution on the 5.11a moves above the 2nd bolt, because there is ankle breaking fall potential from hitting a shelf. The crux is above the 3rd bolt. This climb would be much more difficult by staying on the face and avoiding reaching around the left side of the arete. This direct face variation has 5.12 moves leading to the last bolt, followed by a crux finish & still awaits a first free ascent.
First ascent: Jason Haas & David Johnson in February 2008.

43. **PIGEON PILE PINNACLE.** * 5.11a or 5.10c 5 bolts / 2 coldshuts. The direct line climbs a vertical face, past 3 bolts, using a thin crack on the left (.11a). The line of least resistance climbs the blunt arete to the right & then moves back left to 3rd bolt (.10c). A moderate finish leads to the anchor below a precarious, perched pinnacle. F.A.: Dennis McCarron in 1994.

GOLDEN CLIFFS
TABLE TOP AREA * RIGHT SIDE

41. **BEER BARREL BUTTRESS.** * 5.10c/d PG-13

A. **TOAST AND JAM.** * 5.8

43. **PIGEON PILE PINNACLE.** * 5.11a or 5.10c

42. **THE GROUND DOESN'T LIE.** *** 5.10c/d

B. **INTUITION.** * 5.5 to 5.7

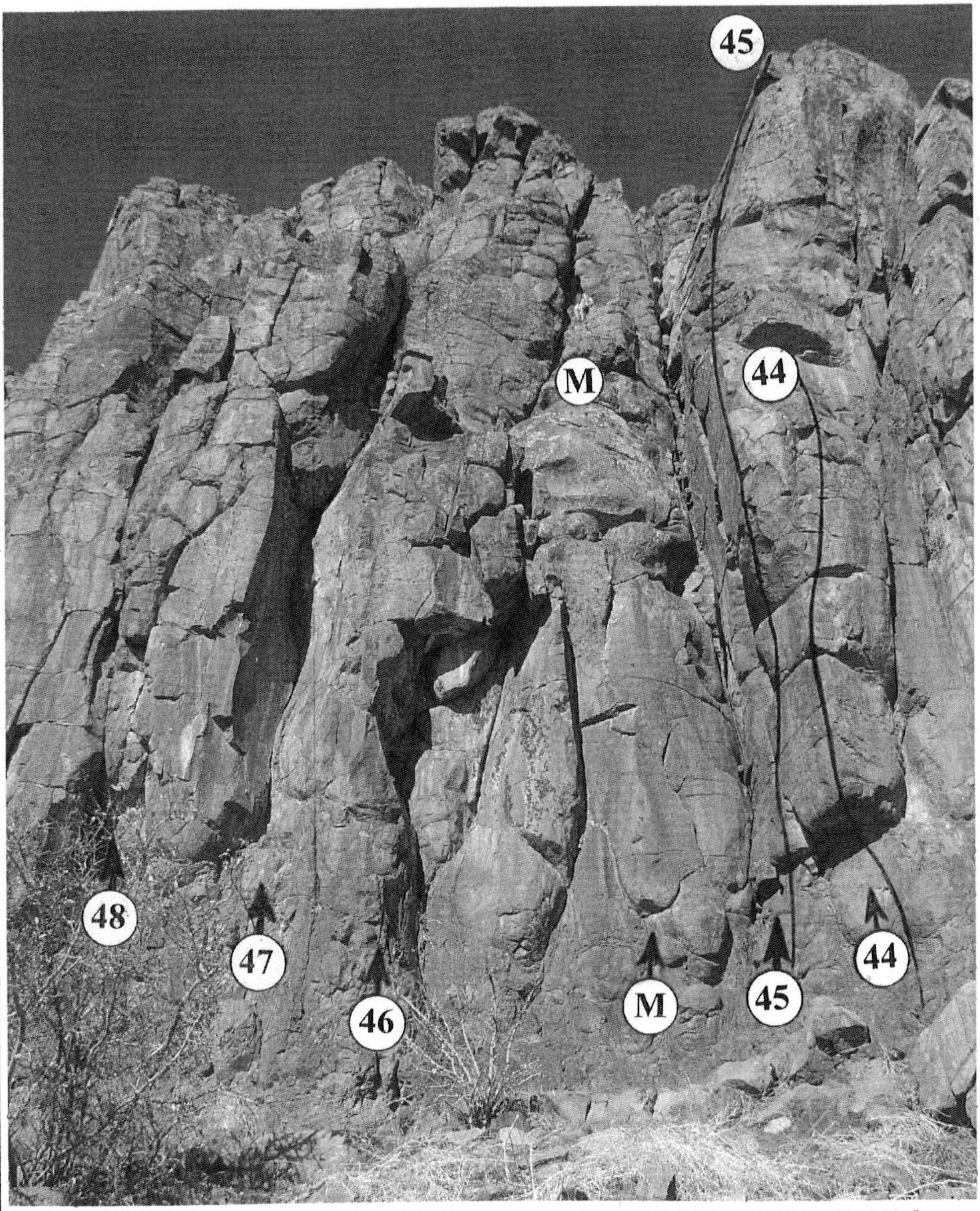

44. **LYING ON THE GROUND.** *** 5.11d/12a

45. **D'S DRY DREAM.** *** 5.10a/b

M. **MOMENT OF WEAKNESS.** ** 5.10c/d

46. **RISKY ONE.** * 5.10c/d

47. **WHISKY RUN.** ** 5.10a/b

48. **UNKNOWN THIN CRACK.** ** 5.11 or 5.12a

GOLDEN CLIFFS * TABLE TOP AREA * CENTER

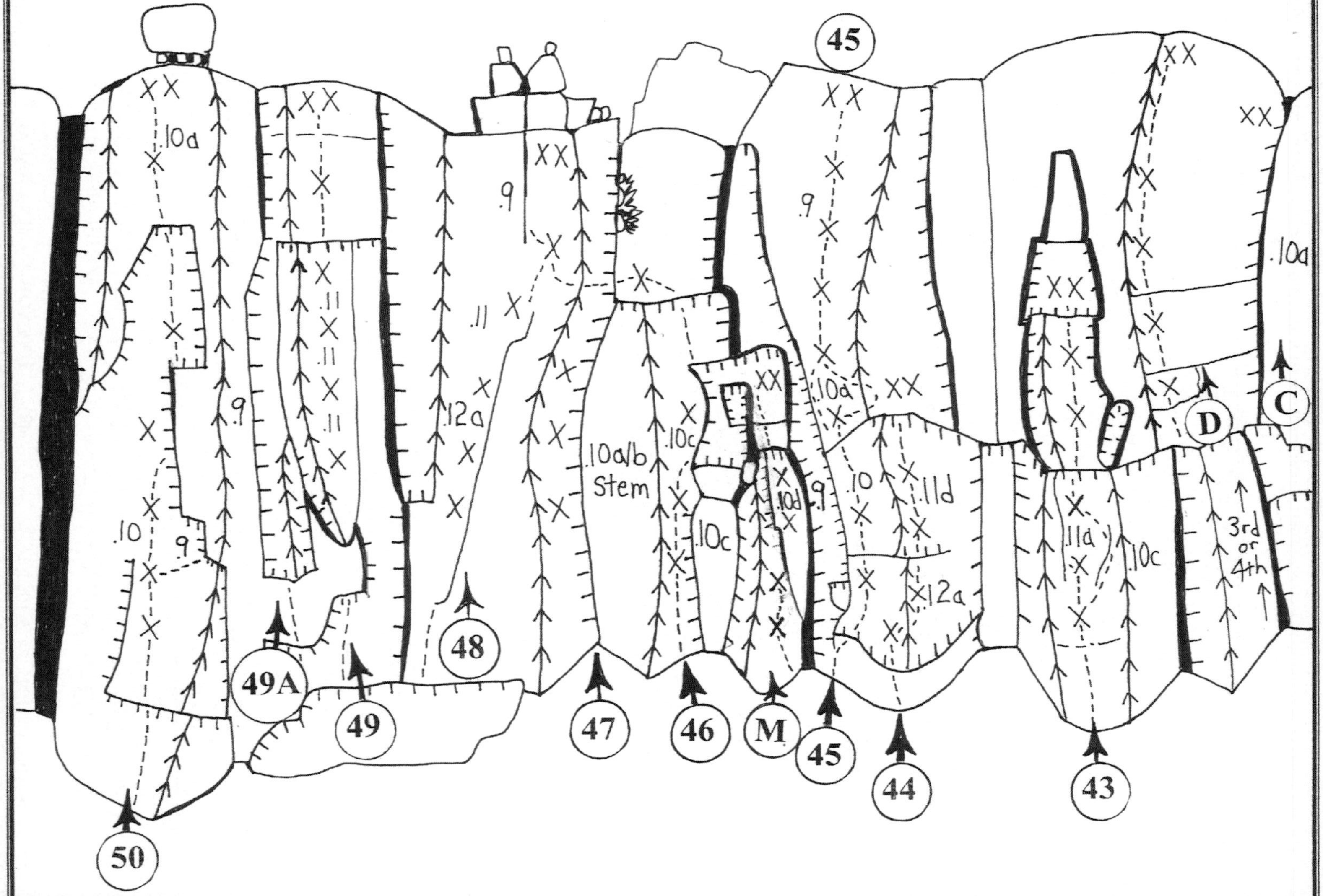

GOLDEN CLIFFS * TABLE TOP AREA * CENTER

C. **THE PLUMBERS CRACK.** ** 5.10a #3 steel nut to a #3. A #4 Friend or larger is optional / 2 Fixe rings. Scramble 20 ft. up to the same ledge as **Pschyasthenia.** Stem & jam up the large dihedral with a crux finish. F.A.: Dan Hare, Cary Griner & Roland Fortin on March 8, 2008.

D. **PSCHYASTHENIA.** ** 5.12b PG-13 4 bolts / 2 Fixe rings. Scramble 20 ft. up a ledge. Ascend the blunt arete up the left side of an overhanging east face. Take caution on the 5.11a moves above the 2nd bolt, because there is ankle breaking fall potential from hitting a shelf. The crux is above the 3rd bolt. This climb would be much more difficult by staying on the face and avoiding reaching around the left side of the arete. This direct face variation has 5.12 moves leading to the last bolt, followed by a crux finish & still awaits a first free ascent.
First ascent: Jason Haas & David Johnson in February 2008.

43. **PIGEON PILE PINNACLE.** * 5.11a or 5.10c 5 bolts / 2 coldshuts. The direct line climbs a vertical face, past 3 bolts, using a thin crack on the left (.11a). The line of least resistance climbs the blunt arete to the right & then moves back left to 3rd bolt (.10c). A moderate finish leads to the anchor below a precarious, perched pinnacle. F.A.: Dennis McCarron - 1994.

44. **LYING ON THE GROUND.** *** 5.11d/12a 4 bolts / 2 rings. Short & stout. Pull over a small bulge & climb the right side of a blunt arete, past the 2nd bolt. Continue up an overhung face that ends on a slab. The climb is 5.12a avoiding the drilled pocket, above 1st bolt.
F.A.: Guy Lords & Ken Trout in 1990.

45. **D'S DRY DREAM.** *** 5.10a/b 7-8 bolts / 2 rings. It is possible to clip 1st bolt on **Lying On The Ground** for lower protection. A reachy 5.10b (or harder) crux past 2nd bolt is climbed up the bulging face. Use the crack to the left and this section is easier. At 3rd bolt, move right on a horizontal break to a stance on the arete or continue up the crack to the 4th bolt. A slab leads to the top. F.A.: Dennis McCarron in 1994.

M. **MOMENT OF WEAKNESS.** * 5.10c/d 4 bolts / 2 Fixe rings. This route climbs the face just left of **D's Dry Dream**. Ascend a left-leaning edge or seam to below 3rd bolt. Balance up the face & stem left to a small right-facing corner. Move up the corner using the arete to reach a shelf past the last bolt. Move up left to a huge detached block & the anchor to its right. F.A.: Dan Hare & Tom Kohlmann in April 2008.

46. **RISKY ONE.** * 5.10c/d 5 bolts / 2 Fixe rings. Climb the right side of a blunt arete to a small roof. Pull over the left side of the roof and continue up the face to a good ledge. Traverse left & join **Whisky Run**. F.A.: Alan Nelson & Richard Wright on June 4, 1997.

47. **WHISKY RUN.** ** 5.10a/b 4-5 bolts / 2 Fixe rings. Stem up a V-shaped dihedral with some jams in the back. Gain a ledge on the right & 4th bolt. Traverse left around an arete & ascend a face to the anchor. F.A.: Alan Nelson and Richard Wright on June 4, 1997.

48. **UNKNOWN THIN CRACK.** ** 5.11 or 5.12a 5 bolts / 2 Fixe rings. Climb the thin crack up the face (.12a). This route is much easier (5.11) by stemming left to a crack corner, past the first 2 bolts.

49. **CHICK FILET.** *** 5.11b to 5.11d 5 bolts / 2 chains. This climb follows a thin crack right of an arete. There are three choices to climb this route. Use the thin crack & the arete for maximum difficulty. Climb the thin crack, the arete, & also use a thin crack around the left side of the arete. The easiest possibility is to climb the thin crack & use holds along the wide crack corner to the right.
F.A.: Alan Nelson & Richard Wright on June 4, 1997.

49A. **THE JIZZLER.** **? 5.9 Medium nuts & cams / 2 chains. Climb the crack corner just left of **Chick Filet** to its anchor.

50. **HENRY SPIES THE LINE.** *** 5.10a/b 6 bolts / 2 Fixe rings. This climb ascends a narrow west-facing wall. Clip the 1st bolt off a tiny ledge. Move up a short right-facing corner. Climbing directly up the face past 2nd bolt is the 5.10b crux. An easier variation traverses right to reach a tiny ledge & a thin crack. Both variations join past 3rd bolt. Ascend a small right-facing crack corner to a small overlap. Pull over the overlap, past 5th bolt, to a good ledge. Climb a vertical face past the last bolt to the anchor. First ascent by Dennis McCarron in 1994.

GOLDEN CLIFFS * TABLE TOP AREA * LEFT SIDE

50. **HENRY SPIES THE LINE.** *** 5.10a/b 6 bolts / 2 Fixe rings. This climb ascends a narrow west-facing wall. Clip the 1st bolt off a tiny ledge. Move up a short right-facing corner. Climbing directly up the face past 2nd bolt is the 5.10b crux. An easier variation traverses right to reach a tiny ledge & a thin crack. Both variations join past 3rd bolt. Ascend a small right-facing crack corner to a small overlap. Pull over the overlap, past 5th bolt, to a good ledge. Climb a vertical face past the last bolt to the anchor. F.A.: Dennis McCarron in 1994.

50A. **KEVIN SPIES THE LINE.** *** 5.6 5 bolts / 2 Metolius Rap hangers. #1-1.5 Friend or red & orange Aliens provide additional pro before 1st bolt. This is possibly the most popular climb at the Golden Cliffs. Start from a small ledge 2 feet above the ground, right of a large block & left of an arete. Either climb directly up the face along a shallow seam or climb onto a ledge atop the large block & then step right onto the face. The crux is getting past the 1st bolt using the thin seam crack to reach a block on the arete. Continue to a good ledge & 3rd bolt above. Ascend a juggy face with cracks on each side of it. Pull onto a small shelf above the last bolt & reach the anchor. F.A.: Unknown.

51. **TABLE TOP.** ** 5.10b 4 bolts / 2 Fixe rings. F.A.: Tod Anderson & Dave Field in 1990?

52. **MIND MANTLE ARETE.** ** 5.11b (arete) or 5.10 5 bolts / 2 Fixe rings. This route ascends a narrow east-facing wall. Climb up the arete on the left for a direct line with 5.11 moves or find an easier way up thin cracks right of the 2nd & 3rd bolts. F.A.: Dennis McCarron in 1994.

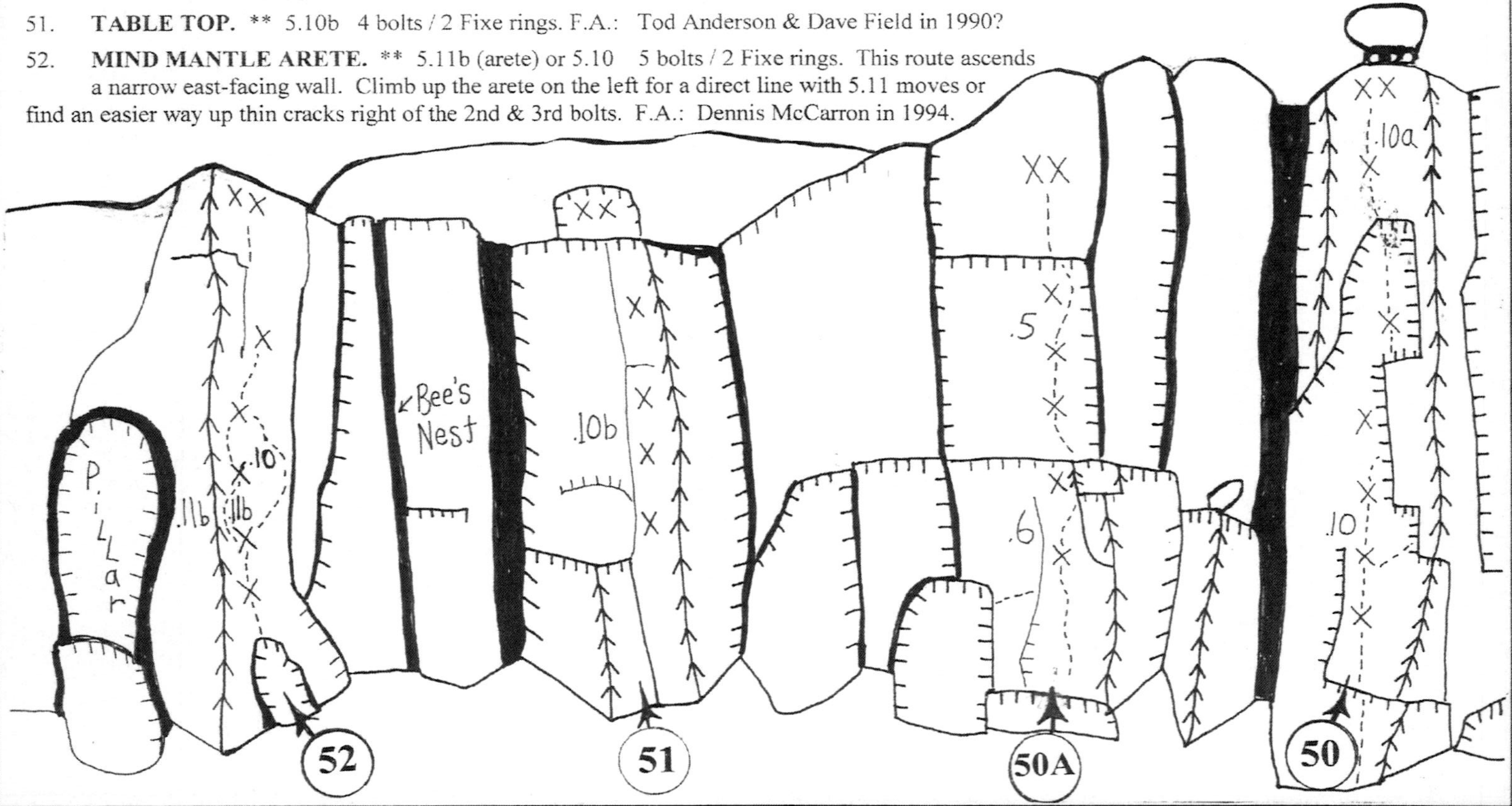

50A. **KEVIN SPIES THE LINE.** *** 5.6 The climber is at the 3rd bolt.

51. **TABLE TOP.** ** 5.10b

41. **BEER BARREL BUTTRESS.** * 5.10c/d PG-13

42. **THE GROUND DOESN'T LIE.** *** 5.10c/d

45. **D'S DRY DREAM.** *** 5.10a/b

49A. **THE JIZZLER.** **? 5.9

50. **HENRY SPIES THE LINE.** *** 5.10a/b The climber is top-roping a crack just left.

50A. **KEVIN SPIES THE LINE.** *** 5.6

UNDER THE TABLE AREA

53. **ALAN'S SEAM.** *** 5.10a

54. **UNDER THE TABLE.** ** 5.10 or 5.11d

55A. **UNKNOWN ARETE.** 5.7 to 5.10

TRADLANDS

A. **RESIDENT BUSH.** ** 5.8 to 5.10a

G. **X IT.** ** 5.10a

K. **LITTLE OX.** * 5.9 PG-13

E. **LIAR LIAR.** 5.7

I. **BIG O FLYER.** * 5.8 PG-13

GOLDEN CLIFFS * UNDER THE TABLE AREA

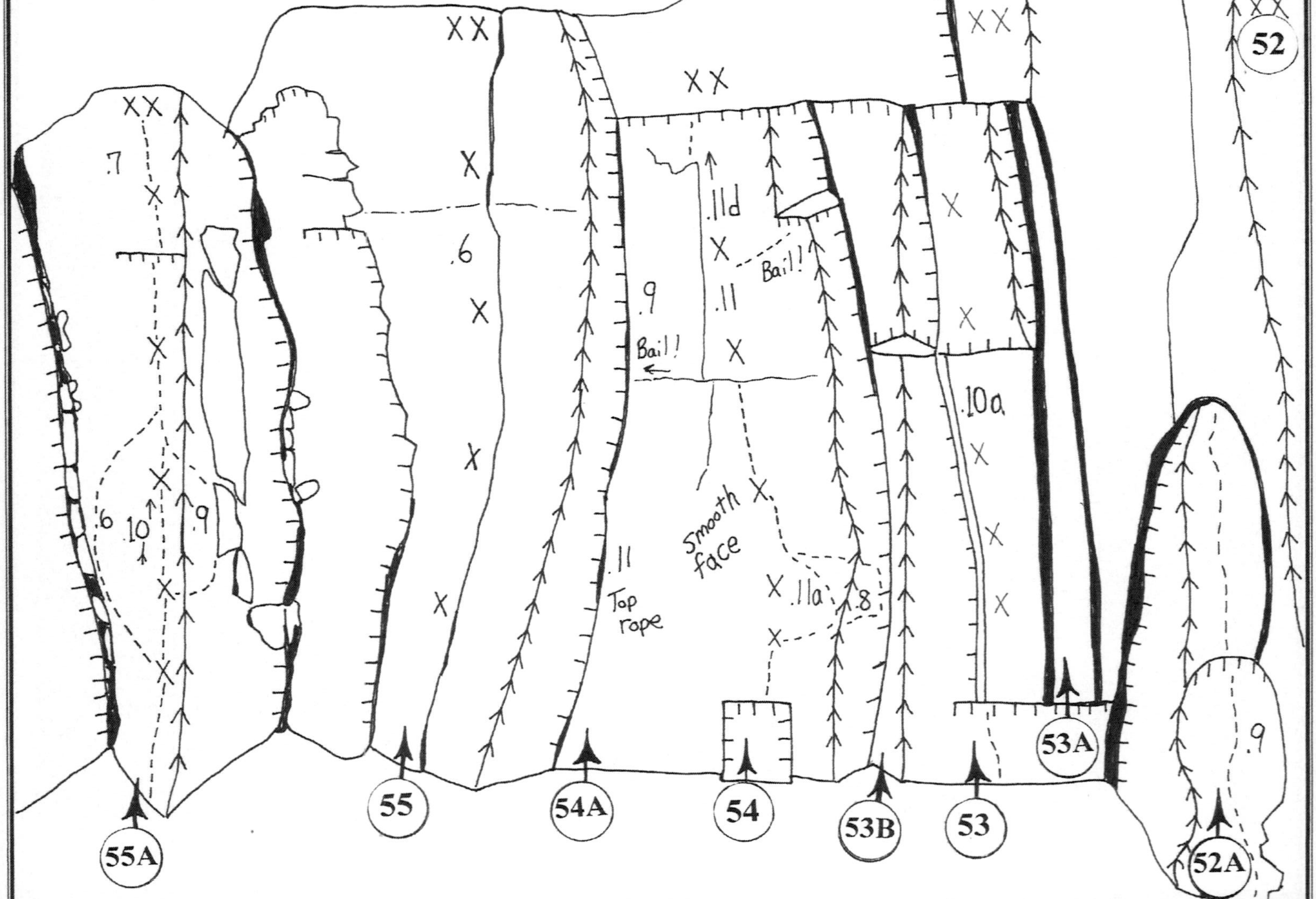

GOLDEN CLIFFS * UNDER THE TABLE AREA

Natural rockfall has occurred here. In Spring 1998, big blocks forming an entire route fell down in a big rock slide. In December 1999, a new route named **Under The Table** was established on the freshly exposed, cleaned rock that used to be under the surface. In March 2008, a large block fell off the **Unknown Arete** on the left side of wall. Could this entire route fall down? Freeze thaw conditions in the Spring, wet weather, or small earthquakes or tremors could potentially contribute to future rockfall.

52. **MIND MANTLE ARETE.** ** 5.11b (arete) or 5.10 Only the anchors are shown. See page 52 for the description & topo drawing of this climb.

52A. **PILLAR.** B5.9

53A. **MEAT IS MURDER.** * 5.8 Gear to 3.5" (#4 Friend)/ 2 bolt anchor. Climb double cracks to the anchor on **Alan's Seam**.
F.A.: Scott Berk & Dave Hart in 1987.

53. **ALAN'S SEAM.** *** 5.10a 5 bolts / 2 bolt anchor. Liebacking & face moves lead up this shallow crack.
First ascent by Alan Nelson in 2001.

53B. **UNNAMED CRACK.** *? 5.7

54. **UNDER THE TABLE.** ** 5.10 or 5.11d 5 bolts / 2 Fixe rings. This route ascends clean, smooth rock left after a major rock slide in early 1998 that removed a previous route. The climb is 5.10 if you wander up the line of least resistance, that finishes either right or left of the last 2 bolts. The direct finish (5.11d) climbs a hairline seam next to the bolts. The direct start staying just left of the first 2 bolts probably hasn't gone free yet. First ascent by Moe Hershoff, Claire Mearns and Dan Hare in December 1999.

54A. **DIHEDRAL.** *? 5.11 Top rope to anchor on **Under The Table**.

55. **TOOTSIE ROLL.** ** 5.6 4 bolts / 2 bolt anchor. This route climbs a perfect thin crack that is possible to climb with gear.

55A. **UNKNOWN ARETE.** (A.k.a.: **BM ROUTE.**) 5.7 to 5.10 5 bolts / 2 Fixe rings. There is a 5.10b crux past the 2nd bolt if this route is climbed directly up the face. Use the crack to the right up the detached block and this section is 5.9. Climb the corner on the left and this section is easy 5th class. This route gets my vote for the most likely climb to fall down on North Table Mountain. A large block fell off this route in March 2008, due to natural causes. This route gets done quite often, but it isn't recommended. F.A.: Unknown.

GOLDEN CLIFFS * THE TRADLANDS

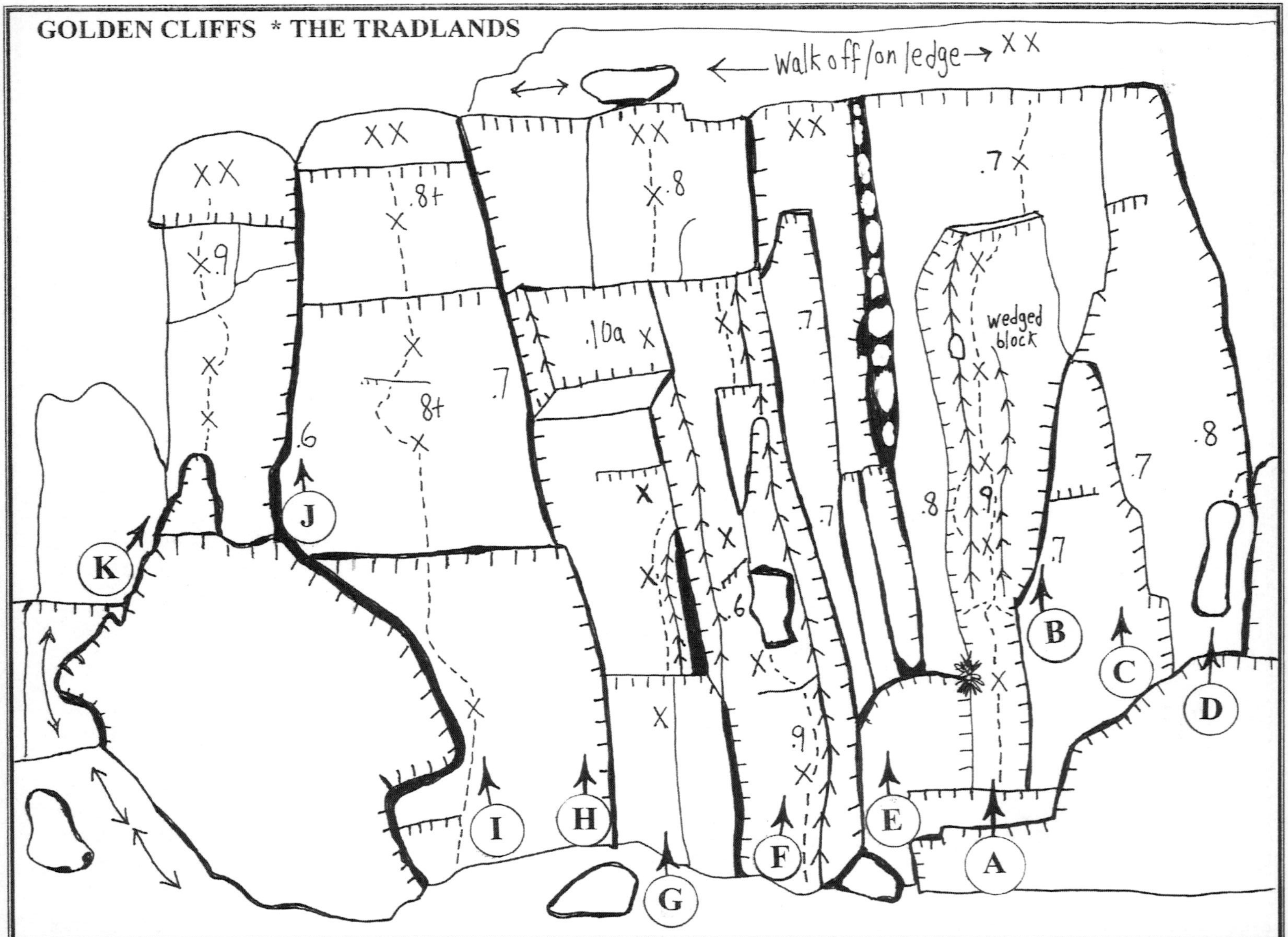

GOLDEN CLIFFS * THE TRADLANDS

This 60 ft. wide section of cliff can be crowded on a busy day, in spite of the fact that it could described as mediocre. There are two good moderate cracks & two sport routes worthy of two stars. It is easy to access the anchors for these climbs by walking around the left (west) side of the cliff and uphill on a trail, where there is a large break in the cliff-band. After 50 feet, walk east on a large ledge, just below the top of this cliff. Most of the anchors are just below the ledge. It is easy to walk to the right side of the ledge to the anchor for **Resident Bush**. Tie off a large boulder to safely reach down to the anchor for **X It**.

A. **RESIDENT BUSH.** ** 5.8 to 5.10a 6 bolts / 2 bolt anchor. Start from a ledge & move up the right crack of **Traditions** to clip 1st bolt, just right of a bush in a right-facing corner. The direct start up the face, past the 1st bolt, is the crux & can be avoided by climbing up **Traditions** to reach 2nd bolt. Ascend a blunt prow. It is easier to climb up the left side of the prow along a shallow crack & more difficult to stay just right of the 2nd & 3rd bolts. Gain a ledge & the last bolt. A short face leads to a large ledge & the anchor. This anchor is safely accessible for setting up a top-rope, because it is possible to easily walk onto this ledge from its left (west) side. F.A.: Alan Nelson in January 2001.

B. **TRADITIONS.** ** 5.7 Small nuts to 2.5 Friend to 1 bolt / 2 Fixe rings. Climb the crack corner that is just right of **Resident Bush**. The crack starts out as a hand crack & thins down, passing a small overlap Reach a small shelf & move up left along a short shallow seam to join **Resident Bush** at the last bolt. It is also possible step right & finish up **Chopless**. First ascent by Alan Nelson in January 2001.

C. **CHOPLESS.** ** 5.7 Small to medium nuts & cams / 2 Fixe rings. Start by scrambling up the ledge. Climb a corner with a thin crack, that is right of **Traditions**. First ascent by Alan Nelson in Fall 2000.

D. **CORN FLAKE.** 5.8 R Medium to #4" cams / 2 Fixe rings. Top-rope recommended. Start on the right end of the ledge. Climb up a short, scary, exfoliated flake & then follow a right-facing hand & fist crack corner that angles up left. First ascent by Alan Nelson in January 2001.

E. **LIAR LIAR.** 5.7 #.5 Alien (green) to #3 Friend (1/2" to 3" gear) / 2 Fixe rings. Scamble up to a ledge 20 ft. above the ground. Climb double thin cracks (the right of which is formed by a pillar) to a small ledge. Continue past a short thin section to a small right-facing corner. Follow the corner that widens from finger to hand size & ends atop a large pillar. Reach the anchor 5 ft. higher & just below the large ledge. This route offers fun crack climbing, but it is composed of large detached pillars that could eventually fall down. F.A.: Alan Nelson in January 2001.

F. **STARTLED.** * 5.9 5 bolts / 2 Fixe rings. A crux start, past the 1st bolt, climbs a blunt arete with a thin crack on its right side. Reach good jugs before the 2nd bolt. Climb up a scary looking exfoliated flake, to reach the 3rd bolt. Don't get startled! Continue up broken terrain to a ledge & join **X It** at its last bolt. First ascent by Alan Nelson in January 2001.

G. **X IT.** ** 5.10a 5 bolts / 2 Fixe rings. A small medium stopper may be useful between 3rd & 4th bolt. Climb a slab with a wide finger crack, past the 1st bolt, to a ledge. Climb up an arete on the left, past the 2nd bolt, to avoid a chimney section in the crack. Join the crack where it thins down & climb a left-facing corner to a small roof. The crux, past the 4th bolt, climbs the thin crack to get over the roof & reach a ledge. A short face leads past the last bolt to reach the anchor below the top. First ascent by Alan Nelson in January 2001.

H. **LINE IT UP.** *? 5.7 Nuts & cams / 2 rings. Climb a left-facing crack corner between **X It** & **Big O Flyer**. F.A.: Alan Nelson January 2001.

I. **BIG O FLYER.** * 5.8 PG-13 4 bolts / 2 rings. Start with a small bulge leading up the right side of a boulder. Climb a steep face past two ledges. Both the 2nd & 4th bolt are a long reach above the ledge. There is ledge fall potential above the bolts. F.A.: Alan Nelson in Jan. 2001.

J. **OXYMORON.** *? 5.6 Nuts / 2 rings. Climb a right-facing crack corner between **Big O Flyer** & **Little Ox**. F.A.: Alan Nelson in Jan. 2001.

K. **LITTLE OX.** * 5.9 PG-13 3 bolts / 2 Fixe rings. Climb the arete on the left side of the wall. There is a run out with bad fall potential, above the 2nd bolt to reach the 3rd bolt. The crux is past the 3rd bolt. First ascent by Alan Nelson in January 2001.

GOLDEN CLIFFS * MAJOR BOLT ACHIEVEMENT BUTTRESS * SOUTH FACE (or right side)

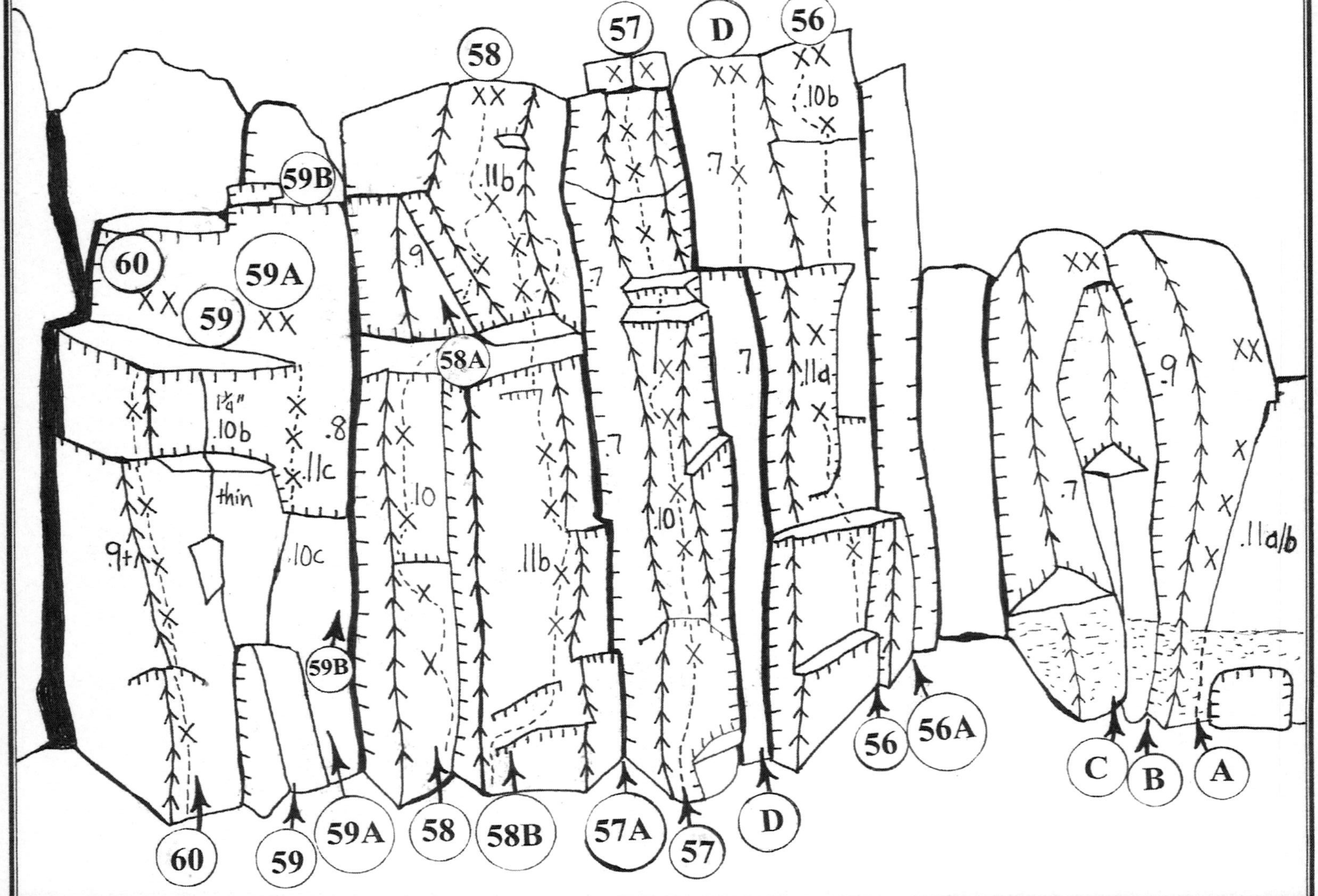

GOLDEN CLIFFS * MAJOR BOLT ACHIEVEMENT BUTTRESS * SOUTH FACE (or right side)

A. **THE MINI ME.** * 5.11a/b 3 bolts / 2 Fixe rings. The shortest climb at the Golden Cliffs. Climb a thin crack using the blunt arete on the left to start. F.A.: Dan Hare & Johnathan Degenhart in April 2000.

B. **BUCHANAN.** * 5.9 #.4 (blue) to 1.5 (orange) Aliens, #6 stopper, #3 Friend optional / 2 Fixe rings. Climb the flared dihedral via a thin crack. The difficulty eases off for the finish, due to a hand crack on the right wall.

C. **NADER.** 5.7 medium to 3" cams / 2 Fixe rings. Climb double thin cracks for a few feet to the top of a wedged block. Continue up a crack into a left facing dihedral that ends on a ledge with the anchor.

56A. **NO MANNERS.** *? 5.9 Gear / 2 Fixe rings. Climb a hand & fist crack up the right side of the east face of the buttress.

56. **OVER THE TOP.** * 5.11a 5 bolts / 2 Fixe rings. This route ascends the bulging east face of the buttress. Climb a short face past the 1st bolt to a large ledge. Stretch up & clip 2nd bolt. Execute a tricky .11a crux to gain a tiny stance in a small corner. Move up to jugs & a small ledge on the left. Climb a bulging face to the anchor below the top. First ascent by Alan Nelson in Spring 2001.

D. **OBLIVIOUS.** *? 5.7 Bring gear to 1 bolt / 2 bolt anchor. Climb a crack corner to a ledge. Finish up a face with 1 bolt. First ascent by Alan Nelson in Spring 2001.

57. **GOOD MAN DAN.** *** 5.10b/c 8 bolts / 2 Fixe rings. Climb the face of the prominent prow to ledges. Moderate climbing leads to the anchor. First ascent by Alan Nelson in Spring 2001.

57A. **LEFT BEHIND.** *? 5.7 Bring gear / 2 bolt anchor. Ascend a crack up the obvious dihedral.

58B. **RESTLESS HEART.** ** 5.11b or 5.11d 7 bolts / 2 bolt anchor. Climb the left side of an arete (.11b) to a ledge. Clip 5th bolt above a small roof. Climb directly over the roof & past 6th bolt for a .11d crux. An easier variation moves right at 5th bolt & up an easy corner. Traverse back left to the 6th bolt. Join **Table Manners** at its last bolt. F.A.: Moe Hershoff, Jim Erickson & Dan Hare in April 2000.

58. **TABLE MANNERS.** * 5.11c 6 bolts / 2 bolt anchor. Start up a left-facing corner. Move up left onto the arete & 3rd bolt. Follow the arete to a ledge. Reach right around a small roof to clip 5th bolt. Turn the lip & climb the face & arete past the last bolt. F.A.: Unknown.

58A. **BAD MANNERS.** *? 5.9 RPs to Friends / 2 bolt anchor. This is a gear variation to **Table Manners**. Climb the left-facing dihedral, that **Table Manners** starts with to the ledge. Finish to the left of **Table Manners**, climbing a left-leaning overhung crack corner. F.A.: Nevada Montagu, Richard Wright in 2001.

59B. **STONEY MIDDLETON.** *? 5.8 Mostly medium gear. Climb the left-facing corner just right of **Broken Arrow** to its anchor or the top

59A. **BROKEN ARROW.** *** 5.11c A few small-medium stoppers & #.4 - 1 Aliens (blue, green, yellow, red) to 3 bolts / 2 Fixe rings. Climb a thin right-leaning crack to its end. Ascend a tricky crux face, past 3 bolts, to a good ledge & the anchor. Avoid stepping right in the easy left-facing crack corner. F.A.: Dan Hare & Claire Mearns in February 2000.

59. **SHADOW OF A HANGDOG.** **** 5.10b Small-medium stoppers to a #2 Friend / 2 chains anchor. Two #.5 Aliens (green) and two #1.5 Friends (or # 1 Camalots) are useful. Follow a thin crack to a stance atop a large flake or wedged block. Ascend a short fingertip crack to a tiny roof. The crux ascends a 1-1/4" splitter crack over the roof via off-size finger jams. Reach good holds for the finish along the thin crack. The best crack climb at the Golden Cliffs. F.A.: Scott Berk, Rick Berk & Dave Hart.

60. **BRAIN CLOUD.** **** 5.9+ 5 bolts / 2 chains anchor. Ascend the excellent arete with a crux above the 3rd bolt. Gain a ledge & the 5th bolt. Continue up the left side of the arete to a large ledge & the anchor. F.A.: Charles Tabor & friends around 1990.

A. **THE MINI ME.** * 5.11a/b

B. **BUCHANAN.** * 5.9

C. **NADER.** 5.7

57. **GOOD MAN DAN.** *** 5.10b/c

58B. **RESTLESS HEART.** ** 5.11b or 5.11d

59. **SHADOW OF A HANGDOG.** **** 5.10b

60. **BRAIN CLOUD.** **** 5.9+

60. **BRAIN CLOUD.** **** 5.9+

61. **MAJOR BOLT ACHIEVEMENT.** *** 5.11a/b

62. **FEEDING FRENZY.** *** 5.11d

63. **SPIKE** *** 5.10a

64. **CLIFF HANGER.** ** 5.9

GOLDEN CLIFFS * MAJOR BOLT ACHIEVEMENT BUTTRESS * WEST (left) SIDE

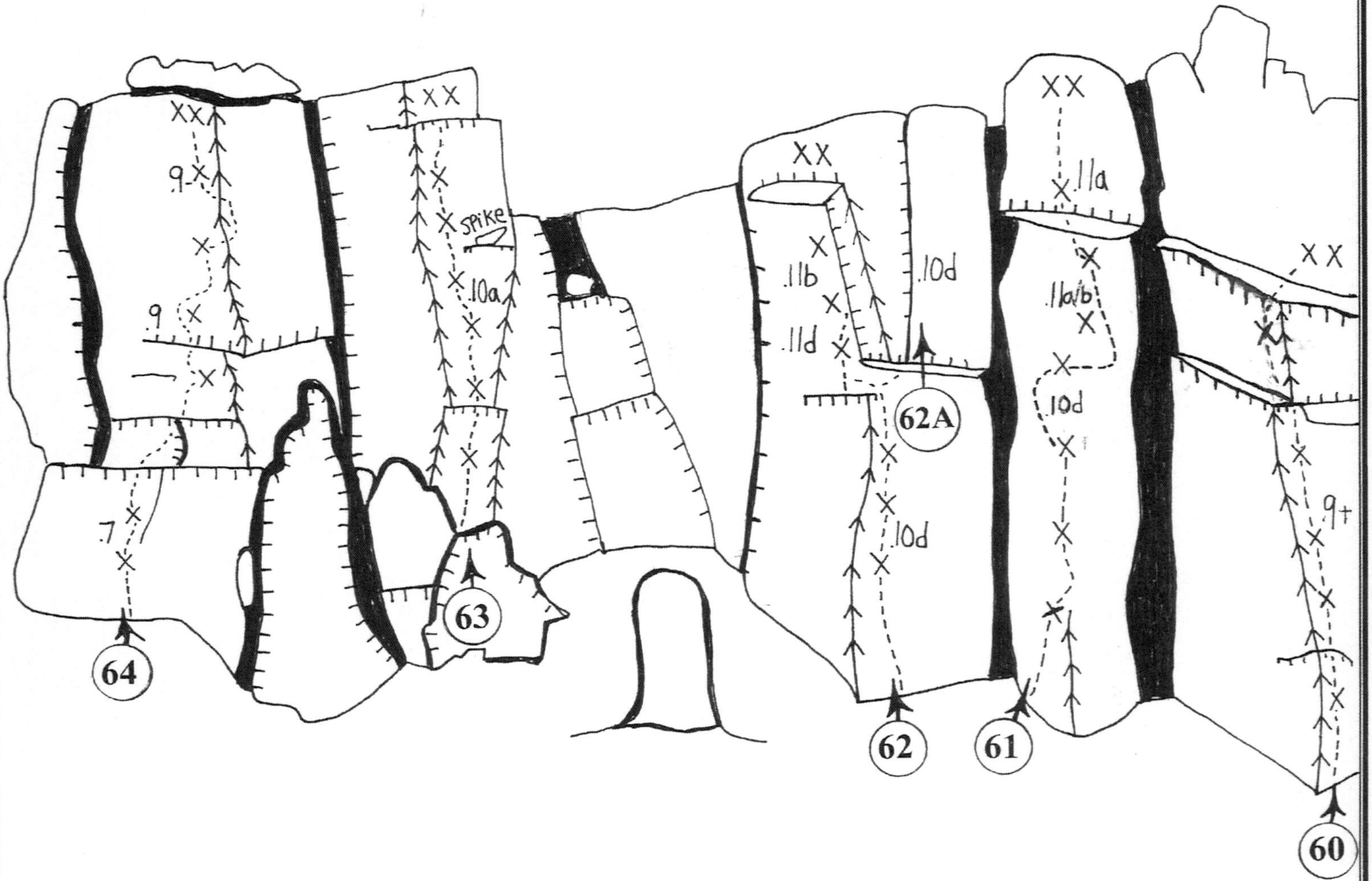

60. **BRAIN CLOUD.** **** 5.9+ 5 bolts / 2 chains anchor. Ascend the excellent arete with a crux above the 3rd bolt. Gain a ledge & the 5th bolt. Continue up the left side of the arete to a large ledge & the anchor. F.A.: Charles Tabor & friends around 1990.

61. **MAJOR BOLT ACHIEVEMENT.** *** 5.11a/b 7 bolts / 2 chains. This route wanders up a face between two chimneys and finishes with a roof. Move up the arete on left side of the face, past the 3rd & 4th bolt. Traverse right to the arete on the right side of the face. The crux ascends this arete past the 5th bolt. Pull over a roof, past the last bolt and finish up jugs.
F.A.: Tod Anderson, Dave Field & Richard Wright in 1990.

62. **FEEDING FRENZY.** *** 5.11d 6 bolts / 2 bolt anchor. Climb a fun arete to a good stance. The crux is entering a left facing dihedral. Tricky stemming leads up the dihedral. F.A.: Tod Anderson, Dave Field & Richard Wright in 1990.

62A. **SHARK ATTACK.** **? 5.10d 3 bolts. Nuts to #2.5 Friend. This is a trad finish to **Feeding Frenzy**. From the good stance below the left-facing dihedral on **Feeding Frenzy**, move right and climb a crack. F.A.: Tod Anderson in 1994.

63. **SPIKE** *** 5.10a 6 bolts / 2 bolt anchor. Start just right of a small pillar. Climb a face between two aretes. Continue up the face following the left arete. F.A.: Alan Nelson in 2001.

64. **CLIFF HANGER.** ** 5.9 6 bolts / 2 bolt anchor. Climb a short face with 2 bolts, to a large ledge. Climb a bulging face, left of the arete. Climbing directly past the 3rd bolt is 5.10 and may seem contrived. Move left, then back right to avoid this crux. Continue up the vertical arete (5.9-). First ascent by Alan Nelson in 2001.

GOLDEN CLIFFS * INDUSTRIAL BUTTRESS

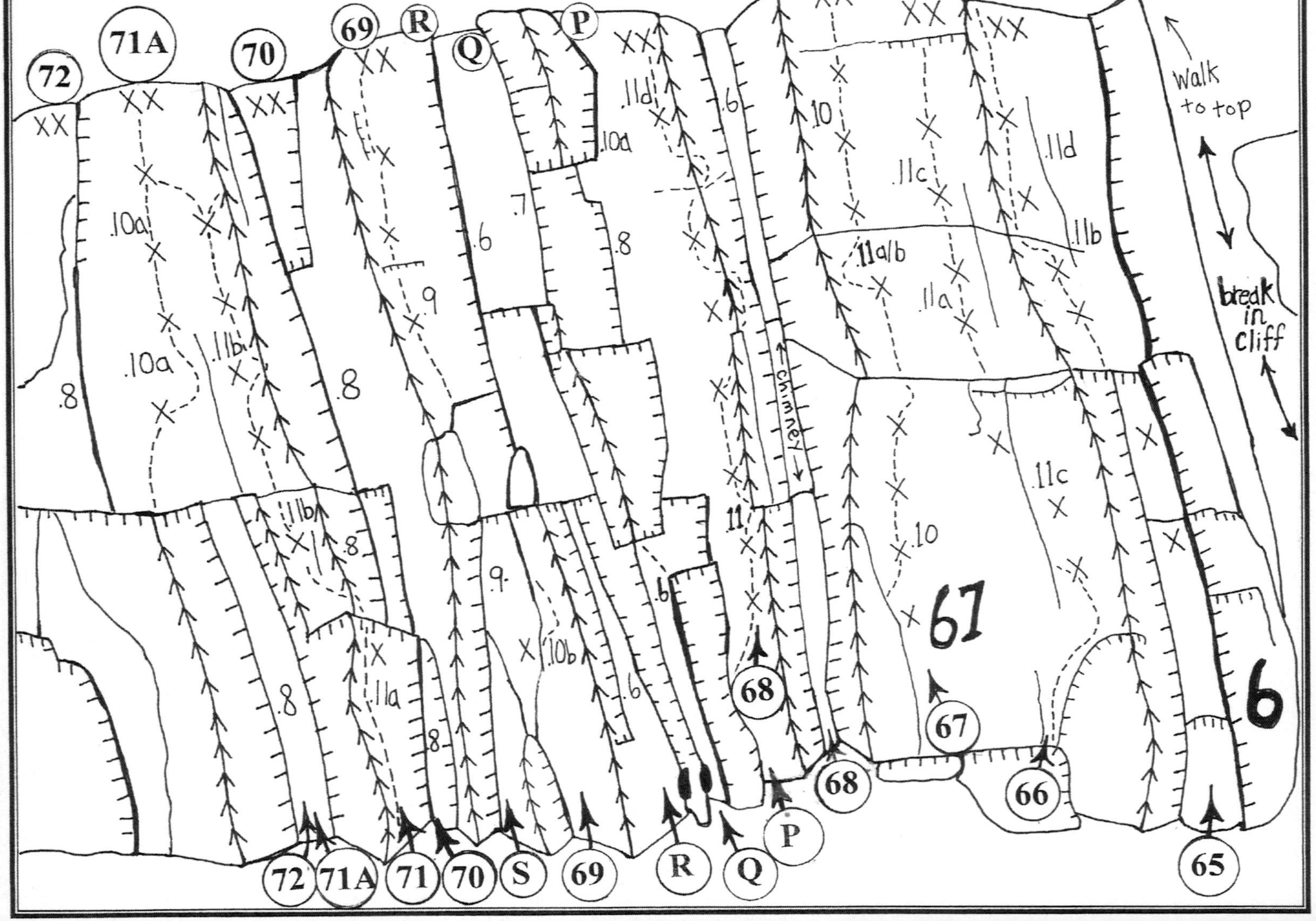

65. **FORGOTTEN NAMES.** *** 5.11d 6 bolts / 2 chains. Start just left of the white painted number 6. Climb a moderate left-facing crack corner to 2nd bolt. Step left into a small corner & move up to a ledge & 3rd bolt. The lower section of the route appears to have streaks of white bird shit. Don't worry, it is actually old white paint. Ascend the arete via a tricky sequence of moves. A few of the holds are on the left side of the arete. The crux past 5th bolt uses the arete & seam on the right side. F.A.: Richard Wright & Tod Anderson in June 1997.

66. **INDUSTRIAL DISEASE.** **** 5.11c 7 bolts / 2 Fixe rings. This route has been retrobolted. Scramble up right on easy terrain to the 1st bolt. Climb a tricky thin crack, past 2nd & 3rd bolt, to a very sloping shelf below a horizontal break. Ascend a sustained overhung face to the top. F.A.: Tod Anderson, Dave Field & Richard Wright in 1990.

67. **FLIGHT '67.** **** 5.11a/b 8 bolts / 2 mussy hooks. This route has been retro-bolted. Start along a thin crack, just below & left of the white painted numbers 67. Climb a vertical face, past 4 bolts, to a tiny stance below a horizontal break. Reach the 5th bolt & ascend overhung face moves with a height dependent reach crux. Continue up a vertical face to the anchor. First ascent by Scott Berk.

68. **ARETE OR GULLY.** * 5.11d or 5.6 7 bolts / 2 coldshuts. This arete is very close to a chimney. Climb the left side of the arete following the bolts for a difficult line with the crux getting to a jug above the anchor. Climb the chimney to the right for an easy pitch.

P. **POLYVINYL CHLORIDE** ** 5.10a/b #4-6 steel nuts, medium stoppers, #.3 (black) Alien to # 4 Friend or #3.5 Camolot (two are useful) / 2 coldshuts. The first 3 bolts on **Arete or Gully** can be used. Ascend the obvious right-facing dihedral. The middle section is a thin seam crack with face holds. The crux is the smooth fist crack finish. For climbers with small hands this crux will be harder & involve an offwidth.

Q. **MONKEY WRENCH.** * 5.7 PG-13 #2-6 steel nuts, #.3 (black) Alien to #2 Friend, #9 stopper. Start right of a small tunnel. Climb cracks to a ledge. Move left around a tiny roof. Follow a left-facing corner, past ledges, with a thin seam. The seam widens to a crack for the finish.

R **NIPPLE PHYLE.** * 5.6 Medium nuts & cams. Start left of a small tunnel. Climb a shallow corner to a ledge. Continue up a good crack.

69. **SALAD BAR.** *** 5.10b 4 bolts / 2 chains. Bring #.3 (black) - 1.5 (orange) Aliens. Climb a short tiny corner to a jug. Follow a thin flake crack to the 1st bolt. The crux moves right & up. Follow a crack to a ledge. Ascend a face right of the arete, past 3 bolts, to the top.

S. **NOODLE FACTORY.** ** 5.9- Small to 2.5" nuts & cams. Climb the right-facing corner left of **Salad Bar**. Gain a good ledge on **Salad Bar**. Step right & follow a crack that is also the upper section of **NIPPLE PHYLE**. It is also possible to finish up **Salad Bar.**

70. **FAST BOAT TO CHINA.** *** 5.8 #.4 Alien (blue) - #3 -3.5 Friend, #6-12 stoppers / 2 Fixe rings. Climb a crack corner with double cracks, via stemming & jamming. There is an alternate right hand finish leading up a tiny right-facing corner. This is one of the better crack climbs at the Golden Cliffs. F.A.: Scott Berk

71. **UNKNOWN ARETE.** *** 5.11b 6-7 bolts / 2 bolt anchor. Climb the right side of an arete past 1st bolt to a ledge. Negotiate a tricky prow, past 2nd bolt, to good holds. Ascend the left side of the bulging arete past 3rd bolt & 4th bolt & continue up the face. Finish up a thin crack to the anchor for **Fast Boat to China** or move left to join **Politicians, Priests & Body Bags** at its last bolt.

71A. **POLITICIANS, PRIESTS AND BODY BAGS.** *** 5.10a A few stoppers (#7-9) or #5-.75 Aliens (green & yellow) to 4 bolts / 2 chains. Climb two facing crack corners to a ledge & the 1st bolt. Wander up a devious vertical face. F.A.: Rick Berk & Dave Hart in 1990?

72. **HIEDI HI.** *** 5.8 #.5 Alien - #2 Friend (two #1.5 & 2 Friends are useful), #7-11 stoppers / 2 rings. Climb the double crack corner start of **Politicians, Preists & Body Bags** to the ledge. Step left & ascend a straight-in thin hand crack that leads into a corner. This is one of the better crack climbs at the Golden Cliffs. F.A.: Ryan Nassimbene & Dave Sams.

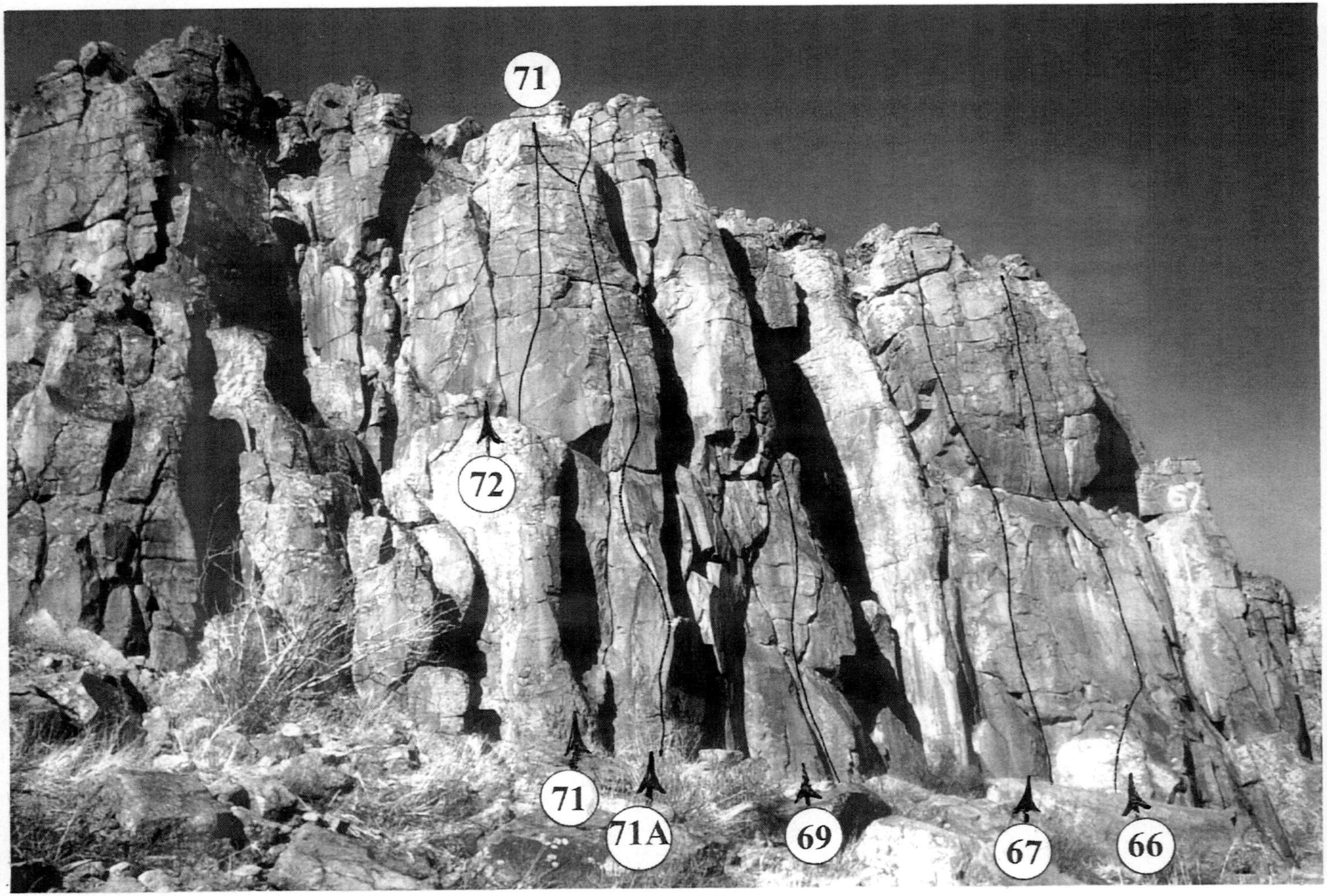

66. **INDUSTRIAL DISEASE.** **** 5.11c
67. **FLIGHT '67.** **** 5.11a/b
69. **SALAD BAR.** *** 5.10b
71. **UNKNOWN ARETE.** *** 5.11b
71A. **POLITICIANS, PRIESTS & BODY BAGS.** *** 5.10a
72. **HIEDI HI.** *** 5.8

73. **CHUNKY MONKEY.** ** 5.9

74. **HONEY, I SHRUNK THE HEMORRHOIDS.** *** 5.7 PG-13

75. **THE CRUX OF THE BISCUIT IS THE APOSTROPHE.** *** 5.10a to 5.10d

76. **UNKNOWN ARETE.** ** 5.10a

77. **PSYCHO BETA BUCK DOWN.** * 5.11d or 5.12

GOLDEN CLIFFS * TWELVE PACK WALL

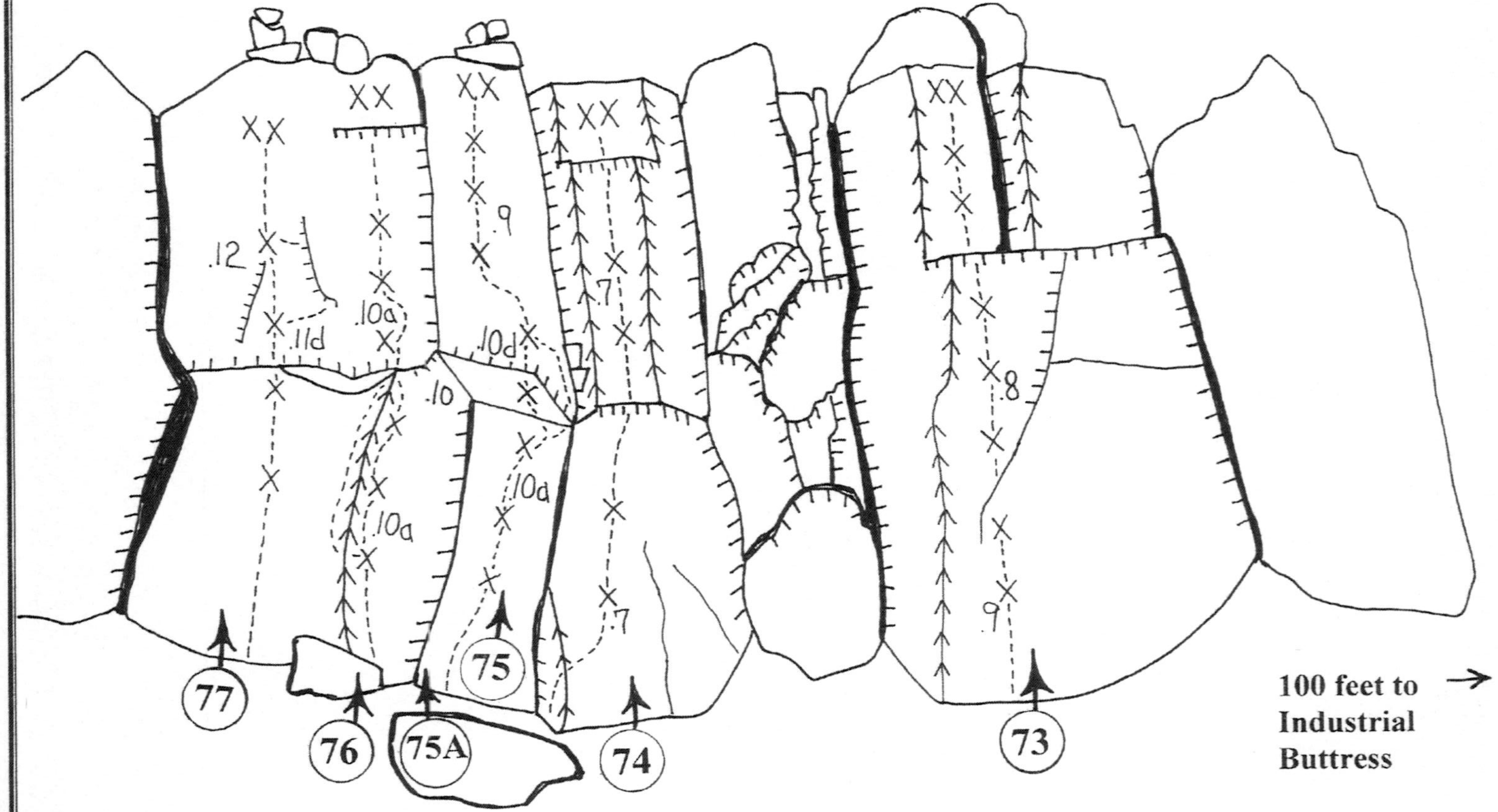

100 feet to Industrial Buttress →

GOLDEN CLIFFS * TWELVE PACK WALL

73. **CHUNKY MONKEY.** ** 5.9 7 bolts / Fixe rings. The crux is the start. Climb a tricky face to a right-leaning thin crack. Continue up the face on the right side of the arete. Gain a good ledge. Finish along a corner. F.A.: Charles Tabor and friends in 1992.

74. **HONEY, I SHRUNK THE HEMORRHOIDS.** *** 5.7 PG-13 4 bolts / chains anchor. Climb over a short bulge to reach the 1st bolt. Continue up a moderate run-out slab past the 2nd bolt to a ledge. The crux ascends a vertical prow past the 3rd & 4th bolt to a small ledge & the anchor just below the top. F.A.: Charles Tabor and friends in 1992.

75. **THE CRUX OF THE BISCUIT IS THE APOSTROPHE.** *** 5.10a to 5.10d 8 bolts / 2 Fixe rings. Climb a slab past 3 bolts to a roof. The route's difficulty depends on how you tackle the roof. Climb directly over the roof for a tricky crux or avoid it by stepping into the corner on the right. Above the roof traverse left & ascend a vertical face to the anchor. First ascent by Pat Thompson in 1996.

75A. **RAW FISH AND RICE.** *? 5.10 Nuts & cams / 2 Fixe rings. Ascend a right-facing dihedral with a roof crux in the middle. Use the anchor for **The Crux Of The Biscuit is The Apostrophe** to descend. F.A. Scott & Richard Berk in 1986.

76. **UNKNOWN ARETE.** ** 5.10a 6 bolts / chains anchor. Climb an arete past 3 bolts to a tiny roof. Avoid the roof on the right & ascend a vertical face to the anchor.

77. **PSYCHO BETA BUCK DOWN.** * 5.11d or 5.12 4 bolts / welded coldshuts anchor. The direct line climbs straight up, staying just left of the 3rd bolt via powerful moves. The less obvious, easier choice involves a using crimps below the 3rd bolt to dyno up and right to a good sidepull. Move up and back left to finish. First ascent by Dennis, Mark and Mike McCarron in 1994.

The author on **WIDESPREAD SHELFISHNESS** *** 5.12b on the Hot Spot Area. Photo by Mike Dallin.

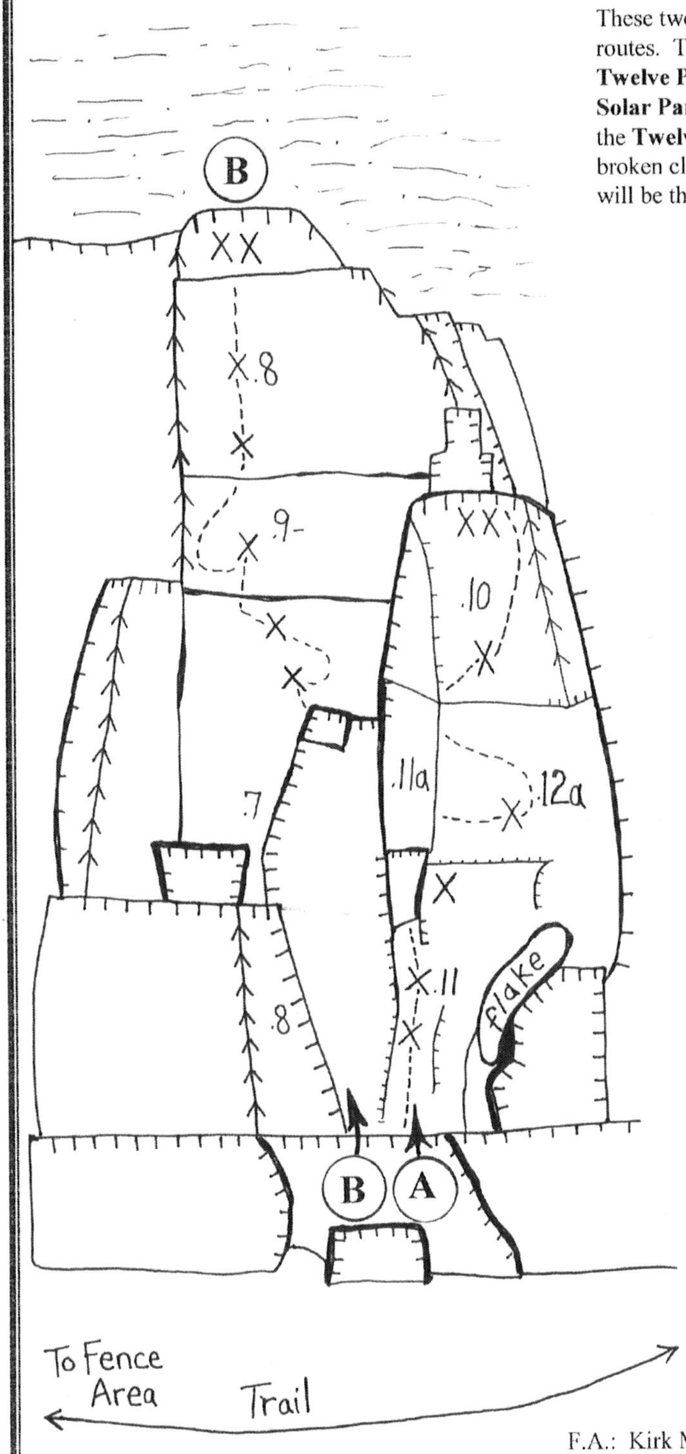

These two climbs stand alone & separated from other routes. They are located 250 feet left (north) of the **Twelve Pack Wall** & 35 feet right (south) of the **Solar Panel** in the **Fence Area**. After walking past the **Twelve Pack Wall**, there is a wide section of broken cliff void of bolted routes. These two climbs will be the first bolted routes to be encountered next.

A. **UNKNOWN.** 5.11 or 5.12a

5 bolts / 2 chains. Bring some gear for easier variation. #5-7 stoppers or #.3 - .5 Aliens (black, blue, green) & #1-2 Friends or Aliens (red, orange). Scramble 10 feet up to a ledge to start this route. Climb up a vertical face (5.11) past 2 bolts, avoiding a large, perched, guillotine flake to the right. Gain a crack & continue with greater ease, past 3rd bolt, up a wedged flake to a stance on its top. The easier direct line climbs a thin crack with gear (5.11) to jugs. Continue up the crack, & reach right to the last bolt. Run it out up a vertical face to the anchor. The less direct line is contrived, but makes for a difficult sport route (requiring no gear & all bolt protection). From the stance at the start of the thin crack, traverse right with the 3rd bolt at your feet. Reach large holds & clip the 4th bolt. The .12a crux uses small holds to move up the face & get stood on the large holds. Move left & join the crack leading to the last bolt.

B. **SLOT TO TROT.** * 5.9-

Small to medium nuts & cams, such as #.3 - 1.5 Aliens (black, blue, green, yellow, red, orange) to 5 bolts / 2 bolt anchor. Scramble 10 feet up to a ledge & climb a right-facing corner that begins a few feet right of **Unknown**. The corner leads 20 feet to a slot between a large block perched on a ledge & the wall to the right. Pass through the slot, onto the ledge. Climb a moderate left-facing corner for 20 feet to a bolt & then move onto a ledge on the right. Wander up the face protected by bolts to the anchor.

F.A.: Kirk Miller & Jeroen Van Wolferen in April 2007.

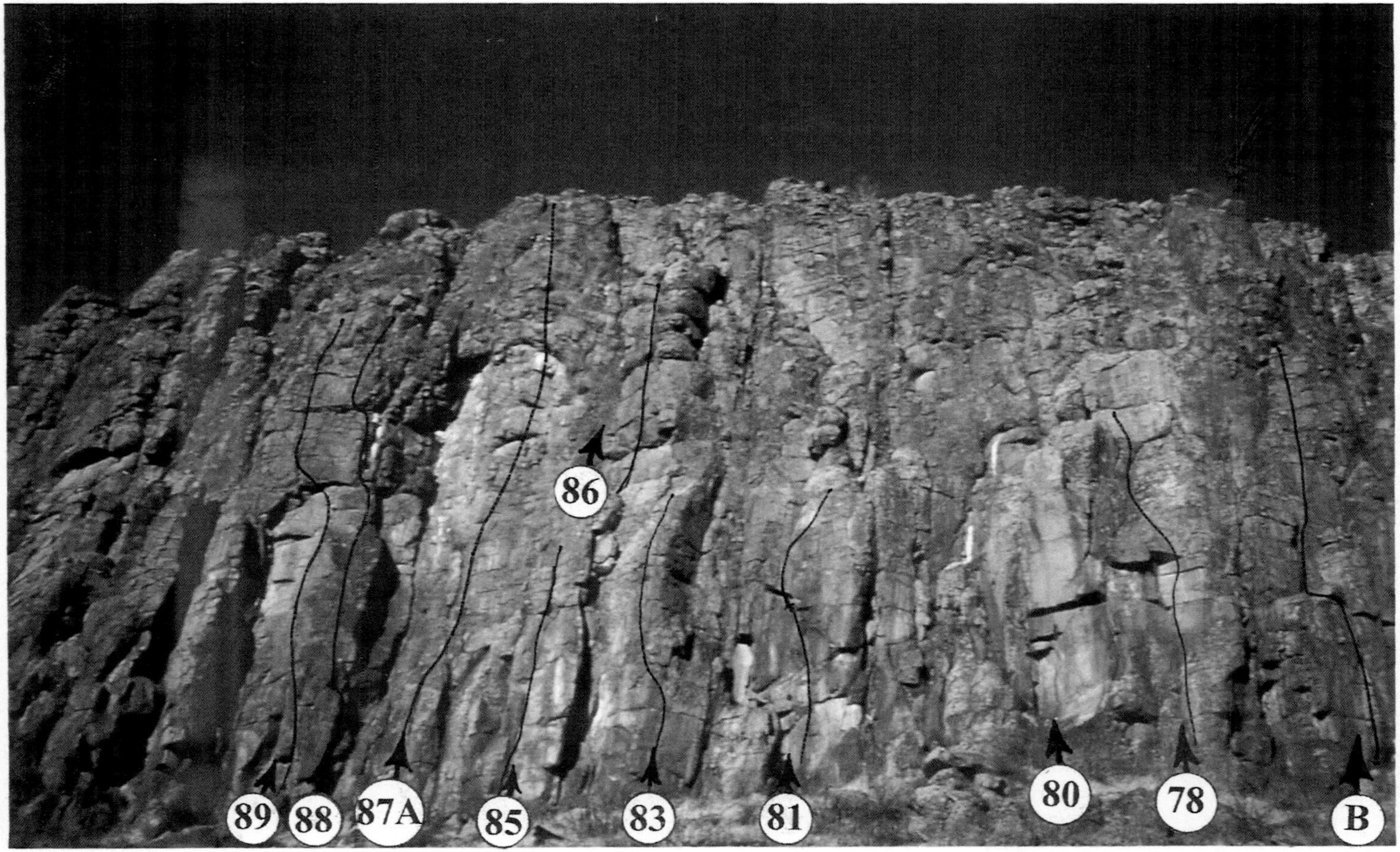

B. **SLOT TO TROT.** * 5.9

78. **POWER OF TOWER.** * 5.10d/11a R

80. **SOLAR PANEL.** *** 5.12c/d

81. **ELECTROCUTICLES.** *** 5.12a/b

83. **KLIMBINK IS FORBOLTEN.** *** 5.11d

85. **BASALT & BATTERY.** **** 5.10d/11a

86. **INSULT & FLATTERY.** * 5.12a PG-13

87A. **UGLY STICK.** *** 5.10b

88. **STICKIN' TO THE MAN.** ***** 5.10b

89. **WINTER WARMER.** ***** 5.10d

78. **POWER OF TOWER.** * 5.10d/11a R

79. **G-SPOT.** * 5.8 PG-13

80. **SOLAR PANEL.** *** 5.12c/d

81. **ELECTROCUTICLES.** *** 5.12a/b

82. **F.A.T.A.L.** *** 5.10a or 5.10c

83. **KLIMBINK IS FORBOLTEN.** *** 5.11d

85. **BASALT & BATTERY.** **** 5.10d/11a

86. **INSULT & FLATTERY.** * 5.12a PG-13

GOLDEN CLIFFS * FENCE AREA

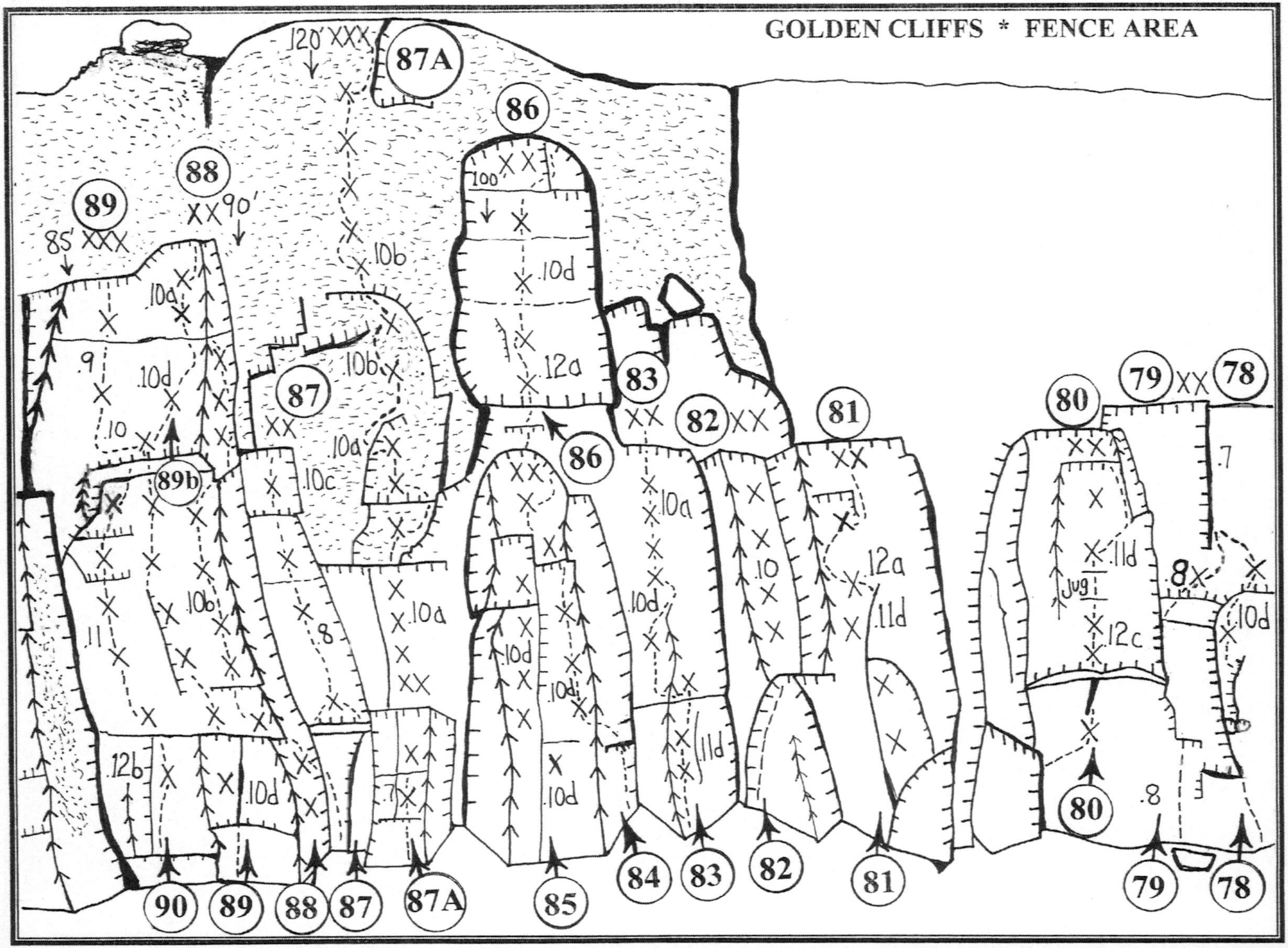

GOLDEN CLIFFS * FENCE AREA

The **Fence Area** has several 3 to 5 star classics. It has the longest climb on the Golden Cliffs, known as **Ugly Stick** (5.10b), at 120 feet. It has the area's two 5 stars routes, **Winter Warmer** (5.10d) & **Stickin' It To The Man** (5.10a/b), that are each 85 to 90 feet long. This area also has one of the hardest routes on the mountain, known as **Solar Panel** (5.12c/d).

78. **POWER OF TOWER.** * 5.10d/11a R 2 bolts, RPs, #. 4 -1.5 Aliens / 2 chains. Climb moderate moves along a right-facing corner without much protection. Step right to a shallow corner leading to a bolt. The crux climbs up & over the right side of a roof. Above the roof, move left & finish up a right-facing dihedral with a good crack, that is shared with **G-Spot**. F.A.: Alvino Pon - 1990?

79. **G-SPOT.** *** 5.8 R 1 bolt, two sets of #3-5 micro-stoppers, #.4 Alien - 2.5 Friend / 2 chains. Climb a face left of a tiny roof to a small right facing corner. Climb the corner to a small roof & a bolt at its lip. Pull over the roof & climb a right-facing dihedral. F.A.: Alvino Pon - 1990?

80. **SOLAR PANEL.** *** 5.12c/d 5 bolts / 2 Goldshuts. Climb up to a small roof. Reach a sharp hold above the roof on the left. The crux is past 3rd bolt, using small edges to lunge to a jug. Dyno up right past 4th bolt & finish up a thin crack. F.A.: Mark Rolofson in November 1993.

81. **ELECTROCUTICLES.** *** 5.12a/b 5 bolts / 2 open coldshuts. Climb a short crack that peters out into a seam. Lieback up the fading seam to the 4th bolt. Move left onto the arete. The crux uses tiny holds to reach big edges. Follow the arete, then move right & up to the anchor. Even though this route sees very few ascents, it is an excellent route for its grade. F.A.: Ken Trout & Rick Leitner in 1991.

82. **F.A.T.A.L. (FEMURS AND TIBIAS ALTERNATING LATERALLY)** *** 5.10a (use crack in back of dihedral) or 5.10c (wide stems up outside) 4 bolts / 2 bolt anchor. Scramble to a ledge. Ascend the obvious dihedral. F.A.: Ralph Bidwell & Leon Henkleman in January 1994.

83. **KLIMBINK IS FORBOLTEN.** *** 5.11d 8 bolts / 2 bolt anchor. A desperate crux start climbs a blunt arete & a vertical seam to the right. Clipping 2nd bolt is difficult & pre-clipping it may be wise. Reach a horizontal break & the 3rd bolt. Strenuous moves lead up left, past the 4th bolt. Continue up a fun face that slabs out for the finish. F.A.: Guy Lords & Ken Trout in 1990. Retro-bolted by M. Rolofson - Feb. 2003.

84. **AT FAULT FOR CHATTERY.** * 5.10d R- 5 bolts / 2 Fixe rings. Run-out above the 1st bolt. Start in a corner right of the arete. Move left & climb the arete to join **Basalt & Battery** at its 6th bolt. F.A.: Tod Anderson in 1990?

85. **BASALT & BATTERY.** **** 5.10d/11a 7 bolts / 2 Fixe rings. Stick clip is useful for the 1st bolt or place a #1.5 Friend or Alien (orange). Climb a thin seam crack to a jug past the 1st bolt. Continue up a right-facing seam corner that turns into a left-facing flared corner & ends at tiny roof. Pull past the roof to gain a ledge. Finish up easier climbing to the anchor. First ascent by Ernie Moskovics & Martin Birch in 1990.

86. **INSULT & FLATTERY.** ** 5.12a PG-13 4 bolts / 2 coldshuts. A #1.5 - 3 Friend is optional before 1st bolt. Begin with **Basalt & Battery**. Continue up run-out easy climbing to a reachy clip to 1st bolt over a bulge. The crux pulls the bulge on small edges. Reach good holds & cruise up the juggy headwall. The crux can be avoided to the left but there is loose rock. F.A.: Alan Nelson, Richard Wright & Tod Anderson - 1994.

See The following pages for detailed route descriptions of the climbs list below.

87A. **UGLY STICK.** *** 5.10b 16 bolts / 3 mussy hooks. This is the longest climb on the mountain at 120 feet. .

87. **NO GUMBIES.** * 5.10c PG-13 4-7 bolts / 2 Goldshuts. A few small to medium nuts & cams provide additional protection.

88. **STICKIN' TO THE MAN.** ***** 5.10a/b 12 bolts / 2 mussy hooks. This is the new version of **Right Hand Warmer**, that is 90 feet long.

89. **WINTER WARMER.** ***** 5.10d 9 bolts / 3 mussy hooks. This is an 85 feet long classic.

89b. **WINTER MAN.** **** 5.10d 11 bolts /2 mussy hooks. This variation links **Winter Warmer** to **Stickin' It To The Man**.

90. **GRUESOME GROOVE.** ** 5.12b/c 9 bolts / 3 mussy hooks. This squeezed route ascends the face left of **Winter Warmer**.

GOLDEN CLIFFS * FENCE AREA * LEFT SIDE

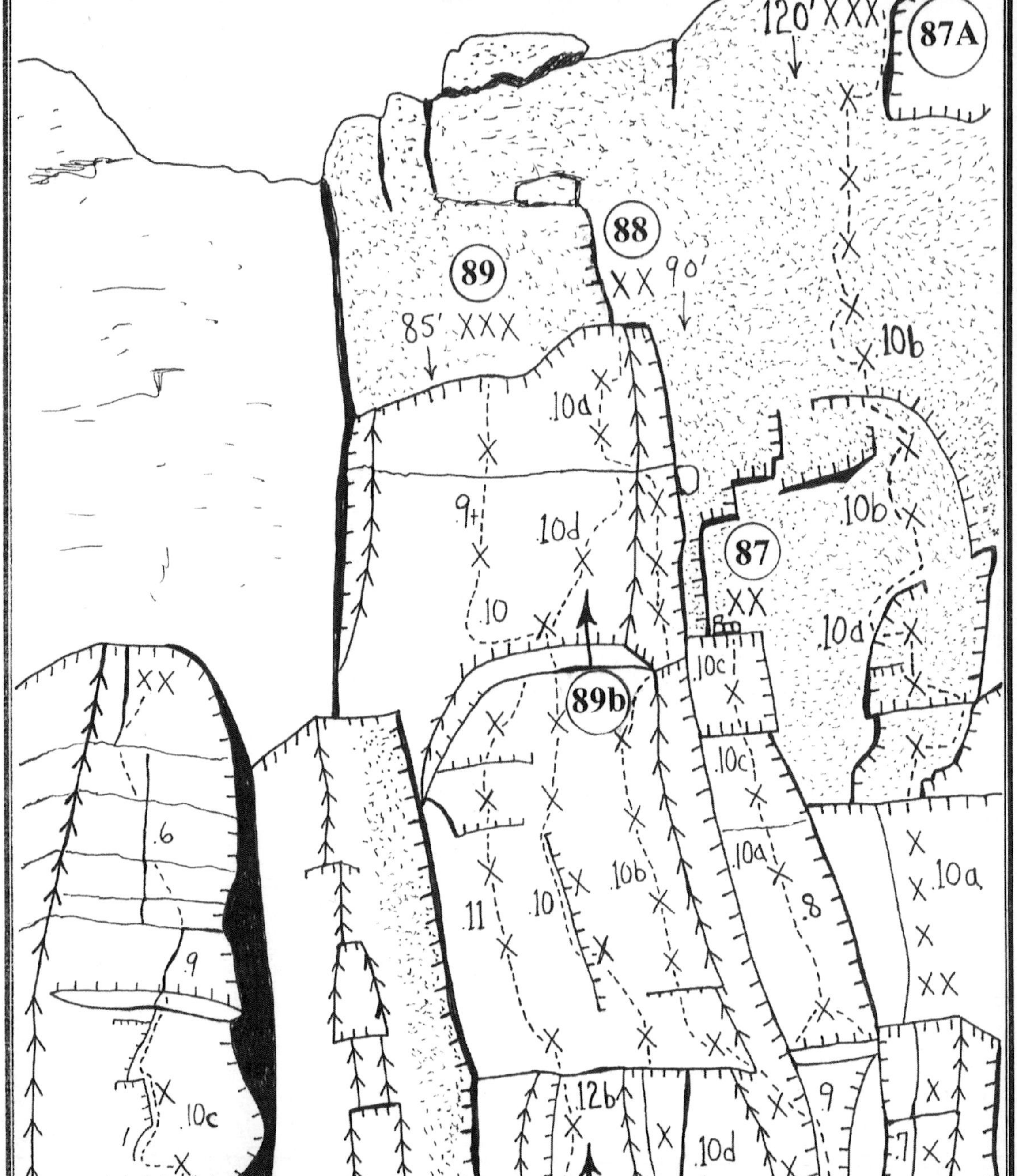

87A. **UGLY STICK.** *** 5.10b 16 bolts / 3 mussy hooks. This is the longest climb on the mountain at 120 feet. Descend with a 70 meter rope or do two lower-offs with a 60 meter rope. Start up solid stone that turns to crumbly dark chocolate rock. A well-bolted route with lots of 5.10 sections between good rests. The climb is becoming cleaner & more solid after repeated ascents. Climb up to the 1st bolt & follow a crack to 2nd bolt. Easy moves gain a ledge with a 2 bolt anchor, to use if you have a 60 meter rope. Follow a crack to another ledge & the 7th bolt. Move right & then up & left, past the 8th bolt Wander up the face with the most difficult moves between the 10th & 12 bolts. F.A.: Kirk Miller on April 15, 2006.

87. **NO GUMBIES.** * 5. 10c PG-13 4-7 bolts / 2 Goldshuts. A few small to medium nuts & cams provide additional pro. Start with the first 3 bolts of **Stickin' It To The Man,** then step right to the 1st bolt on **No Gumbies**. It is also possible to climb a thin crack on the right, protected by gear, to reach the 1st bolt. Climb a moderate red slab, just right of a large right-facing dihedral, to the 2nd bolt. If this seems too run-out, place gear in the dihedral. The slab becomes more difficult past the 2nd bolt & uses the edge of a shallow crack on the right. At the 3rd bolt, the wall steepens to vertical. Continue up the vertical face between two corners, to a bulging finish, past the last bolt. Gain a wide ledge & the anchor. Avoid grabbing some loose blocks on the far left side of the ledge. F.A.: Jim Burtle - 1990?

88. **STICKIN' TO THE MAN.** ***** 5.10a/b 12 bolts / 2 mussy hooks. This is the new version of **Right Hand Warmer**, creating an independent line, that is 90 feet long. This route is popular & destined to be a classic. Start with a right-facing crack corner, past the first 2 bolts. At 3rd bolt pull onto a ledge on the left side of the arete. Continue over a short bulge, past the 4th & 5th bolts, & climb a clean, steep slab left of the arete. Gain a stance on the arete at the 8th bolt. Climb a corner just right of the arete to a horizontal break. Traverse a few feet left. A final crux pulls over a small bulge, past the 11th bolt. Finish up jugs on the arete. F.A.: Ken Trout, Marsha Trout, Tim Slater, Kirk Miller & Jeroen Van Wolferen on January 4, 2008.

89. **WINTER WARMER.** ***** 5.10d 9 bolts / 3 mussy hooks. This is an 85 feet long classic. The crux start liebacks over a tiny bulge, past 1st bolt, to jugs. Gain a stance & the 2nd bolt. Move left & climb a small left-facing corner, past 3rd & 4th bolt. At the corner's end, move right & climb up the face. Clip 7th bolt, just above a small roof. Traverse left underneath a roof. Pull over the left side of the roof & climb up a vertical face, past the upper 2 bolts, with an exciting run-out finish. F.A.: Dave Field & Ernie Moskovics in 1990.

89a. **RIGHT HAND WARMER.** *** 5.10d (Not shown on topo drawing). This route was a variation to **Winter Warmer**. The original 6 bolts that protected this variation have been removed & replaced with **Stickin' It To The Man**. This climb starts with the first 2 bolts of **Winter Warmer**. Continue over a small bulge, past the 4th & 5th bolt of **Stickin' It ....** Continue straight up the slab (also the same as **Stickin' It ...**). Pull over to a tiny roof & finish up the left side of the arete. F.A.: Dave Field & Ernie Moskovics in 1992.

89b. **WINTER MAN.** **** 5.10d 11 bolts /2 mussy hooks. This variation links **Winter Warmer** to the finish of **Stickin' It To The Man**. Climb **Winter Warmer** to the 7th bolt. Move right & pull over a tiny roof to a bolt on the vertical face. A crux moves lead past this 8th bolt. Join **Stick'n It ...** at the 10th bolt. Avoid doing this variation if someone is climbing **Stickin' It ...,** because you will have a traffic jam. It is also possible to access this finish by climbing **Stickin' It ...** for 7 bolts, then move left to the 6th bolt on **Winter Warmer**. This variation was bolted by Ken Trout in January 2008.

90. **GRUESOME GROOVE.** ** 5.12b/c 9 bolts / 3 mussy hooks. This squeezed route ascends the face left of **Winter Warmer**. A puzzling 5.12 crux start, past the 1st bolt, climbs a small corner using tiny crimpers. Continue up a tricky 5.11 face that steepens from a slab to a vertical face. Pull over a small overlap, at the 6th bolt, to join **Winter Warmer** at the roof & its 7th bolt.
F.A.: Keith Ainsworth, accompanied by Mary Riedmiller & Mark Rolofson (equippers) on Feb. 1, 1997.

91. **NIMBY.** 5.10c R 2 bolts, plus #3-5 steel nuts or RPs, #3-1.5 Aliens 7-8 stoppers / 2 Fixe rings. Start from a small sloping ledge on the right. Grab a thin crack to clip the 1st bolt at the lip of a bulge. Move left, then up over the bulge, past crux moves. Reach good holds & clip the 2nd bolt. Continue up a small crackless right-facing corner to another small bulge. Place gear, that is in questionable, friable rock. Reach a good horizontal crack on the left side of the arete. Finish up a moderate slab. F.A.: Tod Anderson - 1989?

87A. **UGLY STICK.** *** 5.10b

88. **STICKIN' TO THE MAN.** ***** 5.10b

89. **WINTER WARMER.** ***** 5.10d

90. **GRUESOME GROOVE.** ** 5.12b/c

91. **NIMBY.** 5.10c R

Photo: Kirk Miller

93. **NINE TO FIVE.** *** 5.9

94. **FIVE TO ONE.** *** 5.11a

95. **DAY OF RECKONING.** ** 5.12a

96. **THE WORLD THROUGH A BOTTLE.** ** 5.10

GOLDEN CLIFFS * HOT SPOT AREA

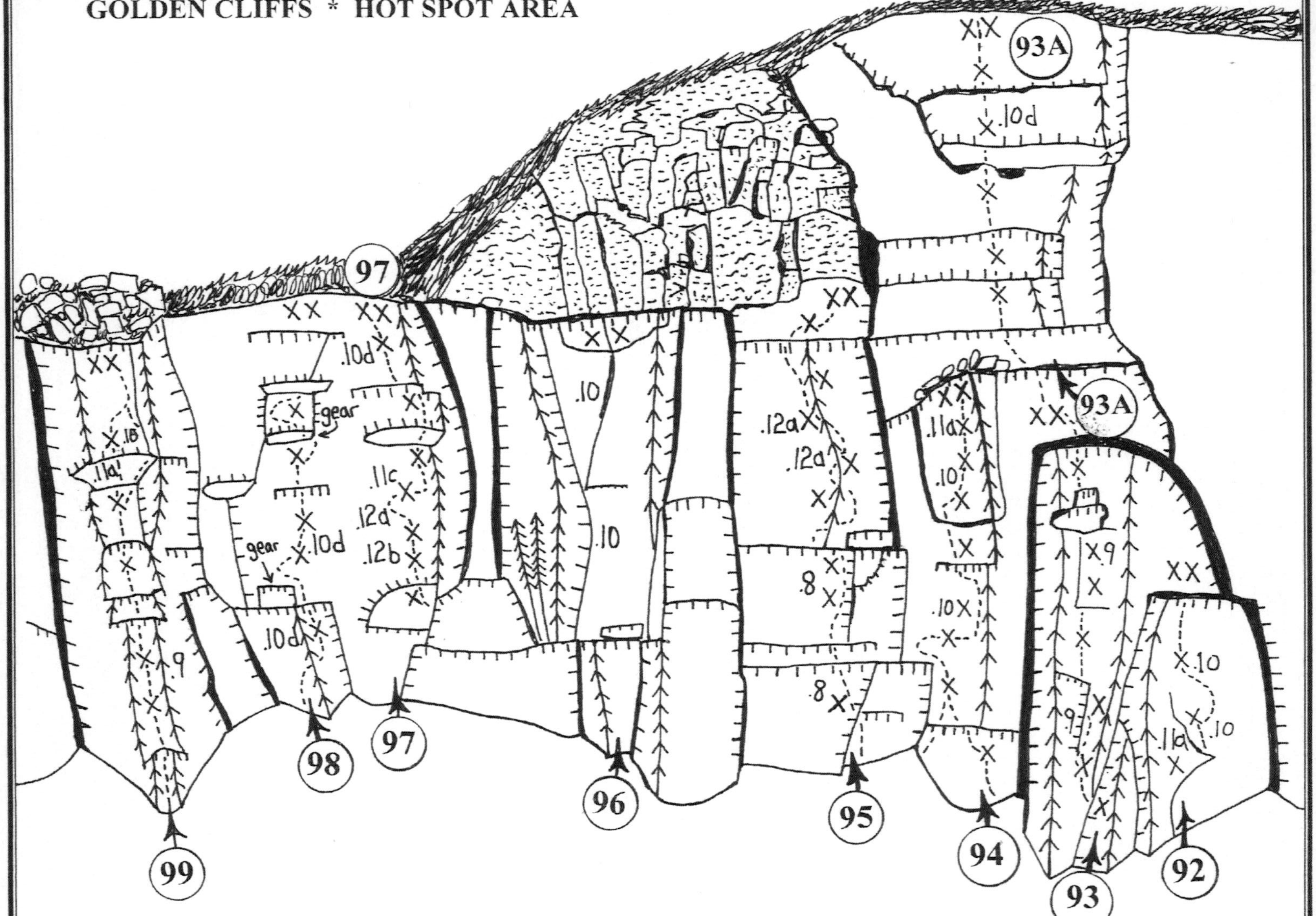

GOLDEN CLIFFS * HOT SPOT AREA

The **HOT SPOT AREA** and the **WINTERFEST WALL** combined, provide one of the best selection of routes from 5.9 to 5.12b on the **GOLDEN CLIFFS**. The average route is 60 feet in length. The majority of routes here receive three stars and are 5.10 or 5.11. The **WINTERFEST WALL** receives the last rays of sun before dusk, making it an ideal winter spot. The exception to this rule is on windy days, since the area is not blocked from a wind blowing from the north or west. The **Hot Spot Area** is often more sheltered from the wind than other areas on the west face.

92. **UNKNOWN.** * 5.10 or 5.11a 3 bolts / 2 Goldshuts. The direct line is 5.11a, which can be avoided by traversing right.

93. **NINE TO FIVE.** *** 5.9 6 bolts / 2 Fixe rings. Climb up a small corner to 2nd bolt. Move left onto the face & up into a short right-facing corner. Reach the 3rd bolt, then move up & left to a small shelf. Continue up a tricky face to a short thin crack that leads to a shelf. Climb over a block & up moderate terrain, past the last bolt, to a ledge. Step left to the anchor. First ascent by Alan Nelson in 1993.

93A. **DISAPPEARING MAN.** *? 5.10d 5 bolts / 2 bolt anchor. 2nd bolt hanger may be missing. Start with **Five To One** & continue in the same pitch or climb **Nine to Five**, belay at its anchor & continue in a 2nd pitch. Climb past an old bird's nest below top. F.A.: Alvin Pon - 1990?

94. **FIVE TO ONE.** *** 5.11a 7-8 bolts / 2 Fixe rings. Start with a short face, past 1st bolt, to gain a ledge. It is possible to avoid this start & 1st bolt, by starting to the left & moving right, past a bush, onto the ledge. Climb up a short, crackless right-facing corner past 2nd bolt to a ledge. At 3rd bolt, move right onto the arete & climb up to a shelf. Climb up & then right on a vertical face to the last bolt. The crux finishes up the face. It is possible to avoid the crux by finishing to the left along a wide crack. F.A.: Kirk Miller & Lindie Brink on Nov. 22, 2006.

95. **DAY OF RECKONING.** ** 5.12a 8 bolts / 2 Fixe rings. The upper part of this route ascends a blunt, bulging arete with two cruxes in a row. Start with a tiny right-facing corner to reach the 1st bolt & gain a low-angle slab. The slab leads a ledge. Climb a moderate vertical face along a tiny right-facing corner past 2 bolts. Gain a good ledge & the 4th bolt. Ascend the arete, using small holds on the right side. There is a difficult clip to 5th bolt & then the first crux. Reach a jug & 6th bolt. The second crux uses poor holds to pull up & stand on the jug. Continue up jugs to a good ledge & the anchor. F.A.: Mark Rolofson & Kirk Miller on November 25, 2007.

96. **THE WORLD THROUGH A BOTTLE.** ** 5.10 #4 RP or #5 Steel Nut, #.3 Alien (black) to #2.5 Friend / 2 bolt anchor. Scramble 20 ft. up to a large ledge. Stem & lieback up a right-facing dihedral with small pro for 20 ft. to a tiny shelf & a straight-in thin crack on the right wall. The dihedral angles to the left, becoming crackless. Ascend the crack up the bulging wall. After a few moves the crack widens to hand jams leading to face holds & the anchor at the top of the wall. F.A.: Unknown. The crack was cleaned of loose blocks & anchor added by Kirk Miller on November 25, 2007.

97. **WIDESPREAD SHELFISHNESS.** *** 5.12b 7 bolts / 2 Fixe rings. Start with easy terrain up shelves along a thin crack. Gain a ledge right of the 2nd bolt & the blunt arete. Step left & climb the bulging, blunt arete, past the 2nd bolt, via sidepulls to a crux dyno for a jug. Clip 3rd bolt & execute tricky sidepull moves to stand on the jug. This is the second crux. Move right, past 4th bolt & climb the arete to small roof. Jugs lead over the roof to a ledge. A short face leads past the last bolt to the anchor. This climb is technical with two cruxes in a row. F.A.: Ken Trout in 1991. F.F.A.: Unknown.

98. **THE CRACK & FACE ROUTE.** **** 5.10d GP-13 5 bolts / 2 Fixe rings. A small rack is useful. Place #.3,.4, or .5 Aliens (black, blue, green) before 2nd bolt or place #5-6 Steel nuts or small stoppers. Above the 4th bolt, # .75, 1, 1.5 Aliens (yellow, red, orange) & a 2.5 Friend are useful. Climb a steep slab up an arete, with a crux past the 1st bolt, to a ledge. Ascend a vertical face past 2nd & 3rd bolt. Gain a ledge & the 4th bolt. Climb up to a crack. Step left & then up past 5th bolt. Reach a short crack leading over a tiny roof to a ledge & the anchor. F.A.: Dave Field & Ernie Moskovics around 1990.

99. **CROWBAR COWBOY.** * 5.10 or 5.11a 5 bolts / 2 Fixe Rings. Ascend a prow to a ledge below a roof. The easier variation moves around the right side of the roof. The direct line climbs directly over the middle of the roof at 5.11a. F.A.: Unknown in 1994.

96. **THE WORLD THROUGH A BOTTLE.** ** 5.10

97. **WIDESPREAD SHELFISHNESS.** *** 5.12b

98. **THE CRACK & FACE ROUTE.** **** 5.10d GP-13

99. **CROWBAR COWBOY.** * 5.10 or 5.11a

100. **WHOLE LOTTA DRUNK.** *** 5.11a

102. **THE DISSOLUTION.** **** 5.11d/12a

103. **LEANING PILLAR (Right Side).** *** 5.10c

106. **UNDER THE WIRE.** ** 5.10c PG-13

111. **BIMBO IN LIMBO.** *** 5.10b

112. **CRAWLING UP ROSEANNE'S BELLY.** *** 5.11b/c

114. **PSEUDO BULLET.** *** 5.12a

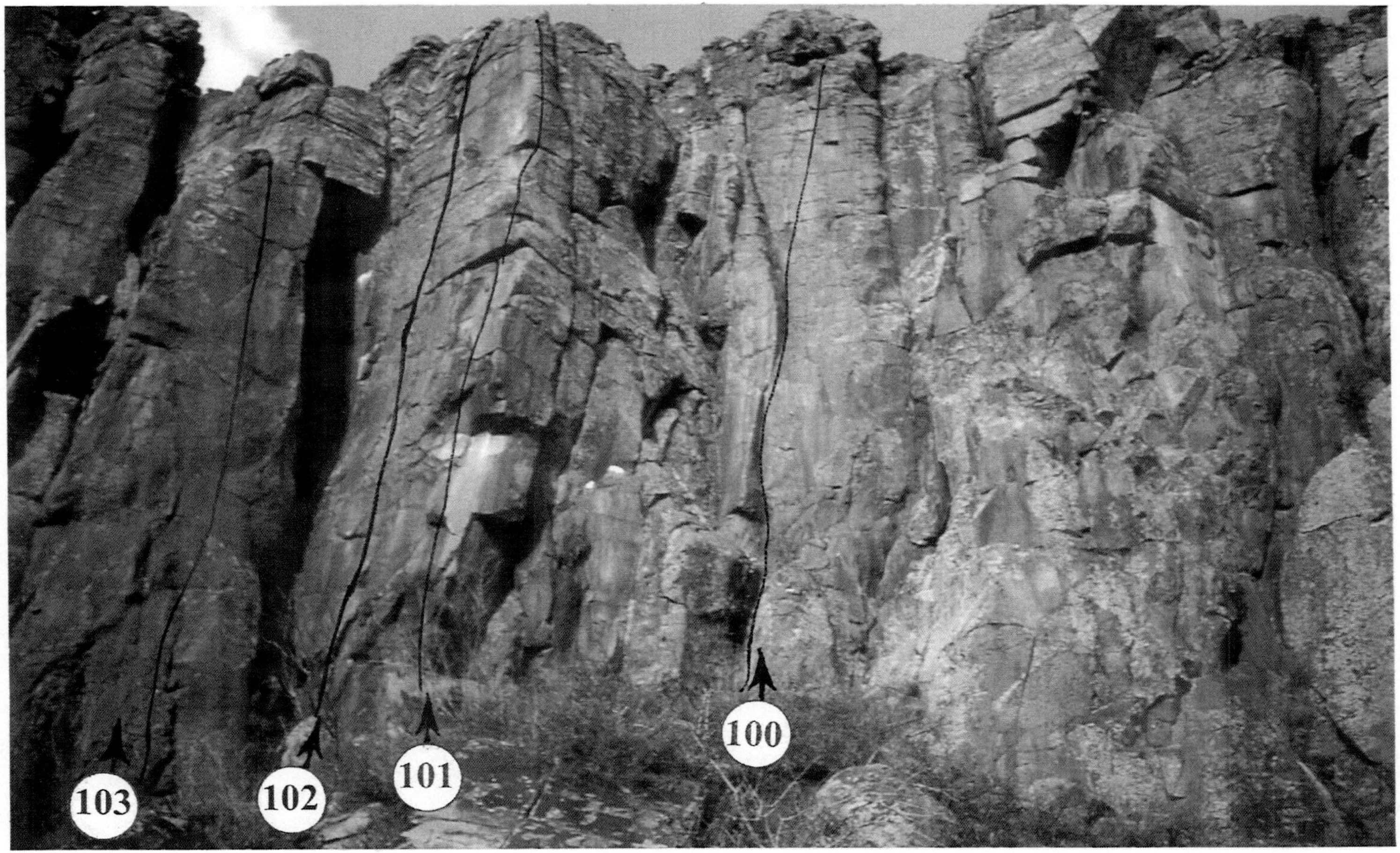

100. **WHOLE LOTTA DRUNK.** *** 5.11a

101. **THE RESOLUTION.** *** 5.11c

102. **THE DISSOLUTION.** **** 5.11d/12a

103. **LEANING PILLAR (Right Side).** *** 5.10c

GOLDEN CLIFFS * WINTERFEST WALL * RIGHT SIDE

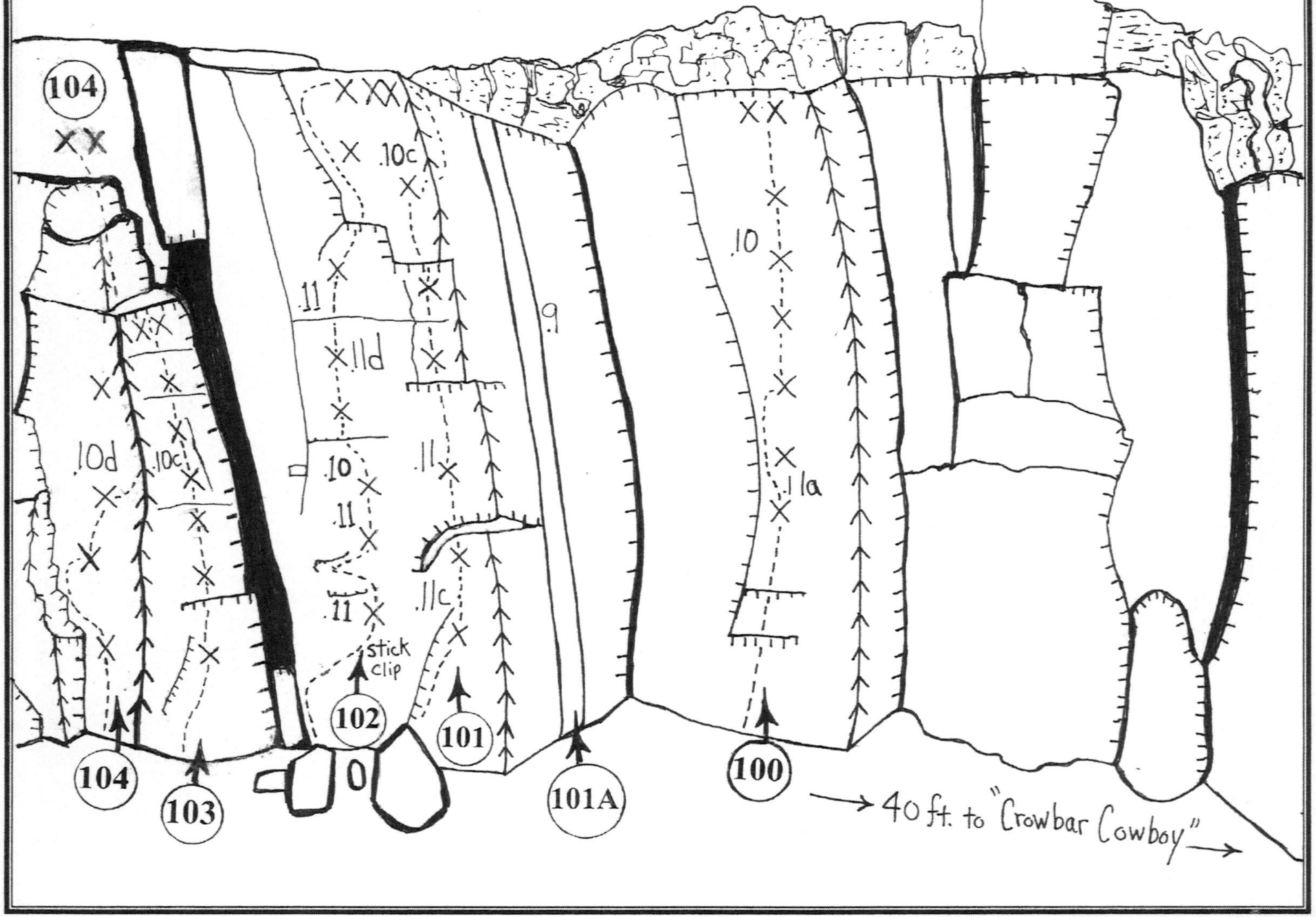

GOLDEN CLIFFS * WINTERFEST WALL * RIGHT SIDE

The **WINTERFEST WALL** and the **HOT SPOT AREA** combined, provide one of the best selection of routes from 5.9 to 5.12b on the **GOLDEN CLIFFS**. The average route is 60 feet in length. The majority of routes here receive three stars and are 5.10 or 5.11. The **WINTERFEST WALL** receives the last rays of sun before dusk, making it an ideal winter spot. The exception to this rule is on windy days, since the area is not blocked from a wind blowing from the north or west.

100. **WHOLE LOTTA DRUNK.** *** 5.11a 6 bolts / 2 bolt anchor. Scramble up to a high 1st bolt. A hard bouldery start past the 1st bolt, leads to fun moderate climbing above. First ascent by Tod Anderson & Richard Wright.

101A. **JELL-O BRAND NAPALM.** ***? 510. Small to medium nuts & cams / 3 mussy hooks. Climb double cracks right of the arete to the anchor on **The Resolution**. F.A.: Richard & Scott Berk in 1989.

101. **THE RESOLUTION.** *** 5.11c 6 bolts / 3 bolts & mussy hooks. Tricky and powerful moves lead past the first 3 bolts to good holds & the 4th bolt. Gain a good ledge. Finish up the arete past the last bolt. F.A.: Ken Trout, Guy Lords and Jim Garber around 1989.

102. **THE DISSOLUTION.** **** 5.11d/12a 7 bolts / 3 bolts & mussy hooks. A stick clip is useful for the 1st bolt, or stretch to clip from a wide chimney stem. A sustained and forearm pumping route for the Golden Cliffs. Tricky moves lead to 3rd bolt. Reach jugs & shake out below 4th bolt. Avoid the off-route rest in the vertical crack left of the 4th bolt. The crux past the 5th bolt, deadpoints from tiny edges to a good hold. Continue past a final redpoint crux to reach a ledge below the last bolt. Move up a tiny right-facing corner & then right to the anchor. F.A.: Tod Anderson & Richard Wright in 1993.

103. **LEANING PILLAR.** *** 5.10c 6 bolts / 2 mussy hooks. Start with a juggy face, past 2 bolts, to gain a small shelf. Continue up a clean, steep face along a hairline seam, with crux moves past the 4th bolt. Finish up jugs. F.A.: Dave Hart & Pete Wisnie in 1989. Originally led with 1 bolt & a piton. Retro-bolted & new start added by Ken Trout in December 2007.

104. **FRACTIONS.** (**Left Side Of Leaning Pillar**). * 5.10d 4 bolts / 2 Fixe rings. Start up a small right-facing corner to gain a ledge. Traverse right across the face & climb the arete. Gain a stance above the last bolt & just left of the mussy hook anchor for the **Leaning Pillar**. Lowering off this anchor will run your rope across the arete & is too far right to effectively clean the pitch. Continue up easy terrain for 10 feet to a blocky ledge & the anchor. F.A.: Richard Wright & Tod Anderson in 1993.

GOLDEN CLIFFS * WINTERFEST WALL * CENTER

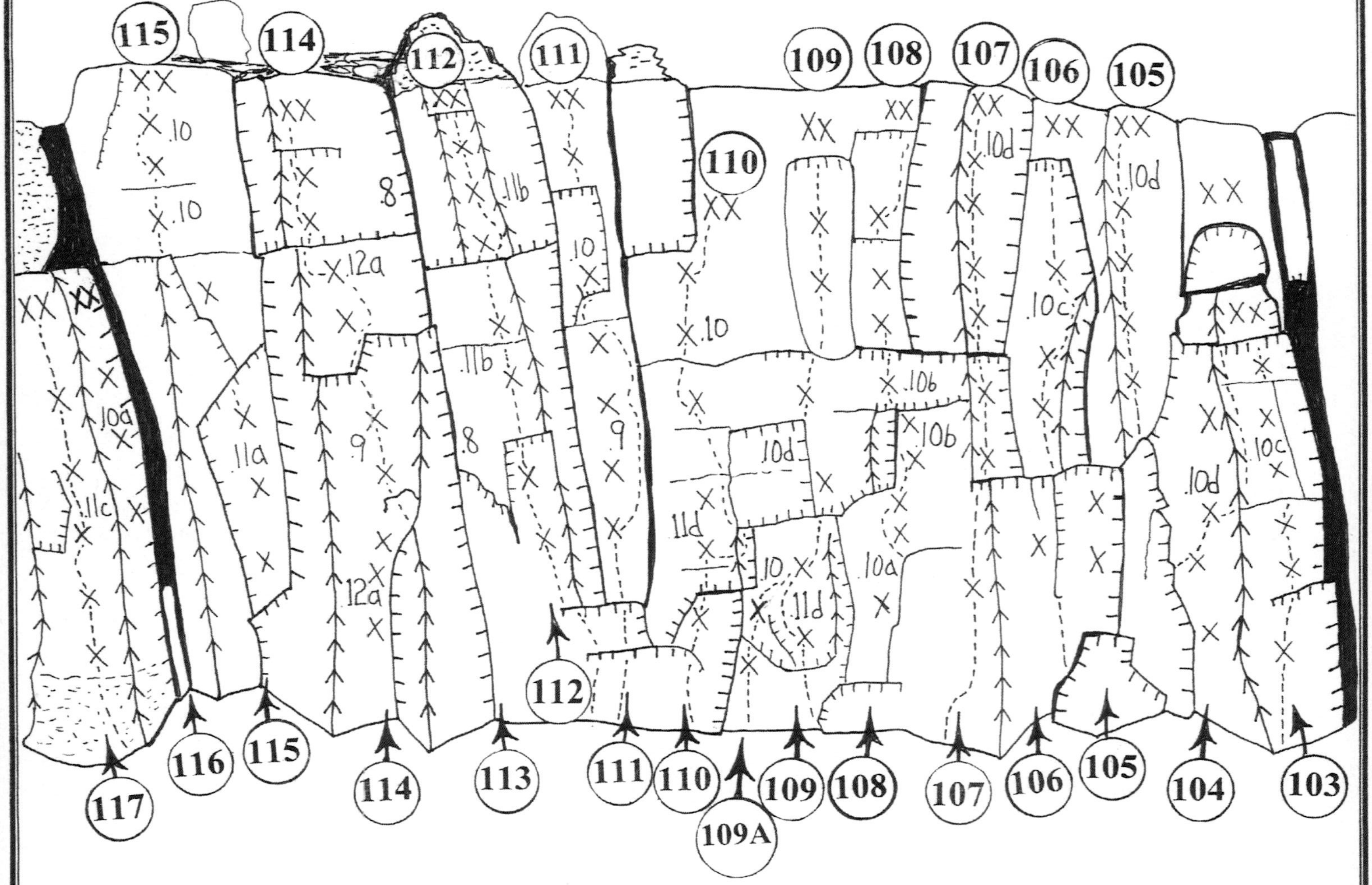

103. **LEANING PILLAR.** *** 5.10c 6 bolts / 2 mussy hooks. See previous page for description & first ascent information.

104. **FRACTIONS.** (**Left Side Of Leaning Pillar**). * 5.10d 4 bolts / 2 Fixe rings. See previous page for description & first ascent information.

105. **GENERICA.** * 5.10d 6 bolts / 2 chains anchor. Climb a dihedral to a ledge. Climb the face up the right side of the arete, avoiding the easier gully corner to the left. First ascent by Alan Nelson in 1993.

106. **UNDER THE WIRE.** ** 5.10c PG-13 4 bolts / 2 Fixe rings. A piece of gear (#.5 Alien to #3 Friend) is useful before 2nd bolt. A stick clip is useful for 1st bolt. No longer the easiest sport route on the **Winterfest Wall**, since holds have broken. Follow cracks past 1st bolt to a ledge & 2nd bolt. Climb a tricky arete past 3rd bolt. At 4th bolt move left & climb a face to a ledge & the anchor. F.A.: Richard Wright in 1993.

107. **AN ARTICHOKE.** * 5.10d 7 bolts / 2 bolt anchor. Climb a face left of the arete to a ledge. Continue up a corner to another ledge. Climb the arete with a crux finish up its right side. First ascent by Alan Nelson in 1993.

108. **SILVER BULLET.** *** 5.10b/c 9 bolts / 2 Fixe rings. Start up a flake with a thin crack. Climb up the face & up a small right-facing corner. Pull past a small bulge & gain a ledge. Finish up a moderate crack corner. It is possible to move left to the anchor on **Tanning Butter** before reaching the anchor for **Silver Bullet**. F.A.: Rick Leitner, Brian Hansen, Mike & Tom Carr in 1990. Retro-bolted by Ken Trout in Jan. 2008.

109. **TANNING BUTTER.** ** 5.11d 6 bolts / 2 mussy hooks. A desperate crux pulls over a bulge, past the 1st bolt, to gain a slab. Pass a roof on the right & ascend a short right-facing crack corner to a ledge. Finish up a moderate prow. First ascent by Alan Nelson in 1993.

109A. **PASS THE TANNING BUTTER.** *** 5.10d 7 bolts / 2 hooks. This is a 2 bolt variation to the start of **Tanning Butter** up a right-facing corner that avoids the crux & joins at its 2nd bolt. F.A.: Ken Trout, Kirk Miller, Adam Schroeder & Jeroen Van Wolferen on January 13, 2008.

110. **KILIAN'S RED.** *** 5.11d 6 bolts / 2 mussy hooks. Scramble to 1st bolt. The crux, past 2nd bolt, moves right & up the right-facing corner. At a roof, step back left to 3rd bolt. The crux also goes directly up the red face. Finish up dark rock. F.A.: Mike Carr & Tom Carr - 1990.

111. **BIMBO IN LIMBO.** *** 5.10b 6 bolts / 2 hooks. She wanders around a bit taking the line of least resistance up varied climbing. Scramble up ledges to 1st bolt. Move right, past 2nd bolt & follow a wide crack to 4th bolt. Traverse left across the face to the dihedral. Ascend the face to 5th bolt. The crux gains a tiny right-facing corner leading to a small ledge & last bolt. Finish up easy climbing. F.A.: Alan Nelson - 1993.

112. **CRAWLING UP ROSEANNE'S BELLY.** *** 5.11b/c 7 bolts / 2 mussy hooks. Clip first 2 bolts & climb straight up overhung moves to a good ledge & 3rd bolt. It is easier to move left to **Bush Loves Detroit**, then up & right to this ledge. The first crux climbs a rounded prow past 3rd bolt. Follow the prow to a small roof. The second crux pulls over the roof using the left arete. F.A.: Ken Trout & Rick Leitner in 1990.

113. **BUSH LOVES DETROIT.** *** 5.8 #.5 - 3 Friends (two 2 - 2.5), medium nuts. Jam & lieback up the dihedral. F.A.: Scott & Rick Berk -'80s.

114. **PSEUDO BULLET.** *** 5.12a 9 bolts / 2 mussy hooks. Ascend a disappearing, left-facing corner past the 3rd bolt. A strange crux pinches the arete to reach good holds. 5.9 climbing gains a flat ledge to camp on. Step up right onto a higher ledge & then traverse left across the face underneath a tiny roof, to gain the arete. Finish up the arete. F.A.: Ken Trout in 1989. F.F.A.: Dave Twinam and Annette Bunge in 1990.

115. **INTERSTELLAR OVERDRIVE.** **** 5.11a 7 bolts / 2 Fixe rings. Enter a flared dihedral at 1st bolt. The crux stems or chimneys up the dihedral, past 2nd & 3rd bolt, to gain a ledge. Climb up left to a shelf on the prow. Ascend a steep face to the top. F.A.: Dave Hart led the dihedral to the top without bolts in the late '80s. First ascent of the face finish & retro-bolting of the crux dihedral by Ken Trout in 1990.

116. **CHIMNEY.** * 5.10a R 3 bolts / 2 chains. Run it out up a smooth chimney. At the anchor, it's possible to finish up **Interstellar Overdrive**.

117. **DRIVING OVER STELLA.** *** 5.11c 5 bolts / 2 mussy hooks. See the following pages for description & first ascent information.

GOLDEN CLIFFS * WINTERFEST WALL * CENTER

108. **SILVER BULLET.** *** 5.10b/c

110. **KILIAN'S RED.** *** 5.11d

111. **BIMBO IN LIMBO.** *** 5.10b

112. **CRAWLING UP ROSEANNE'S BELLY.** *** 5.11b/c

114. **PSEUDO BULLET.** *** 5.12a

115. **INTERSTELLAR OVERDRIVE.** **** 5.11a

117. **DRIVING OVER STELLA.** *** 5.11c

118. **REBEL YELL.** *** 5.11b

117. **DRIVING OVER STELLA.** *** 5.11c
118. **REBEL YELL.** *** 5.11b
119. **SUNSET ARETE.** **** 5.11a/b
120. **NOUVEAU REACH.** *** 5.11b
121. **CAT'S MEOW.** *** 5.9/10a
123. **PUMCAT.** *** 5.12b or 5.11b/c

GOLDEN CLIFFS * WINTERFEST WALL * LEFT SIDE

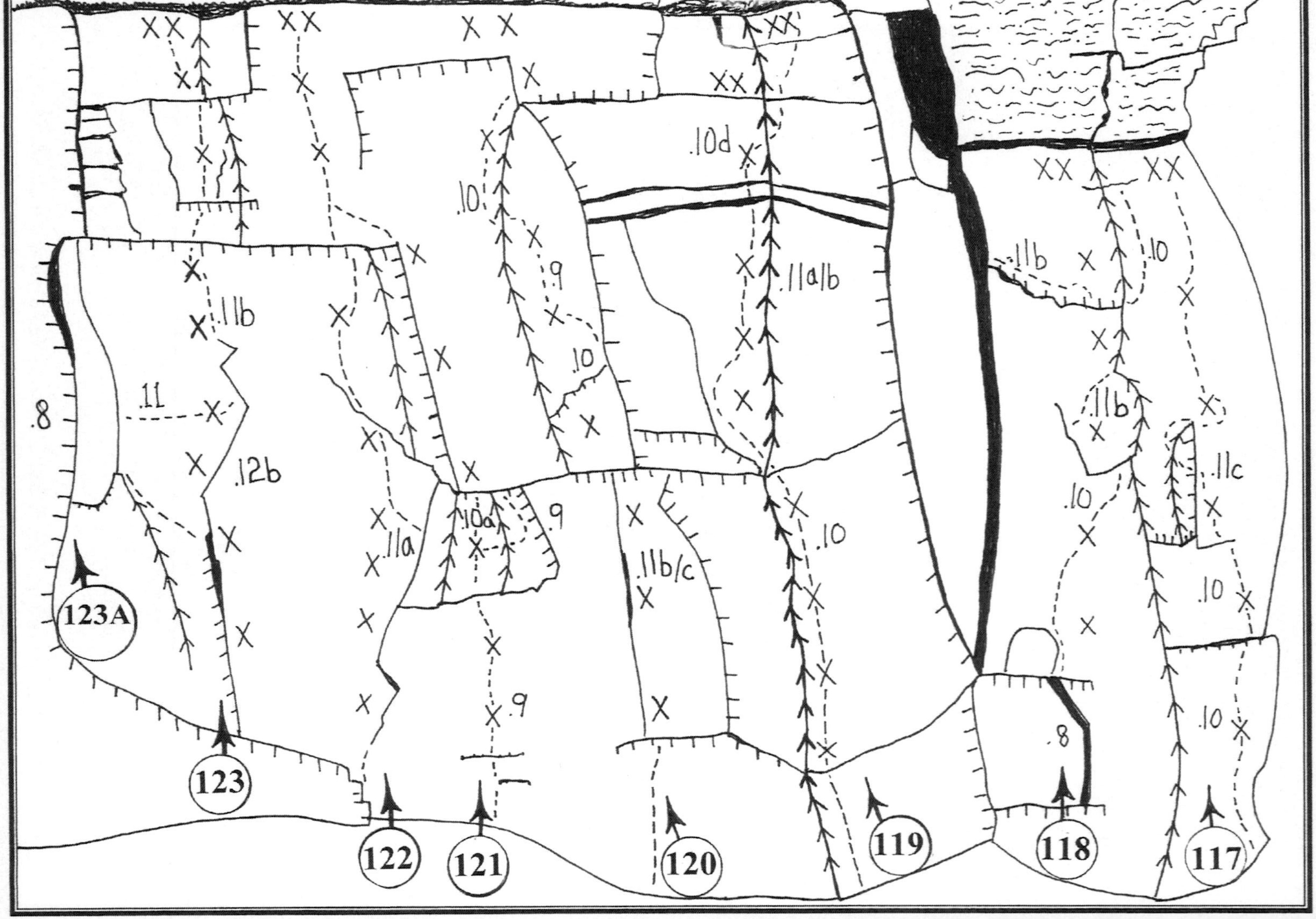

117. **DRIVING OVER STELLA.** *** 5.11c 5 bolts / 2 'biners anchor. Ascend a bulging face with a strenuous crux moving up a tiny right-facing corner past 3rd & 4th bolt. Finish with a steep slab or up the exposed arete on the right.
First ascent by Ken Trout and Guy Lords in 1990.

118. **REBEL YELL.** *** 5.11b 5 bolts / 2 Fixe rings. Start along a wide crack leading to a ledge. Climb the face and left side of the arete to just below the last bolt. To continue up the left side of the arete becomes extremely difficult. Either move right & climb the face up the arete's right side or traverse left across the face (5.11b) to a wide crack, that is followed to the anchor.
First ascent: Tod Anderson & James Donnell in 1990.

119. **SUNSET ARETE.** **** 5.11a/b 8-9 bolts / 2 bolt anchor. Climb a vertical face past 4 bolts to a stance on the left side of the arete. Move up left on a slab to a ledge. The crux ascends the sharp vertical arete using holds on both sides, past the 6th & 7th bolt, to reach a horizontal break. Reach another horizontal break & continue up the arete to jugs above the original anchor. There are currently two anchors. The original anchor is the higher anchor. A new anchor with mussy hooks is 4 feet lower. It was placed here because the equipper didn't trust the block his original anchor is in. He left the original anchor for those climbers who want to end the climb at it. The original anchor has worked fine for over 19 years & I see no reason not to trust it. The climbing is interesting to the holds above this anchor. F.A.: Ken Trout & Guy Lords in 1989. Retro-bolted by Ken Trout in January 2008.

120. **NOUVEAU REACH.** (A.k.a.: **PHOTO ART**) *** 5.11b 8 bolts / 2 Fixe rings. Scramble up to a shelf & the 1st bolt. A deceptively easy looking crux stems up between a thin crack and a left-facing corner, past the 2nd & 3rd bolts. Gain a ledge and ascend a right-facing dihedral for a short distance. Move left and climb the arete to where it joins the crack. Finish up the crack to a good ledge & the anchor.
First ascent led with gear by Jeff Brown in 1988. Retrobolted by Alan Nelson in Spring 2001.

121. **CAT'S MEOW.** *** 5.9/10a 8 bolts / 2 Fixe rings. A bulging start gains a rest. A tricky crux leads up a short arete past the 3rd bolt. It is possible to move right and then up a corner to avoid this crux. Follow a corner to a good ledge. Finish up a face with slightly friable rock. F.A.: Alan Nelson in Spring 2001.

122. **TWINKLETOES.** ** 5.11a 8 bolts / 2 Fixe rings. This route follows the right-leaning thin crack to the right of the bolt line. Move left onto the face at the 4th bolt. Gain a small shelf & 6th bolt. Face moves gain a large ledge. Above the ledge, either finish up **Cat's Meow** or **Pumcat**. First ascent by Alan Nelson in Spring 2001.

123. **PUMCAT.** *** 5.12b (direct line) or 5.11b (indirect variation) 8 bolts / 2 Fixe rings. An excellent route with clean stone. The direct line is sustained & powerful. Climb straight up the hairline seam from the 2nd to 4th bolt. The crux is at the 4th bolt to gain a good hold in a small triangular pod & 5th bolt. The line of least resistance moves left & up a small ramp past the 2nd bolt. Clip the 4th bolt from a small stance. 5.11 moves lead up & right onto the face with hairline seam. Both variations merge above the 4th bolt. Undercling off the triangular pod, at the 5th bolt, to reach edges. Gain a good ledge. A moderate finish leads up a face on the left side of an arete, past the last 2 bolts. First ascent by Alan Nelson in Spring 2001.

123A. **RUNT** *? 5.8 Climb the crack corner left of **Pumcat**. First ascent by Alan Nelson in Spring 2001.

Dianne Dallin leading the stemming crux of **INTERSTELLAR OVERDRIVE** (**** 5.11a) on the Winterfest Wall - Center in 1993. Photo by the author.

The author on **PUMCAT** *** 5.12b on the Winterfest Wall - Left Side. Photo by Mike Dallin.

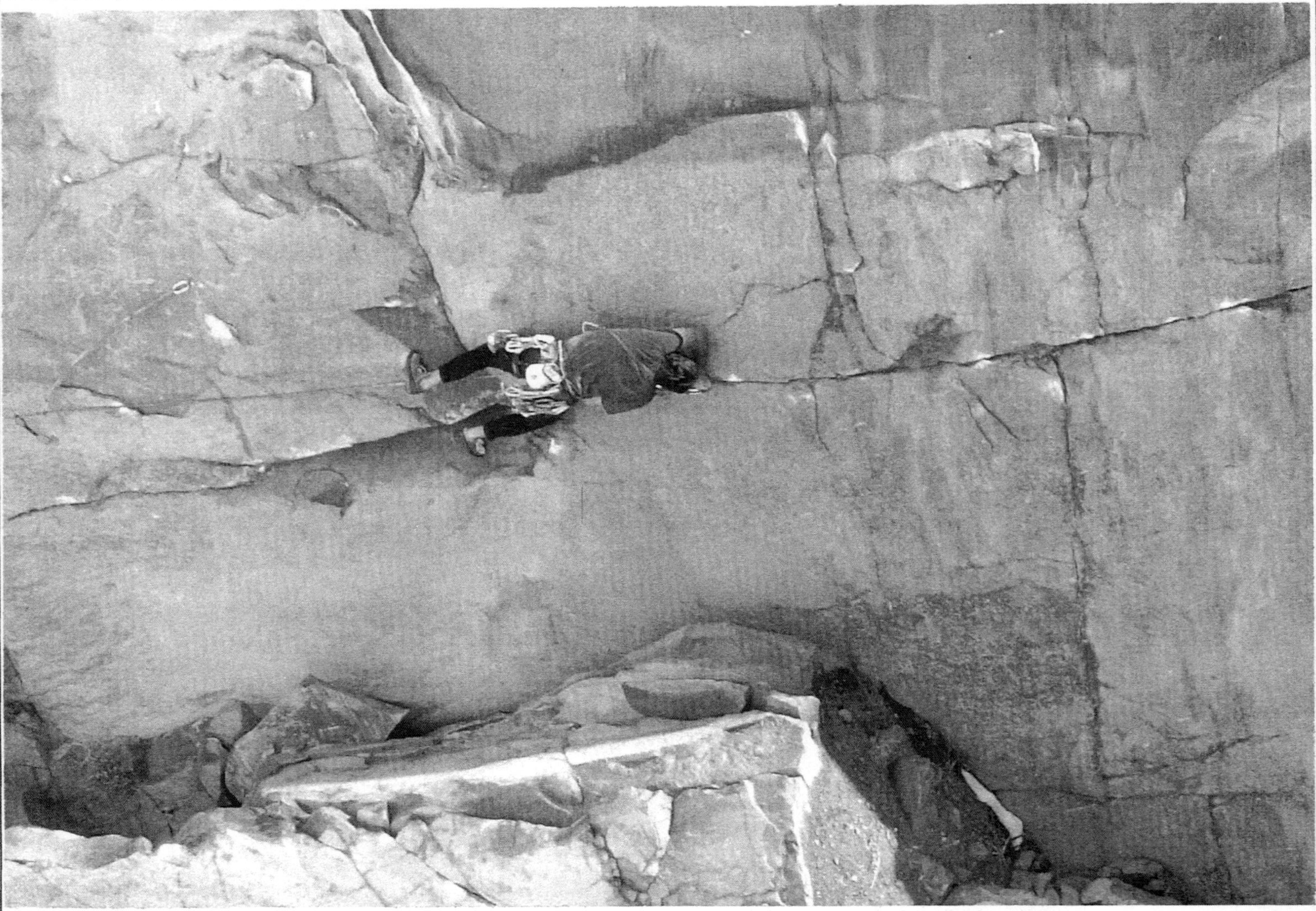

Bob Horan on the first ascent of **Sweet** (*** 5.11a) on the Crater Crag - North Quarries. Tired of the Golden Cliffs? This thin crack is located on the mesa's top, less than 10 minutes from the Risk Area. See page 107.

A. **THE DELEGATE.** ** 5.10d/11a

124. **ROPE TRICK.** *** 5.11a

125. **BABY BEEPER.** *** 5.10

GOLDEN CLIFFS * THE RISK AREA * Right Side

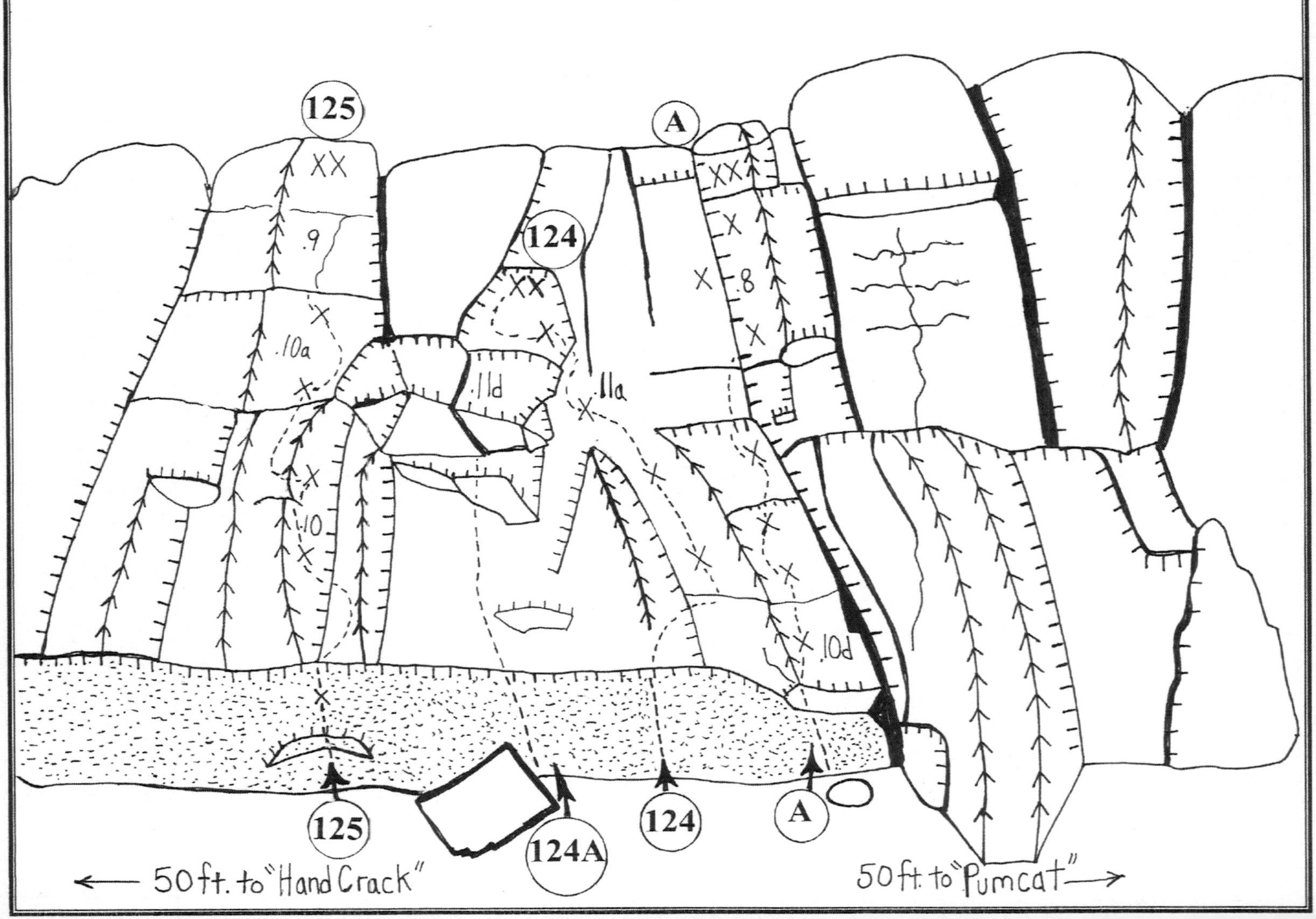

GOLDEN CLIFFS * THE RISK AREA * Right Side

The **Risk Area** is the leftmost section of the west face before the cliffband becomes too small for roped routes. The longer climbs at the **Risk Area** are 50 feet in length and are on the **right side** & middle (right end of the **left side**). The routes on the left end (see following pages) are short. These 20 to 35 foot high climbs are worth doing, offering great stone & fun moves.

A. **THE DELEGATE.** ** 5.10d/11a 7 bolts / 2 Fixe rings. The crux start pulls over a small bulge on an arete, past the 1st bolt, & onto a clean red face. Continue up the face along the right side of the arete, moving right to the 4th bolt. Gain a ledge & the obvious dihedral. Climb the dihedral, past 3 bolts, to the anchor. F.A.: Mark Rolofson, Jeroen Van Wolferen & Tim Slater on February 9, 2008.

124. **ROPE TRICK.** *** 5.11a 4 bolts / 2 bolt anchor. Pull onto a ledge 4 feet off the ground. Traverse right on a thin horizontal break to a jug & clip the 1st bolt. Ascend a shallow corner to the 3rd bolt. The wall above overhangs. Move left & up into a right-facing corner. At the 4th bolt, hand traverse left on a sloping shelf above a roof. Stand up on the shelf to reach the anchor. It can be tricky to find the good holds on this short, strenuous route. F.A: Guy Lords & Ken Trout in 1990.

124A. **SINISTER MINISTER.** *? 5.11d Top-rope / 2 bolt anchor. Climb up to & over a blocky roof to the anchor on **Rope Trick**. F.A.: Guy Lords around 1990.

125. **BABY BEEPER.** *** 5.10c 5 bolts / 2 Fixe rings. Deceptively easy-looking. Start by climbing up jugs over a small bulge to reach the 1st bolt & then a small ledge below a right-facing corner. Step left to the 2nd bolt into another right-facing corner. Climb up the corner for a few feet & move left onto the arete. At the 3rd bolt, pull around the arete to a good stance on the prow. Continue up steep terrain & then step right to a sloping stance & the last bolt. Step back left & run it out on jugs up a vertical face finish.
F.A.: Mike & Tom Ross around 1990.

GOLDEN CLIFFS * THE RISK AREA * Left Side

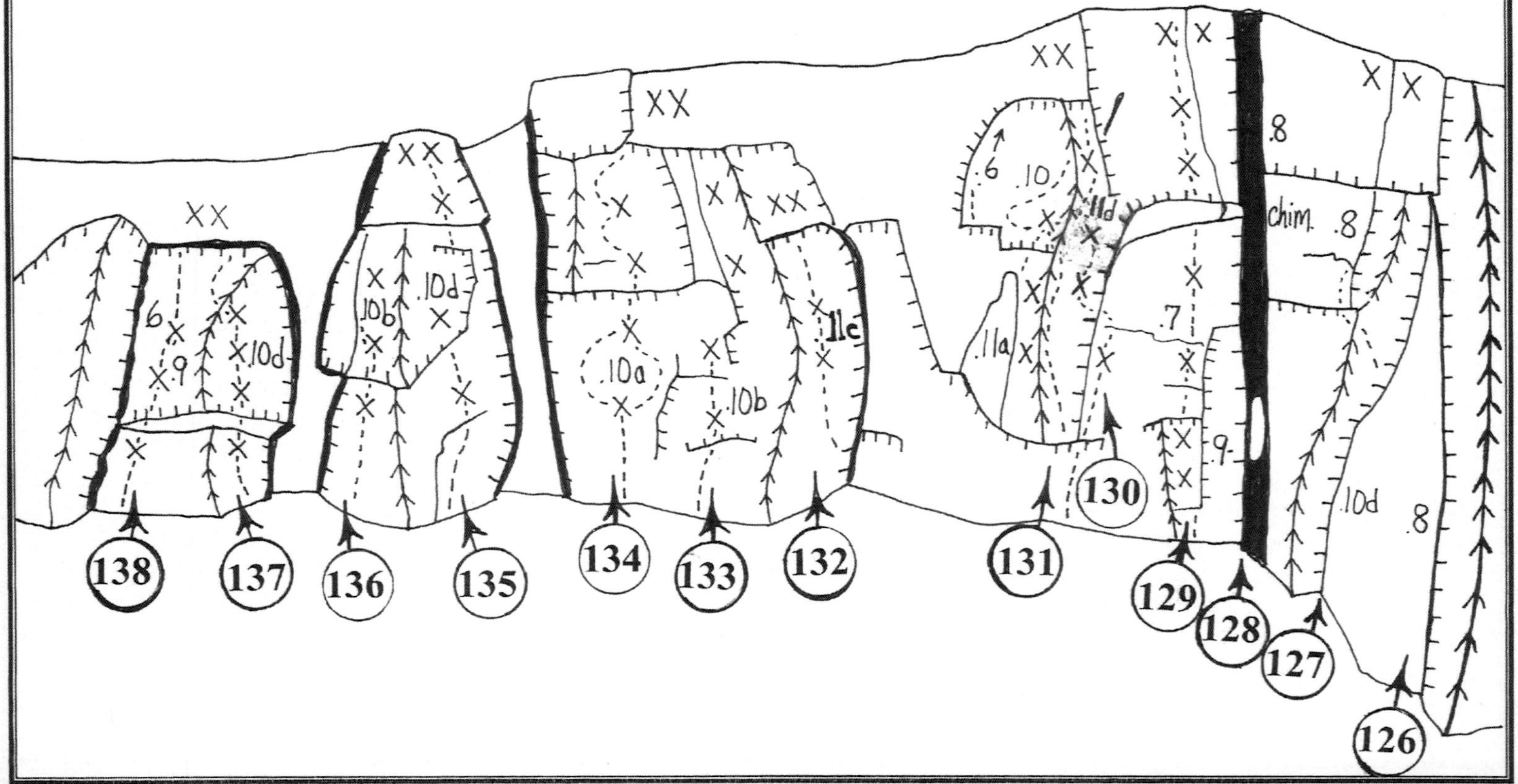

GOLDEN CLIFFS * THE RISK AREA * Left Side

This is the leftmost section of the Golden Cliffs. Further left the cliffband becomes more broken. A trail continues north & then leads through a break in the cliffband to the top of the mesa. The climbs on the right side of the **Risk Area - Left Side** are 50 feet in length. The leftmost routes are 20 to 35 ft. in length, but worth doing, offering great stone & fun moves.

126. **HAND CRACK.** ** 5.8 Gear to 3" (Mainly #2-3 Friends or #1-2 Camalot) / 2 Fixe rings. Climb a hand crack up a left-facing corner.

127. **METTLE DETECTOR.** ** 5.10c/d #3-6 steel nuts, #.3 Alien (black) to #2.5 Friend, small to medium stoppers / 2 Fixe rings. Climb a short right-facing corner with a very thin crack for 20 ft. to where it eases off before joining the **Hand Crack**. Move left onto a ledge. Continue up a left-facing corner. Pull past a tiny roof & onto a small shelf. Finish with easy moves up a thin crack
First ascent: Alan Nelson in Spring 2001.

128. **CHIMNEY ROUTE.** 5.8 Ascend a chimney.

129. **THIS BONE'S FOR YOU.** *** 5.9- 6 bolts / 2 Fixe rings. The crux start ascends the arete & a tiny left-facing corner past the first 2 bolts. Continue with greater ease up a juggy vertical face passing a tiny roof. First ascent by Alan Nelson in Spring 2001.

130. **CHILLIN' AND DRILLIN'.** * 5.11d 4 bolts / 2 Fixe rings. Climb a large right-facing dihedral to 3rd bolt. Ascend a bulging face up the left wall of the corner, moving left to the arete. Join **This Bolt's For You** at the last bolt, finishing up a left-facing corner on the right side of the arete. F.A.: Mike Morley & Alan Nelson on January 16, 2004.

131. **THIS BOLT'S FOR YOU.** ** 5.11a or 5.11d 4 bolts / 2 Fixe rings. The easier variation climbs the face to the left of the bolt line. The harder variation stays on the arete, right of the bolts & finishes up a left-facing corner on the right side of the arete.
First ascent by Tod Anderson, Dave Field, & Ernie Moskovics in 1991.

132. **RISK OF INJECTION.** * 5.11c 2 bolts / chains anchor. Short & bouldery. Climb a small overhang with the crux dyno above the 2nd bolt. F.A. Guy Lords in 1990.

133. **NOT.** ** 5.10b 4 bolts / 2 Fixe rings. Overhung moves lead up brown rock past the 2nd bolt. Gain a small corner leading to a small ledge. Finish up cracks. F.A. Alan Nelson in 1993.

134. **THE PERFECT 10.** ** 5.10a 4 bolts / 2 Fixe rings. Climb up left from the 1st bolt & reach back right to the high 2nd bolt. It may also be possible to do the opposite (move right from 1st bolt & back left to the 2nd bolt). Move right & up to a ledge. Continue up the face to a ledge & the anchor. F.A.: Alan Nelson in 1993.

135. **DADDY DWARF.** * 5.10d 3 bolts / 2 chains anchor. Ascend a bulging face. F.A.: Alan Nelson in 1993.

136. **MAMA MIDGET.** * 5.10b 3 bolts / 2 chains anchor. Climb the left side of a prow to a tiny roof. Follow a thin crack over the roof & up the face to the anchor. F.A.: Alan Nelson in 1993.

137. **MY RED CATCHER'S MITT.** ** 5.10d 4 bolts / 2 bolt anchor. Ascend the overhung right side of the 20 ft. leaning pillar on the left side of the **Risk Area**. F.A.: Top roped by Guy Lords in 1990. Bolted & first led by Alan Nelson in 2001.

138. **LITTLE GREEN APPLES.** * 5.6 or 5.9 3 bolts / 2 bolt anchor. Climb the left side of the 20 ft. leaning pillar via an easy right-facing corner (5.6) left of the bolts or the face & arete (5.9) along the bolts. This climb shares the anchor with **My Red Catcher's Mitt**.
First ascent by Alan Nelson in Spring 2001.

NORTH TABLE MOUNTAIN * Approach Map to North Quarry & THE PINNACLE AREA

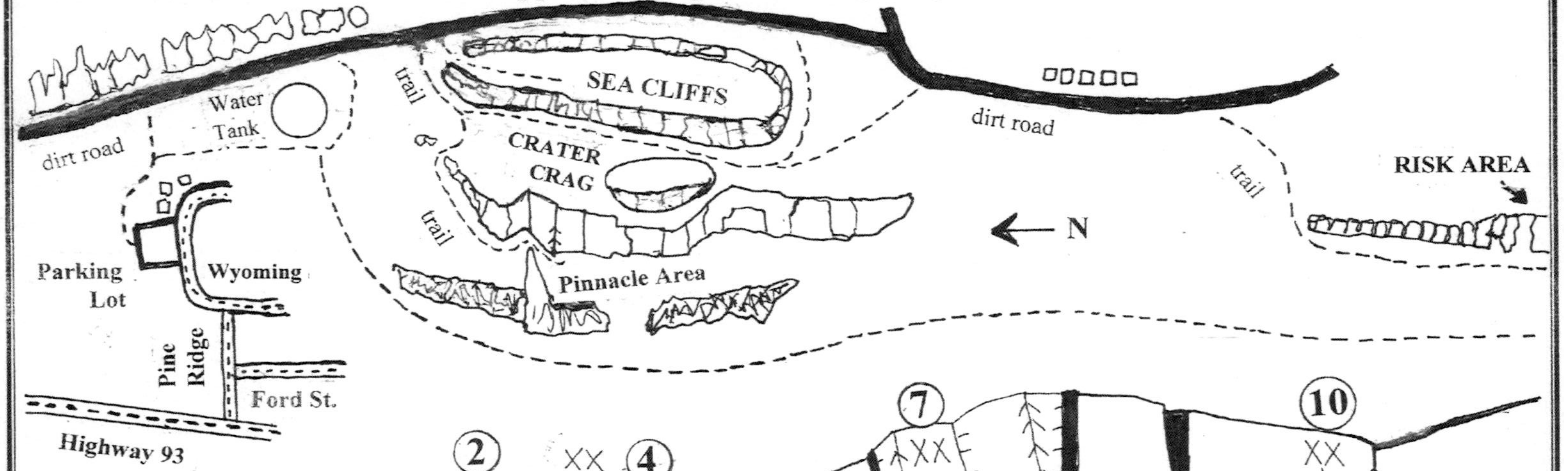

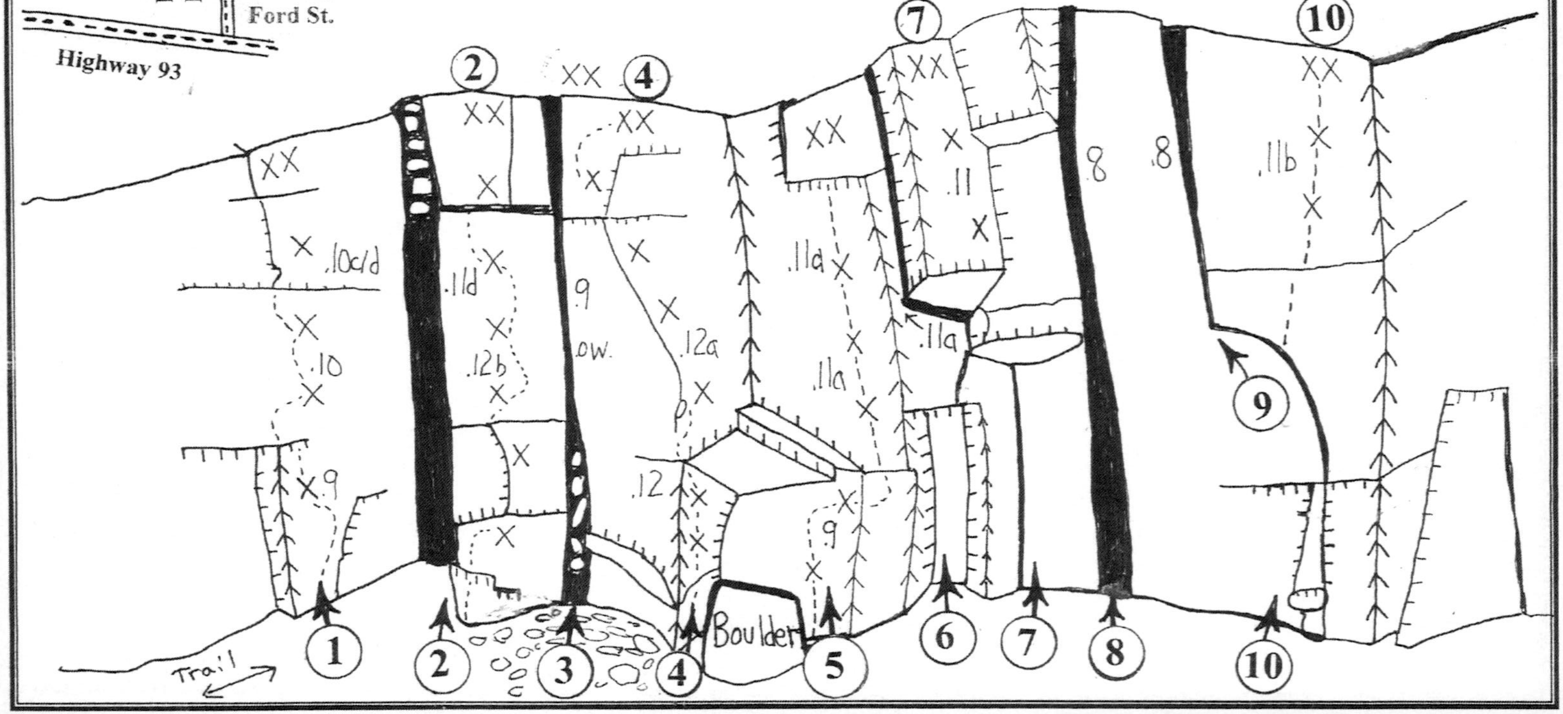

NORTH TABLE MOUNTAIN * Approach to North Quarry & THE PINNACLE AREA

The **Pinnacle Area** is located on the north end of northwest-facing cliff-band behind a prominent free standing pinnacle. The pinnacle & wall below do not have routes. The climbs are on the 50 ft. tall cliff below the rim of the mesa (see routes descriptions below). This area is not popular & has the least comfortable belay zones of any area in this book with sloping scree & talus at the base. It is a good spot to find shade with west & north faces.

There are **two approach options**. The **first & faster approach** begins from the north end of Golden. Turn east onto the Ford St. exit off Highway 93. This is the northernmost exit in Golden. Go straight on Pine Ridge Rd. for one block to a stop sign. Turn left onto Wyoming St., that leads to a paved parking lot on the left at the trailhead. Hike up a trail on the north side of houses to the dirt road. Follow the dirt road to the top of the mesa. The **Sea Cliffs** (pg. 105) are straight ahead. Walk into the flat pit to the climbs. **As of June 2010, there is a new parking area for North Table Mountain Park, north of the Ford St. exit off Highway 93.** This parking lot is at the bottom of the dirt road that leads up the mountain to the **Sea Cliffs**.

To reach the **Pinnacle Area** & the **Crater Crag**, turn right onto a trail leading up a short hill onto the rim. For the **Pinnacle Area**, walk 200 feet on the trail. Turn right & follow a steep path downhill (west) for 50 feet. A trail leads south 200 feet along the base of the cliff to the climbs at the **Pinnacle Area**. To reach the **Crater Crag**, stay on the trail that continues along the west rim of the **Sea Cliffs** to the east side of a second quarry in a narrower, deeper pit. This pit has the **Crater Crag** on its west side (see page 107). Allow 30 minutes for the approach to these crags.

The **second & longer approach option** is from the Golden Cliffs. The **Pinnacle Area** is 1/2 mile north of the **Risk Area - Left Side** (see pg. 101 & map on page 7). Starting from the left side of the **Risk Area**, follow a trail north for a few hundred feet, where it leads up onto the mesa. Continue northeast on the trail to a dirt road. Follow the road north to a quarry with a large flat pit. This is the **Sea Cliffs** (page 105). To reach the **Crater Crag** & **Pinnacle Area**, follow the trail north, between the rim of the mountain & the rim of the **Sea Cliffs**. After 300 feet you will reach the **Crater Crag**.

1. **HOMEMADE.** ** 5.10c/d PG-13 4 bolts (with homemade angle-iron hangers) / 2 chains. The leftmost route. Wander up the face, past the 1st bolt, to a ledge on the left. Step right to 2nd bolt & climb a devious vertical face. The sporty crux is getting to the last bolt.
2. **MANDOLIN WIND.** *** 5.12b 6 bolts / 2 Fixe rings. This route ascends the left side of the north face. Scramble to 1st bolt, then lieback up a flake to its top. The crux moves past 3rd bolt, on small edges to reach a jug. Reachy moves lead up the vertical face to a wide horizontal break & last bolt. Finish up a short crack. F.A.: Kaelen Williams & Mark Rolofson on May 15, 2009.
3. **WIDE PRIDE.** *? 5.9 Gear to 6" / 2 bolts with lowering rings. Ascend an offwidth / chimney crack up the north face. The anchor is on the top.
4. **WAYNE'S ROUTE.** *** 5.12c 6 bolts / 2 Fixe rings. Clip 1st bolt off a boulder & then begin from the ground. Climb a powerful arete to a roof. Reach 3rd bolt above a roof & continue up the vertical north face along a left-leaning thin crack. Move right below the top to the anchor. Partially equipped by Wayne Ingram in 2005? First 2 bolts added by M. Rolofson - May 2009. F.F.A.: Kaelen Williams - May 15, 2009 (flash).
5. **CATCHING THE QUARRY.** *** 5.11a 5 bolts / 2 coldshuts. Ascend the striking west face on perfect rock. Climb up & right to under a roof & 2nd bolt. Traverse right around the arete. Pull over a tiny bulge & climb a sustained vertical face. F.A.: Tod Anderson & Dave Field - 1992.
6. **BURLY MAN.** **? 5.11a Bring several #5 Camalots or giant cams / 2 coldshuts. Start with a shallow chimney with ledges. Undercling left on a wide crack around a roof & continue up the crack to the top & the anchor for **Stem Corner** on the right.
7. **STEM CORNER.** **? 5.11 Gear to #4 Friend, 2 bolts / 2 coldshuts. Climb a hand crack up a north face. Pull over a roof & stem up a corner.
8. **BOOBALATY.** 5.8 Climb the chimney.
9. **UNNAMED CRACK.** *? 5.8 Small to 5" gear / 2 coldshuts. Start with **Cracking Up** & traverse left. Climb a thin crack that becomes wide.
10. **CRACKING UP.** *? 5.11b #5 stopper - 3 Friend to 2 bolts / 2 coldshuts. Start with a short corner to a shelf. Climb a crack to where it traverses left. Ascend the vertical face with horizontal breaks, past 2 bolts. F.A.: Tod Anderson & Dave Field in 1992.

NORTH TABLE MOUNTAIN * NORTH QUARRY * EAST PIT (A.k.a.: SEA CLIFFS)

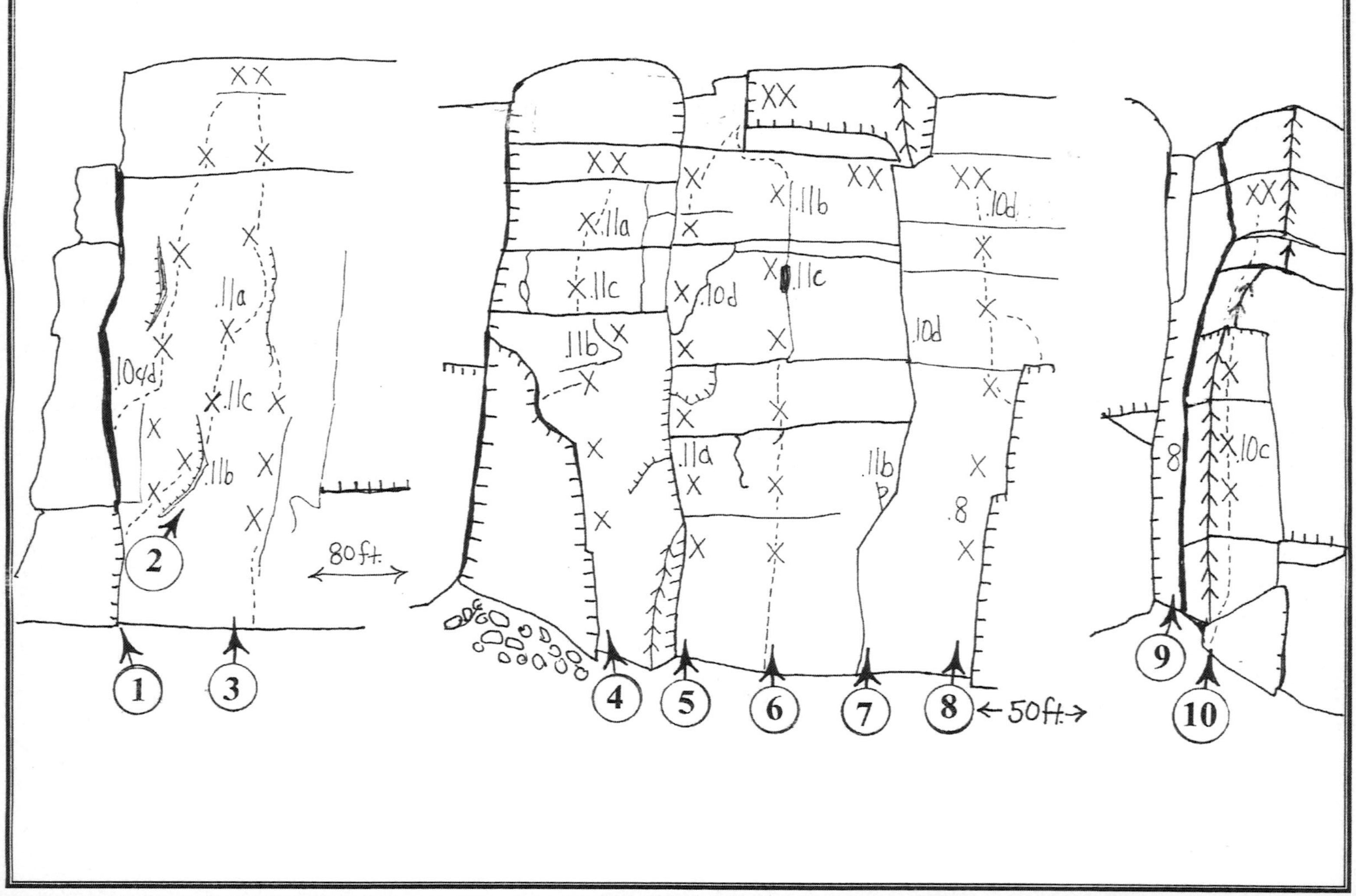

NORTH TABLE MOUNTAIN * NORTH QUARRY * EAST PIT (A.k.a.: SEA CLIFFS)

This wide quarry pit is located on top of the mesa. The dirt road leads up the hillside to this quarry. The climbs are on the east-facing wall, that is described in three sections. The overall rock quality is not as clean as most climbs on North Table Mountain. In other words, expect some friable rock. The better rock is a yellow white color. The darker rock is often very decomposed and rotten. The rock near the top is often worse than the rock on the lower two-thirds of the wall. The routes ascend vertical to bulging faces, that are well bolted & offer a good forearm pump.

MOONSCAPE WALL *

Located on the left side of the cliff, this face has two routes & a direct start that shares the same top anchor.

1. **MOONSCAPE.** 5.10c/d 6 bolts / 2 Fixe rings. Start up a left-leaning dirty crack & then move right onto the face. Climb the face with chossy holds. A well-bolted pile! F.A.: Bob Horan & Gillian Collins in April 2009.
2. **MOON WALK.** *** 5.11c 6 bolts / 2 Fixe rings. Start with the 1st bolt of **Moonscape** & then move right to 2nd bolt. Ascend the middle of the clean white face. Beautiful, balance moves lead to a high step, followed by reaches to good edges. F.A.: Bob Horan in April 2009.
3. **METEOR SHOWER.** 5.12? Project 6 bolts / 2 Fixe rings. This is a hard start to **Moon Walk.**

SUNRISE WALL *

This is the best section of the **Sea Cliffs**, with five routes including one crack climb. The routes have been cleaned of big blocks & most of the holds are solid. Some scaly rock & small pieces of loose rock still fall off, when touched or kicked. The belayer should wear sunglasses to keep rock out of their eyes & a helmet is wise. For a 5.11 climber this is a fun 40 to 50 foot tall face.

4. **DAY BREAK.** *** 5.11b/c 6 bolts / 2 bolt anchor. Ascend a small right-facing hand crack corner. At 3rd bolt, move right onto the bulging face via small holds to reach a jug. Move up to a horizontal crack & 5th bolt. The crux uses small holds to reach a horizontal break. Continue straight up the face with more reach moves off small edges to the anchor. F.A.: Bob Horan in April 2009.
5. **SUNRISE.** **** 5.11a 7 bolts / 2 Fixe rings. The best route on the wall with solid holds. The rock gets dirtier with some decomposed rock above the last bolt, but solid holds can be found. Start up a shallow corner via lieback moves to reach jugs. Continue along a seam up sustained, pumpy climbing with a variety of holds (jugs, lieback flakes, & sidepulls). F.A.: Bob Horan & Kevin Murphy in April 2009.
6. **STAR SHINE.** *** 5.11c 6 bolts / 2 Fixe rings. Excellent sustained climbing, but if you're looking for perfect rock, the finish may disappoint you. The rock around the last bolt is a bit flaky. Climb straight up the vertical face via good holds. The crux at 5th bolt uses small holds to get the horizontal crack above the last bolt. Traverse left on the crack to finish on the final holds of **Sunrise**. F.A.: Bob Horan in April 2009.
7. **SUNSET.** *** 5.11b R 1 fixed pin, RPs, stoppers, tiny cams to #1.5 Friend or Alien (orange) / 2 Fixe rings. Climb the thin crack. The crux is getting to & past the fixed pin. F.A.: Bob Horan & Kevin Murphy in April 2009.
8. **TWILIGHT.** 5.10d? 5 bolts / 2 bolt anchor. Start with moderate climbing up a small left-facing corner. Move left & climb a bulging face with tricky moves on some chossy rock. Don't be surprised if footholds break. F.A.: Bob Horan on April 26, 2009.

SEND FRIEND WALL *

This section of the **Sea Cliffs** is located 50 feet right of **Twilight** on the **Sunrise Wall**.

9. **SEND FRIEND.** *? 5.8 Cams to #2.5 Friend / 2 bolt anchor. Climb a hand crack left of **Send Arete** to its anchor. F.A.: Bob Horan & Gillian Collins in April 2009.
10. **SEND ARETE.** * 5.10c 3 bolts plus a couple .5" - .75" cams / 2 bolt anchor. Well protected moves lead up the right side of the blunt arete. Continue up an easy finish that can be protected with gear in thin horizontal cracks. F.A.: Bob Horan & Gillian Collins in April 2009.

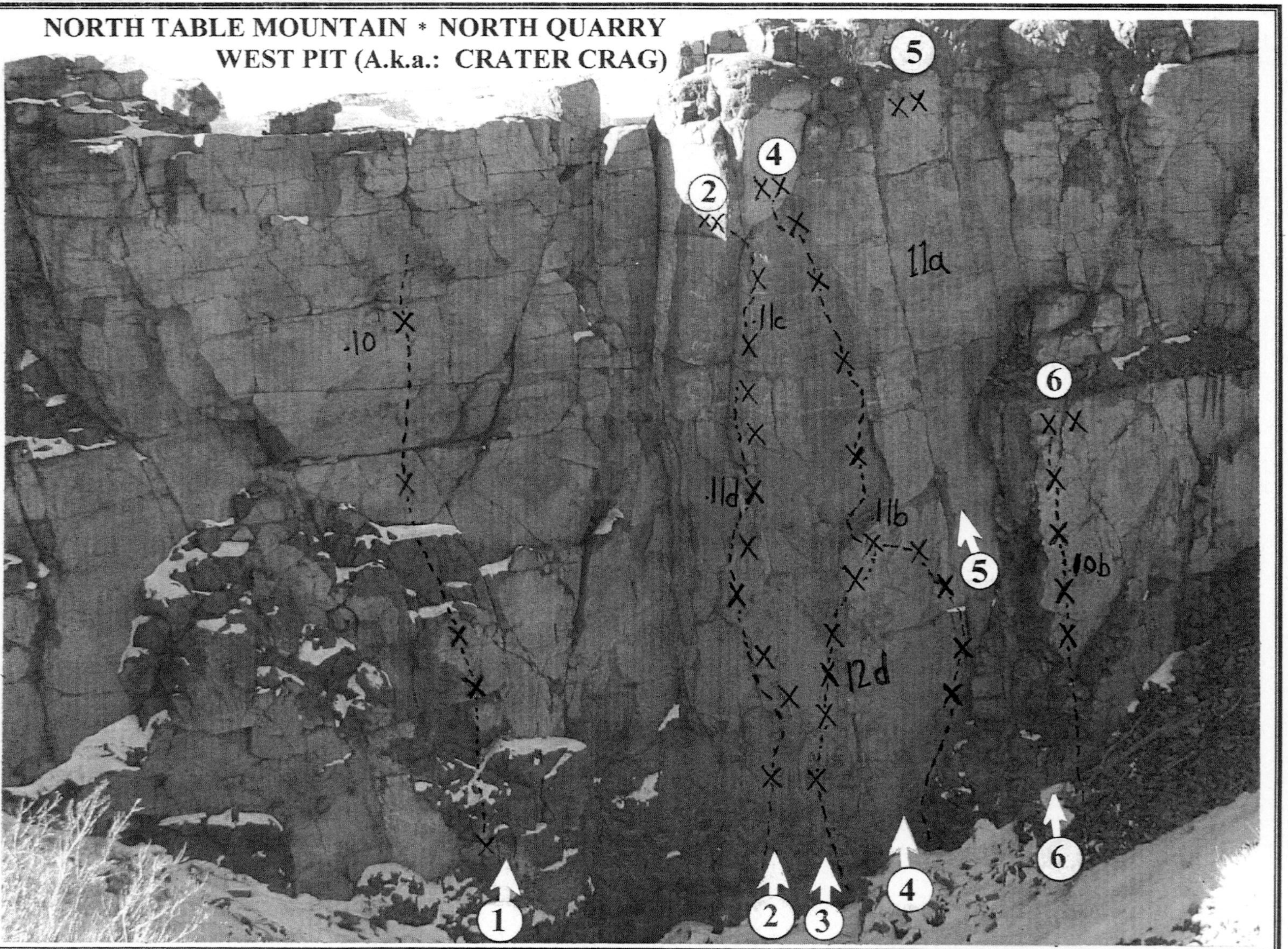
NORTH TABLE MOUNTAIN * NORTH QUARRY
WEST PIT (A.k.a.: CRATER CRAG)
.10
.11c
.11d
11a
11b
12d
10b
1
2
3
4
5
6

NORTH TABLE MOUNTAIN * NORTH QUARRY * WEST PIT (A.k.a.: CRATER CRAG)

The **Crater Crag** is located in a narrow, deep quarry pit just behind the rim of the mesa top south of the **Pinnacle Area**. Except for the east-facing 80 ft. tall wall of the **Crater Crag,** this pit resembles a crater. The rock wall is on the west side of the pit. There are steep dirt & scree slopes on all the other sides of the pit that lead down to its bottom. It is recommended to walk down into the pit on its south side along the base of the rock face. All the other slopes are more unstable with loose rock & scree that can easily be sent downhill into the pit. Be very careful walking down into the pit should people already be down in it. No way down is perfectly stable. See page 103 for the approach information from the parking area to this quarry. The approach takes about 30 minutes.

This quarry has a few great routes, but it's the least aesthetic spot on the mountain with much garbage, old metal pipes, barbed wire & wood planks strewn around the pit. There are a few flat belay zones at the base of **Misty**, **Golden Prow** & **Mountain Lion**.

1. **RANCID.** **? 5.10 5 bolts, plus a few pieces of small to medium gear / No lowering anchor. This route is located in the left side of the pit. Climb up the broken face past two ledges to 4th bolt. Continue up the face along a very thin crack to the last bolt. Finish up a crack. F.A.: Deaun Schovajsa & Dave Gottenborg in 1994.
2. **MISTY.** **** 5.11d 10-11 bolts (with gray hangers) / 2 Fixe rings. Stick clip is useful for 1st bolt. Start up softer rock & stand on a tiny shelf atop a hollow flake to reach 1st bolt. The flake seems intact but is suspect of becoming loose & pulling off. It is possible to clip the 1st bolt on **Golden Prow** with a long sling & station the belayer off right to the side. From 1st bolt, traverse left a few feet & move up to 2nd bolt. Continue angling up & left along lieback holds & tiny shelves to gain a small right-facing corner. Lieback holds lead up to 7th bolt & peter out. The crux involves reaches to positive edges. Ascend the corner past thin fingerlocks. Step right onto a small shelf on the arete & clip the anchor. This route offers sustained climbing from bottom to top. F.A.: Bob Horan & Adam Horan in March 2009.
3. **GOLDEN PROW.** ***? 5.12d 11 bolts / 2 Fixe rings. This variation is a hard direct start to **Mountain Lion** that ascends a rounded, bulging prow past 4 bolts with red hangers. Gain a steep short slab & 5th bolt. Move up & slightly right to join **Mountain Lion** at its 4th bolt. F.A.: (5.12 A0) Bob Horan in March 2009.
4. **MOUNTAIN LION.** **** 5.11b 9 bolts / 2 Fixe rings. Climb onto a ledge & clip 1st bolt. Ascend easy terrain up round blobs or blocks to a small sloping shelf & 3rd bolt. Stand up on the shelf using the start of the thin crack that **Sweet** ascends. Traverse left to 4th bolt. The crux ascends a vertical face, moving left & up, past 5th bolt. Mantle onto a good shelf. Climb a steep slab with nice edges. Move left to the last bolt & onto a shelf on the right side of the arete. Climb up & right to the anchor. F.A.: Bob Horan & Alex Shainman in March 2009.
5. **SWEET.** ***? 5.11a 3 bolts, RPs to #2 Friend (or #1 Camalot) / 2 bolt anchor. Start with the first 3 bolts of **Mountain Lion** to reach the base of a thin crack. Climb the thin crack. F.A.: Bob Horan & Mark Soot in March 2009.
6. **THE GIG.** ** 5.10b 4 bolts / 2 Fixe rings. This short route ascends the arete to a ledge halfway up the wall. Scramble onto a ledge to begin. Move up to face on the arete's right side & then back left onto arete. Climb the arete. F.A.: Bob Horan & Alex Shainman in March 2009.

NORTH TABLE MOUNTAIN * THE SOUTH QUARRY & EAST QUARRY WALLS

The **South Quarry Wall** offers 12 crack climbs up to 80 feet long. Most of the crack climbs have a two bolt anchor at the top. There are two of the best 5.12 crack climbs on the Front Range on this southeast-facing wall, offering continuous finger jamming. There are also five excellent hard sport routes, including **Elephantiasis**, Table Mountain's first 5.13!

The best season is Winter. This south face soaks up sun & is sheltered from wind out of the north. The wall is not sheltered from wind out of the west. It is possible to climb here during Spring & Fall on cooler days when the temperature doesn't reach 70 degrees. November into March are the recommended months. It can get hot here even in the Winter, but by late afternoon the wall gets shade providing cooler temperatures.

Avoid the South Quarry during a wet weather season. The upper part of **Elephantiasis** fell down in May 2009 after weeks of wet snow & rain.

Located 500 feet east is a smaller 50 foot tall quarry wall, known as the **East Quarry Wall**. The routes on the wall started to be established in January 2009. There are currently over 25 routes, including 14 cracks, 8 sport climbs & 4 mixed routes from 5.9 to 5.12d. This wall is very sheltered from the wind out of the north or west & sunny until late afternoon when it goes into the shade.

The quarried Basalt is much less featured with face holds than the nearby, popular **Golden Cliffs**. The rock surface texture at the **Quarry Walls** is also not as slick as the natural surface of the **Golden Cliffs**, making for better friction. The only thing to detract from this area is the noisy Coors Brewery Plant directly below on the other side of the highway. Otherwise, this is a secluded spot below the top of the mesa with excellent climbing.

Driving there: The **South & East Quarry Walls** are located east of the Golden Cliffs. Both walls are easily spotted from Highway 58 or 44th street on the north side of the Coors Brewery. From Ford Street take 10th Street east for 1.5 miles. In that distance it will turn into 44th street and cross underneath Highway 58. Take a sharp left onto Easley Way. Easley Way goes up a hill to a T intersection. Take a right onto Easley Road. If you go left, it turns into the on-ramp for Highway 58 West. Turn left onto Ridge Road and follow it for less than a tenth of a mile to a gate on the left with a Jefferson County Open Space sign. This is a trail head. Better yet, continue driving up Ridge Road, that immediately turns into Ulysses Way. Follow Ulysses Way that turns into 43rd Drive. The street comes to a dead end at a cul de sac & the trail head. The main trail starts here.

The approach: If you park down by the gate on Ridge Road, take the wide trail for a very short distance and then go right onto a trail leading uphill to the start of the main trail from the cul de sac on 43rd Drive. The trail heads north up the valley. This trail traverses up the hillside on the east side of the valley for 400 yards. The trail finally crosses over the drainage in the middle of the valley and then heads back south. The trail gradually climbs up the hillside on the west side of the valley. The trail reaches the ridge line & then heads west paralleling the highway. Walk underneath large power lines & pass 100 feet below the **East Quarry**, where a small path leads north to its base. The main trail continues to the west. To reach the **South Quarry** take a small path that leaves the main flat trail & heads up a small hill Gain a flat terrace, on top of a large scree bank. Walk west leading to the talus pile below the **South Quarry**. A small path leads to the base on the right side of the wall or cross the talus for 50 feet to reach the climbs on the left side of the wall. Allow 30-35 minutes for the approach. This long trail is an easy hike that is never steep.

The direct approach: This approach may be a bit shorter, even though not as aesthetic, since it is much noisier. Snow melts off this slope quicker than sections of the other trail. Park in a large pullout on the south side of Easley Road, just east of the T intersection at Easley Way. Walk west along Easley Road, where it turns to the on-ramp for Highway 58. Follow a trail diagonally west up a steep hillside for 400 feet to where it joins a flat, wide path along an old road bed. This trail heads west & gradually bends uphill and north. This trail continues all the way to the top of the mesa, but you will leave it much sooner. Take a right onto a wide trail, along an old road bed, that leads east. After several hundred feet there is a fallen cottonwood tree across the trail that must climbed over. Continue on the trail to underneath a dirt and scree bank directly below the **South Quarry**. A small trail diagonals up the right side of the steep scree bank to gain the flat terrace below the cliff. To reach the **East Quarry** continue east for 500 feet.

NORTH TABLE MOUNTAIN * SOUTH & EAST QUARRY WALLS * Road and Trail Map

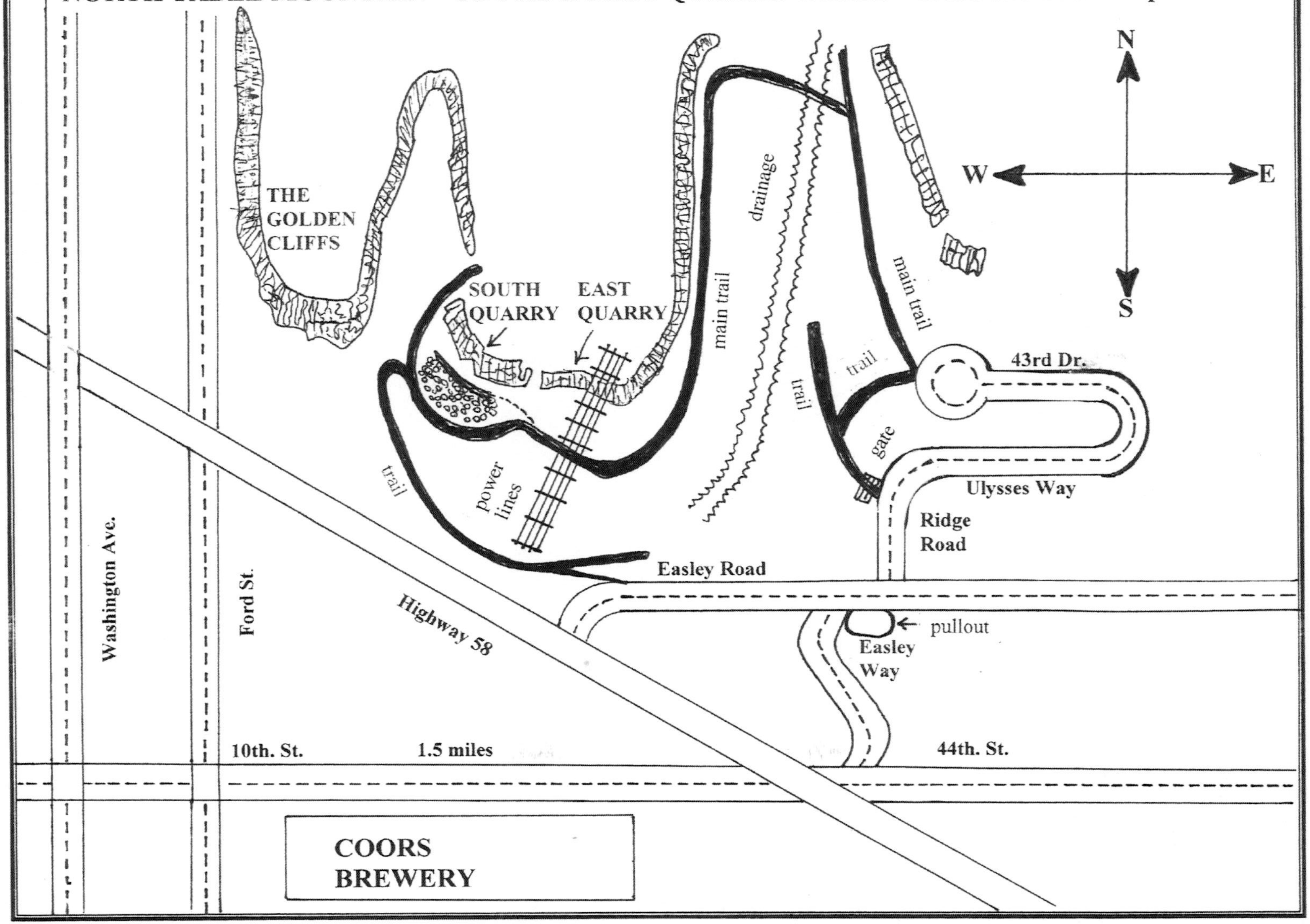

NORTH TABLE MOUNTAIN * SOUTH QUARRY WALL * LEFT SIDE

1. **EASTERN HEART.** *** 5.12a/b
2. **RECESSION.** **** 5.11d/12a
3. **DEPRESSION.** * 5.10a
4. **ELEPHANTIASIS.** **** 5.13b
5. ***KLEPTOCRACY.*** ***** 5.12d/13a
6. **BONE COLLECTOR.** ***** 5.12b/c
7. **SILVER BULLET II.** ***** 5.12a

NORTH TABLE MOUNTAIN * SOUTH QUARRY WALL * RIGHT SIDE

1. THE MUMMY ** 5.8
4 THE BOWELS *? 5.9
5. THE SHORT TOUR *** 5.10b
6. THE GNOME *** 5.12b R-
7. STIMULUS **** 5.12d
8. MARRY ME BECKY ** 5.10c

NORTH TABLE MOUNTAIN * SOUTH QUARRY WALL * LEFT SIDE

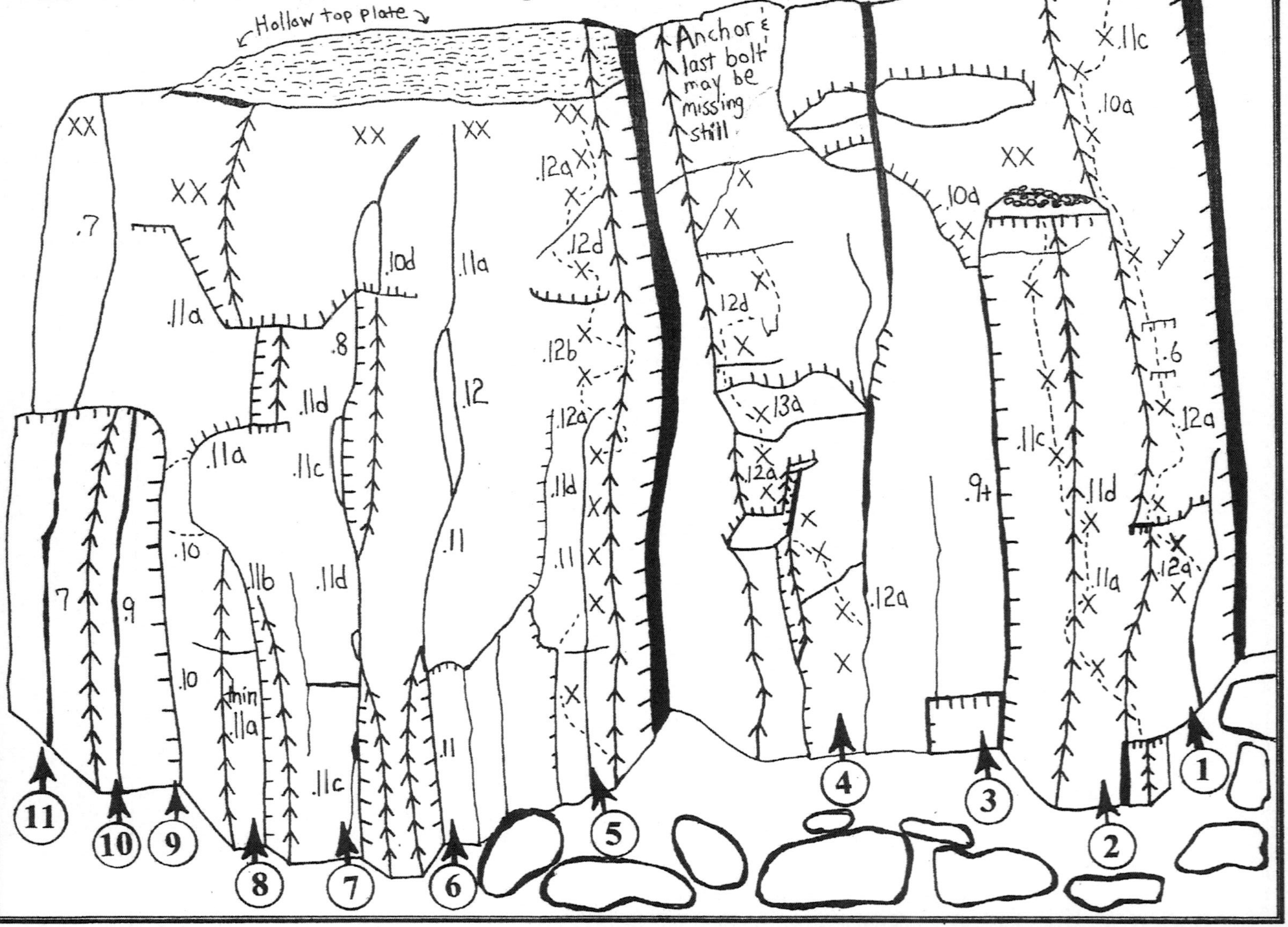

NORTH TABLE MOUNTAIN * SOUTH QUARRY WALL * LEFT SIDE

1. **EASTERN HEART.** *** 5.12a 8 bolts / 2 bolt anchor. This route ascends a sheer east-facing wall. Stick clip 1st bolt. A strenuous start climbs a thin crack & reaches left, past 2nd bolt, to a small shelf. Mantle onto the shelf. The crux ascends tiny edges, past 4th bolt, to jugs. Climb the arete to 7th bolt & move right onto the face. Finish up a tricky vertical face. F.A.: Josh Gross & Mark Rolofson on Dec. 19, 2008.

2. **RECESSION.** **** 5.11d 6 bolts / 2 Fixe rings. This route ascends a blunt prow & the west face on its left side. Start from a block along the arete right of the 1st bolt. Traverse left & up to the prow & 2nd bolt. Ascend the prow with an insecure crimpy crux, past 3rd bolt, to reach a sloping shelf. Climb the face just left the prow to a large ledge & the anchor. F.A.: Josh & Madoline Gross on December 13, 2008.

3. **DEPRESSION.** * 5.10a #.3 (black) & #.4 (blue) Aliens, #.75 - 2.5 Friends (or Camalots to #1) with two #1.5 - 2 Friends to 1 bolt / 2 rings. Jams & jugs lead up a left-facing dihedral. The crack fades away before the bolt. Finish at the anchor shared with **Recession**. There is still some dirt in the crack. This climb may be worth another star when it cleans up. F.A.: Josh & Madoline Gross on December 19, 2008.

4. **ELEPHANTIASIS.** ***! 5.13b 12 bolts / anchor may still be gone! This is Table's hardest climb. Unfortunately, the top of the climb fell down after heavy rains in May 2009! Begin with a vertical face using a thin seam at 2nd bolt to reach left. Traverse left, past 4th bolt, onto a small stance on the arete below a tiny roof. Bear hug up two short aretes to a smooth bulge & 7th bolt. A powerful crux moves left & up to the lip of the bulge. The redpoint crux, pulls over the bulge & moves right. A dicey slab leads to an easier finish. F.A.: Josh Gross on January 30, 2008.

5. ***KLEPTOCRACY.*** ***** 5.12d/13a 10 bolts / 2 Fixe rings. This is a sustained climb with the powerful crux before the finish. Ascend dual thin shallow cracks just left of the arete to start. Follow a seam crack & the arete. Climb up the arete, past 5th bolt, & then move left to reach big holds & 6th bolt. Sidepulls lead to a tiny roof. A gymnastic reach crux, past 8th bolt, gains a diagonal break. Tape the right hand baby finger to avoid cutting it. A fingertip traverse leads right up the break. Tiny holds lead to the anchor. F.A.: Josh Gross & Mark Rolofson on Dec. 31, 2008.

6. **BONE COLLECTOR.** (A.k.a.: **Bone Crusher**) *****? 5.12b/c Three sets of .3"-1.5" cams, two # 1 Camalots or #2 Friends. / 2 rings. Ascend the right of three thin cracks. Begin in a right-facing dihedral that fades away after 20 feet. Step right to a rest on a small shelf. Continue up the crack to a jug. The desperate crux ascends a splitter 1"-1.5" finger crack up the bulging headwall. Fat fingers are an advantage. Gain a stance & finish with up the pumpy 5.11 crack. F.A.: Jimmy Menendez in 2005.

7. **SILVER BULLET II.** ***** 5.12a #.3 (black), two #.4 (blue), two .5 (green), three or four .75 (yellow), 1 (red) Aliens, two 1.5 Friends or Aliens (orange), #2, 2.5 Friends, one each: #6-10 Stoppers. / 2 Fixe rings. Ascend the middle of three thin cracks up a left-facing dihedral. Stem & lieback up a bouldery start, protected by a #.75 Alien & a #9 stopper, to reach a wide hand jam. Ascend finger jams & the occasional hand jam to a rest on small footholds 45 ft. up. Fingertip jams & lieback moves lead up the bulging dihedral to a good rest. 5.8 moves gain jugs below a roof. Pull over the roof to hand jams & the anchor. This fine crack is very sustained for 65 feet offering a great pump. F.A.: Wayne Crill in 2005.

8. **FRANK'S WILD YEARS.** **** 5.11b Two #.3 (black), two .#4 (blue), #.5 (green), #.75 (yellow), two #1 (red) Aliens, two #1.5 Aliens (orange) or Friends, two #2 Friends or #1 Camalots (red), two 2.5 Friends, #6-11 stoppers / 2 bolt anchor. Climb the left of three thin cracks. Begin with a few hand jams, then it's all fingers jams & a few face holds, leading up a tiny left-facing corner, just right of a blunt arete. The crack curves left turning into a hand traverse that leads to a big dihedral. Continue 10 ft. up the dihedral via shallow hand jams to a horizontal crack on the left for pro (#2-2.5 Friends or #1 Camalot). Place a #.3 Alien & crank out jug moves with no footholds along a right-angling thin crack. Gain a wide ledge. A hammered in stopper in the crack before the ledge was fixed to keep the rope from jamming in the crack & not for protection. A wide finger crack leads 10 ft. up a left-facing dihedral to a small roof. A final crux climbs around the roof & up the corner, on thin hand jams. The crack peters out just before a sloping ledge & the anchor. F.A.: Hank Caylor, Wayne Crill, Kevin Gallagher & Jimmy Menendez in 2005.

9-11. Three more cracks are found just left of **Frank's Wild Years**. See the following page 115 for information.

NORTH TABLE MOUNTAIN * SOUTH QUARRY WALL * Right Side

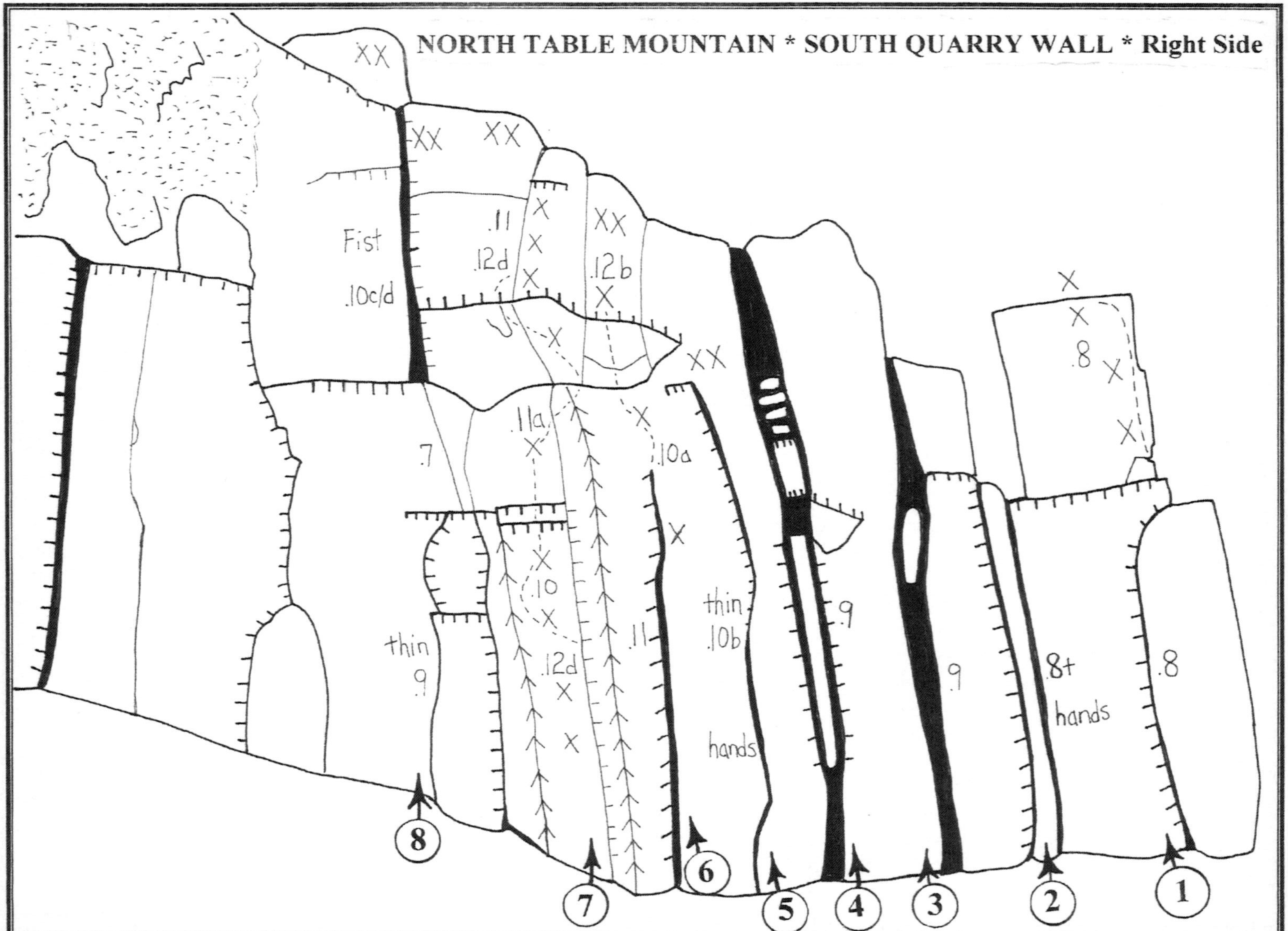

NORTH TABLE MOUNTAIN * SOUTH QUARRY WALL * Right Side

The routes on the right side of the wall are 25 to 60 feet long.

1. **THE MUMMY.** ** 5.8 #.5 - 2 Friends or Aliens, 2 bolts / 2 bolt anchor. Ascend the right side of the pinnacle known as the **Mummy**. Start with a hand & lieback crack to a ledge. Ascend the arete past 2 bolts. F.A.: Free soloed by ?? Bolted by Josh Gross on January 1, 2009.

2. **WARM-UP CRACK.** * 5.8+ # 3 - 4 Friends (or #3.5 Camalot). Ascend 25 foot high double cracks via wide hand & fist jams just left of the **Mummy** pinnacle. Walk off east to descend or step right on a ledge to the last bolt on **The Mummy** to finish. F.A.: Jimmy Menendez in 2005.

3. **OFFWIDTH BULGE.** *? 5.9 Gear? Ascend the squeeze chimney. Grunt, groan & thrash up this one! F.A.: Jimmy Menendez in 2005.

4. **THE BOWELS.** *? 5.9 Mainly large gear to #5 Camalot / 2 Fixe rings. Climb double offwidth cracks formed by giant flake inside a shallow chimney, right of the **Short Tour** to its anchor. This line appears to be quite a grunt. F.A.: Wayne Crill in 2005.

5. **THE SHORT TOUR.** *** 5.10b #.4 (blue), .5 Alien (green) to 2.5 Friend or #2 Camalot. Two #2 friends or #1 Camalots / 2 Fixe rings. Climb a hand & finger crack for 50 ft. to an anchor. Originally rated 5.9, this route is a sandbag at that grade. F.A.: Jimmy Menendez in 2005.

6. **THE GNOME.** *** 5.12b PG-13 #.5-1 Aliens (green, yellow, red), # 2-3 Camalots & #5-7 stoppers to 3 bolts / 2 chains. It is possible to access the top anchor by climbing **The Short Tour** & then continuing above its anchor on jugs or rappel off a 2 bolt anchor on top. Climb a shallow, flared hand crack up a corner that fades away into a steep slab leading to a roof. The crux pulls over the roof, past the last bolt, using a thin seam crack & a pinch hold. First top roped by Jimmy Menendez in 2005. F.A. led by Jimmy Menendez on January 15, 2009.

7. **STIMULUS.** **** 5.12d 9 bolts / 2 Fixe rings. Climb a small left-facing corner with a lieback crux past the 2nd bolt to reach a jug on the arete. It is also possible to climb the arete & then reach back right to the corner. Continue with good holds to a good shelf & the 5th bolt. Continue up right to below the roof. Move left to an undercling flake just below the roof's lip. Execute a powerful crux sequence, past the 7th bolt, to gain lieback holds on the edge of a very thin splitter crack. Climb the crack to jugs & finish up easy moves.
F.A.: Kaelen Williams, Jimmy Menendez & Mark Rolofson on February 6, 2009.

8. **MARRY ME BECKY.** ** 5.10c A few small to medium cams: #.4 (blue) to 1 (red) Aliens. Four large pieces of gear: #3.5- 4 Friends or #3- 3.5 Camalots / 2 bolt anchor. Climb a short hand & finger crack to a ledge. Continue up double thin cracks to a second ledge. The crux ascends a left-facing dihedral via wide hand & fist jams. The hardest moves are off the ledge up a wide flared section with heel & toe jams for the feet. F.A.: Jimmy Menendez & Kevin Gallagher in 2005.

SOUTH QUARRY * FAR LEFT SIDE

The following three crack climbs are located left of **Frank's Wild Years**. See the drawing of **South Quarry Wall - Left Side** on the previous page.

9. **FRANK'S TAME YEARS.** ** 5.11a #.3 Alien (black), mostly medium gear (1.5 to #3 Friends) / 2 bolt anchor. This is an easier variation to the start of **Frank's Wild Years**. Climb the large dihedral 20 feet left of **Frank's Wild Years** (5.10). This is the dihedral that **Frank's Wild Years** steps into & climbs for 10 feet. F.A.: Joseph Crotty & Mike Cichon in January 2009.

10. **SHARKCICLE.** 5.10a Small-medium to 3" nuts & cams / 2 bolt anchor. Climb the finger crack left of **Frank's Tame Years** & just right of the arete to a big ledge. Follow a crack up softer, poor rock. Watch out for loose rock! F.A.: Mike Cichon in January 2009.

11. **SHARK JAW.** 5.7 Small-medium to 3" nuts & cams / 2 bolt anchor. Climb the crack left of the arete up the west face to a big ledge. Continue up a loose, lightning bolt crack on softer rock. Watch out for loose rock! F.A.: Mike Cichon in January 2009.

NORTH TABLE MOUNTAIN * EAST QUARRY WALL * Left Side

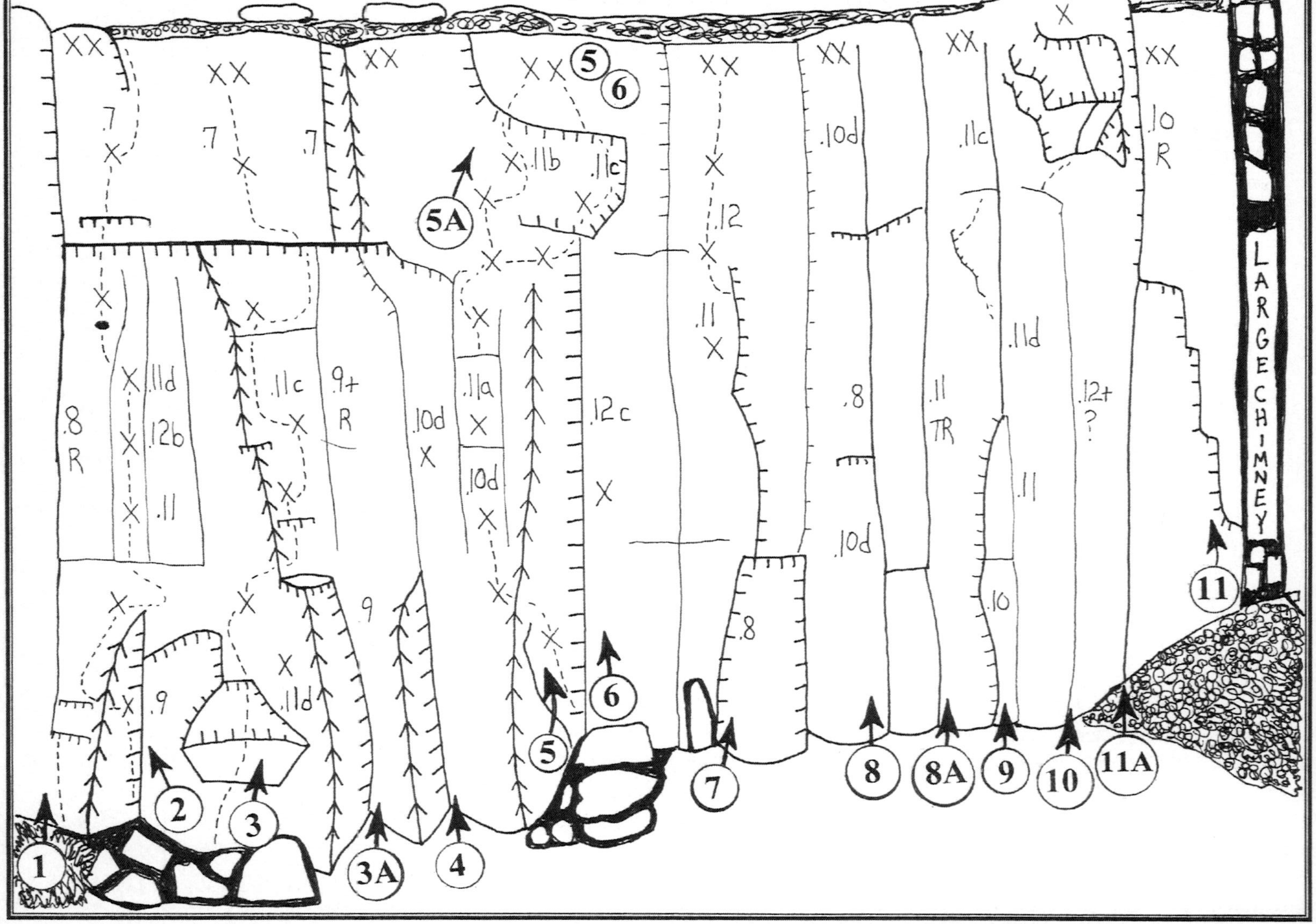

NORTH TABLE MOUNTAIN * EAST QUARRY WALL * Left Side

1. **NATURAL BORN TOP-ROPERS.** (A.k.a.: **Barnacle**). * 5.8+ R/X 1 bolt, gear / 2 bolt anchor. Climb a shallow crack up the slab to the same finish as **Hairless Dog**. F.A. (lead): Mike Cichon in 2009.

2. **HAIRLESS DOG.** *** 5.12a/b 7 bolts / 2 bolt anchor. Start from the left side of the pile of boulders. Climb a short right-facing corner, past 1st bolt. & onto a slab. Ascend technical crux moves up the slab using shallow seams to a jug pocket below 6th bolt. Gain a ledge & finish up easier climbing. F.A.: Mark Rolofson - April 3, 2010.

3. **PINKERTON.** ** 5.11d 6 bolts / 2 chains. Start off a pile of boulders. Stick clip 1st bolt. The crux start pulls over a small roof. Easier climbing leads up & right, past 2nd bolt, to a nice ledge. Climb a steep, tricky slab up the right side of a blunt prow. At 5th bolt, execute a traverse right to good holds. Wander up an easy finish. F.A.: Mark Rolofson & Jimmy Menendez on January 30, 2009.

3A. **SEA URCHIN.** *? 5.9+ R/X RPs, .3" to 2" cams/ 2 bolt anchor. Start with a short, small corner just right the roof on **Pinkerton**. Continue up a steep slab along a seam, just a few feet right of **Pinkerton**. Gain a ledge & finish up a corner. F.A.: Mike Cichon in Spring 2009.

4. **UNKNOWN.** ** 5.10d PG-13 1 bolt, RPs, small stoppers, .3"- 2" cams / 2 bolt anchor. Climb a short corner to its top. Move left & up to a bolt. Continue along a seam. Gain a ledge & finish up a left-facing corner. Reach right to the anchor.

5. **PRETZEL LOGIC.** ***** 5.11c 8 bolts / 2 chains. Fun moves & a good pump. Begin just left of the right-facing dihedral of **Hellhound**. Climb up the left wall past 1st bolt. Traverse left around a rounded prow. Ascend shallow seams to jugs & 6th bolt. Traverse right to 7th bolt & into the dihedral of **Hellhound**. The crux pulls over a small bulge, past last bolt. F.A.: Eric Schmeer & Kirk Miller - February 22, 2009.

5A. **DEFECTIVE AGENCY.** ***** 5.11a/b 8 bolts / 2 chains. This is an easier, direct finish to **Pretzel Logic**. At 6th bolt, continue straight up the face angling slightly right to the last bolt. F.A.: John Langston in Spring 2009.

6. **HELLHOUND.** *****? 5.12c 1-4 bolts, several small cams / 2 chains. Ascend a right-facing dihedral via sustained moves to finish with the same bulge as **Pretzel Logic**. F.A.: John Langston - January 18, 2009. His headpoint ascent avoided using the first & last two bolts on **Pretzel Logic**. He had attempted to establish the route ground up, but pulled pro from breaking rock. He returned to inspect gear on rappel, top rope the climb & remove one of two bolts he drilled on lead. He arrogantly removed three bolts on **Pretzel Logic**, that have since been replaced.

7. **TENDONKEY PUNCH.** * 5.12 .75"-2" cams to 3 bolts / 2 chains. Start off a small boulder & climb a short crack corner to gain a ledge. It is also possible to climb the crack to the right to gain the ledge. Place gear & lieback up a tiny left-facing corner to 1st bolt. Continue up the corner, that fades away, to a vertical face crux past 2nd bolt. Finish up tricky face moves. F.A.: John Langston in January 2009.

8. **SAND SHARK.** * 5.10d R- RPs (one set), .3"-.4" cams, .5" - 1.5" (two each) / 2 bolt anchor. Climb a shallow, dirty crack with a hard start. A juggy midsection ends with a tricky finish. Placing pro in the best fingerlocks increases the grade. F.A.: Mike Cichon on January 17, 2009.

8A. **ASHBURY PARK.** 5.11 Top rope This line is just right of **Sand Shark** & is top-roped from its anchor. F.A.: Mike Cichon - January 2010.

9. **JAWS.** *** 5.11d R #2-5 RPs, two-three each: #.3 Alien (black) to 1.5 Aliens (orange) / 2 chains. Climb the thin shallow crack 15 ft. right of **Sand Shark**, via technical stems, fingertip locks & face holds with tricky pro. Sustained to the finish. F.A.: Mike Cichon in Spring 2009.

10. **Crack Project.** 5.12+? 1 bolt anchor. A difficult shallow crack leads to a roof finish. May have been top-roped.

11A. **Crack Project.** A direct start to **Herringbone**.

11. **HERRINGBONE.** 5.10 R Bring a standard rack. Begin on the left side of the huge chimney. Climb up & left on sloping shelves to a short right-facing corner. The crux finish has poor pro. Watch out for natural rockfall out of the chimney. F.A.: Mike Cichon - January 2010.

NORTH TABLE MOUNTAIN * EAST QUARRY WALL * Right Side

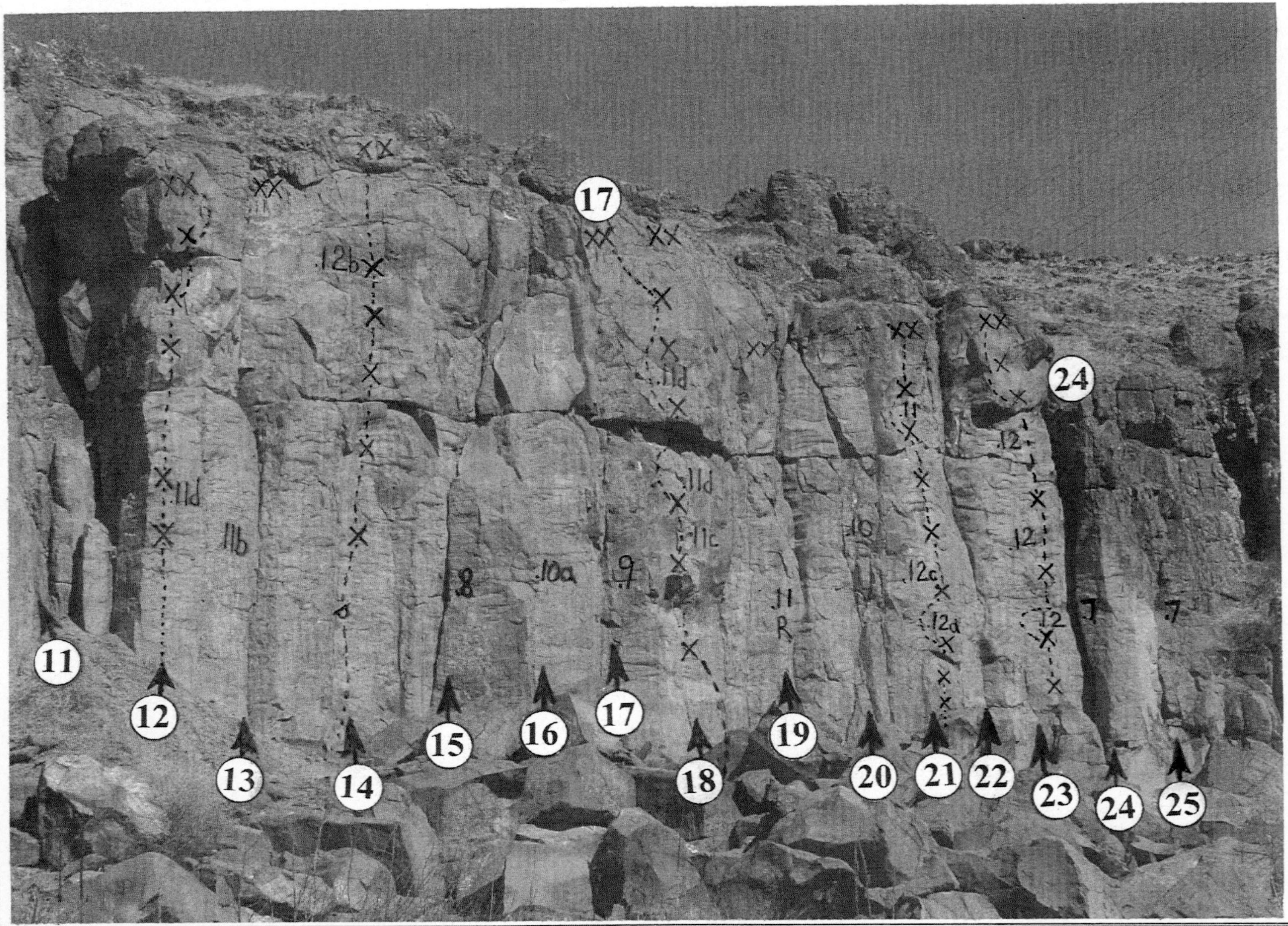

12. **SLAP HAPPY.** **** 5.11d/12a 5 bolts / 2 chains. Start just right of the huge chimney from atop a mound of dirt. Slap up two aretes (one for each hand) that form the outer edges of a narrow column to jugs & 3rd bolt. Continue with greater ease up pumpy moves to a small roof. Move right & then up to the anchor. This climb features excellent moves & a good pump. F.A.: Eric Schmeer in March 2009.

13. ***PLAY WITH YOUR BALLS.*** *** 5.11b R- #.3 (black) to #1.5 Friend, Ball-nuts or RPs / 2 chains. Finger jam & lieback up a small left facing corner with a thin crack to a small shelf. Face moves lead up a right-facing dihedral. F.A.: John Langston & Mike Cichon - Jan. 2009.

14 **FLYING FISH.** ****? 5.12b 1 pin, 5 bolts plus #.5 Alien / 2 chains. Climb up two shallow seams past a knifeblade piton to 1st bolt. Reach a small overlap. Ascend the bulging crux face past bolts. F.A: Mike Cichon in February 2010.

15 **SEA ROBIN.** * 5.8 Medium stoppers & cams to #3 Camalot / 2 chains. Climb a left-facing crack corner to a big ledge. Climb up 10 feet to wedged blocks. Angle right up suspect blocks or traverse right low across the face to the finish of **Nurse Shark**. Use the anchor for **Hammerhead** & **Nurse Shark** to descend. F.A.: Mike Cichon in January 2009.

16. **HAMMERHEAD.** ** 5.9+/10a #.5 (green) - 1.5 Friend (two useful), #2-3 Friends, a few medium stoppers / 2 chains. Climb a thin hand & finger crack up a 25 ft. right-facing dihedral to a big ledge. It is easier to move left 12 ft. up onto the arete & face climb to the ledge. Finish up **Sea Robin**. F.A.: Mike Cichon - January 2009.

17. **NURSE SHARK.** *** 5.9 #.75 Alien (green) to #3.5 Friend (#3 Camalot), a few medium stoppers / 2 chains. Climb a bulging crack via mostly hand jams. F.A.: Mike Cichon in January 2009.

18. **OLD MAN & THE SEA.** **** 5.12a 6 bolts / 2 chains. Start in a short, tiny right-facing corner & reach left to a jug above 1st bolt. Climb over a small roof & up sidepulls to a second roof & 4th bolt. Pull over the roof on the left. At the last bolt angle left to the anchor on **Nurse Shark**. The direct finish still awaits a free ascent. There is an anchor. F.A.: Mike Cichon in November 2009.

19. **LAND SHARK.** ***? 5.11 R #.3 Alien (black) to 2.5 Friend / 2 chains. The crux is the start. A straight-in thin crack leads into & up a left-facing, flared dihedral. F.A.: Mike Cichon in Spring 2009.

20. **BLUEFISH.** 5.10 R Bring a standard rack. Climb the dirty, loose crack to the right of **Land Shark**. F.A.: Mike Cichon in January 2010.

21. **WOOLY BULLY.** ***** 5.12d 8 bolts / 2 bolt anchor. Ascend a clean vertical face. A powerful, fingery crux on small edges & sidepulls, past 4th bolt, leads to slabby midsection. Wander up a tricky 5.11 finish to a ledge. F.A.: Mark Rolofson & Kirk Miller - May 1, 2010.

22. **TIGER SHARK.** ** 5.11a R- Two #.3 Aliens (black), two #.4 Aliens (blue), #1 Alien (red) to 2.5 Friend, #3-6 micro-stoppers (or RPs), #5-10 stoppers / 2 chains. Climb a shallow, flared crack with tricky jams & face moves that turns into a left-facing dihedral with a moderate finish. F.A.: Mike Cichon in Spring 2009.

23. **TIGER'S WOODY.** ***** 5.13a Project 6 bolts / 2 Fixe rings. Start by climbing 15 ft. up a small pillar to 1st bolt. Hard moves lead up the vertical face past 2nd bolt to a sloping, shallow horizontal break. Traverse right & ascend the left side of the arete to a tiny roof & 6th bolt. Move left to another short arete & pull over the roof to find good holds below the top. F.A: (5.12 A0) Mark Rolofson - January 30, 2010.

24. **SS MINNOW.** **? 5.7 Tiny to medium nuts & cams / 2 Fixe rings. Climb up the right side of a short pillar. Ascend a wide chimney. with gear in a thin crack on the left. F.A.: Kirk Miller & Lindie Brink in Spring 2009.

25. **GREAT WIDE SHARK.** *? 5.7 Two #4 Camalots / 2 Fixe rings. Climb a wide crack up the right side of a pinnacle to the anchor for **SS Minnow**. F.A.: Mike Cichon in Summer 2009.

INTRODUCTION TO DUDE'S THRONE & THE GRENDEL IN GOLDEN GATE STATE PARK

Located above 9,000 feet elevation in the mountain pine forests west of Highway 93 and south of Highway 72 are some excellent, secluded granite crags. Unlike the Golden Cliffs or Clear Creek Canyon this area has been largely ignored by climbers until 2003. The exception is Mt. Thorodin, the area's largest rock formation at 500 ft. tall, that has multi-pitch trad routes established before 1990. Much of the rock in the State Park and bordering National Forest land involves a long approach of one hour or more. The most notable exception is **Dude's Throne** located near Dude's Fishing Hole and Aspen Meadow Campground. This crag & its close neighbor **Little Dude's Throne** have a short 15 minute approach walk. Nearby, the **Grendel** sits high up on a pine tree covered hillside above 9,500 feet elevation with a 45 to 60 minute approach hike.

The beauty of climbing here is the lack of highway and city noise associated with so many Front Range sport climbing areas like Boulder Canyon, Clear Creek and the Golden Cliffs. This mountain valley is cut by a dirt road that doesn't run next to the cliffs. There is the small lake (Dude's Hole) below and the vast pine tree forests. There are the aspen groves which display their bright yellow colors in the early Fall. There is the opportunity to get away from the fast pace of the Front Range and relax for a day in a serene setting.

As for the climbing at **Dude's Throne**, the excellent granite is very featured with holds. There are 35 climbs most of which are sport routes ranging in difficulty from 5.9 to 5.13a. There are fun overhanging 5.11 jug hauls & a nice selection of 5.12a to 5.13a climbs to choose from. There are some good 5.9-5.10d warm-ups & three crack climbs, including an 85 foot 5.11 splitter crack, known as **Dude's Jam Crack**, offering a variety of jams.

In Spring 2003, Kirk Miller discovered the cliffs near Dude's Fishing Hole and recruited me to explore them. Prior to our route development, the few cracks had been climbed by unknown climbers, but the area saw almost no climbing activity. Our first route, that we established in June 2003, was a brilliant 5.12a on the south face of **Dude's Throne** that we named **Open Space Cowboy**. This route offers varied terrain from a steep slab to powerful overhanging moves on highly featured granite. After we climbed this route, the June heat drove us off the taller south face onto the shorter overhanging north face to find shade. This face offers a varnished patina surface and a variety of holds. We soon recruited Vaino Kodas who established several routes. We were joined by several other friends who helped us establish over 30 routes and variations, during the next two years.

In 2006, Kirk Miller and I turned our attention to the **Grendel**. Rick Lietner had established the first sport route in Fall 2003. Miller has established most of the routes on this cliff and cairned the excellent approach trail. There is an excellent 100 foot 5.9 and a 120 foot 5.10c. The hardest route thus far is a 5.12b through tiered roofs. For the approach information to **The Grendel** see page 141.

Directions to Dudes Throne: From Highway 93, between Boulder and Golden, take Highway 72 west up Coal Creek Canyon for 6.9 miles. Take a left (go south) onto Twin Spruce Road. There is a small sign for Golden Gate State Park on the north side of the road just before this turn. If you miss the turn, you will come to a Conoco gas station. Follow Twin Spruce Rd. (that becomes Gap Road) for 6.4 Miles and take a left into Aspen Meadow Campground. There is a self service pay station at the entrance, if you don't have an annual Colorado State Parks Pass. Follow the dirt road for a few hundred feet and take the first right leading downhill. Then take the next right that leads around a one-way loop. Be careful to stay to the left and don't take the next right. Park in the designated parking lot for Dude's Fishing Hole, which can fit about a dozen cars.

The approach to Dude's Throne: Walk east on the one-way loop road (the way you would drive out). You will be able to see the cliff to the east. After 200 feet you will pass a gated dirt road on the right that leads downhill to Dude's Fishing Hole. Continue uphill on the loop road for 25 feet to a narrow 5 foot boulder (much like a tombstone) and turn right off the road. Follow a path for 50 feet downhill to a trail (that becomes a stream bed during water run off) and turn left onto it. Walk uphill for 50 feet on this trail and look for cairns that lead off to the east (right). Follow a trail with white quartz stones embedded in the ground that leads gradually uphill and then flattens out. The trail ends at the talus and boulders below the west face of **Dude's Throne**. The north face is easily spotted and is 100 feet uphill through the boulders on the left. Follow the base of the wall around right to the climbs on the south face. **Little Dude's Throne** is directly below the west face. See page 137 for details on its approach.

MAP TO DUDE'S THRONE & THE GRENDEL IN GOLDEN GATE STATE PARK

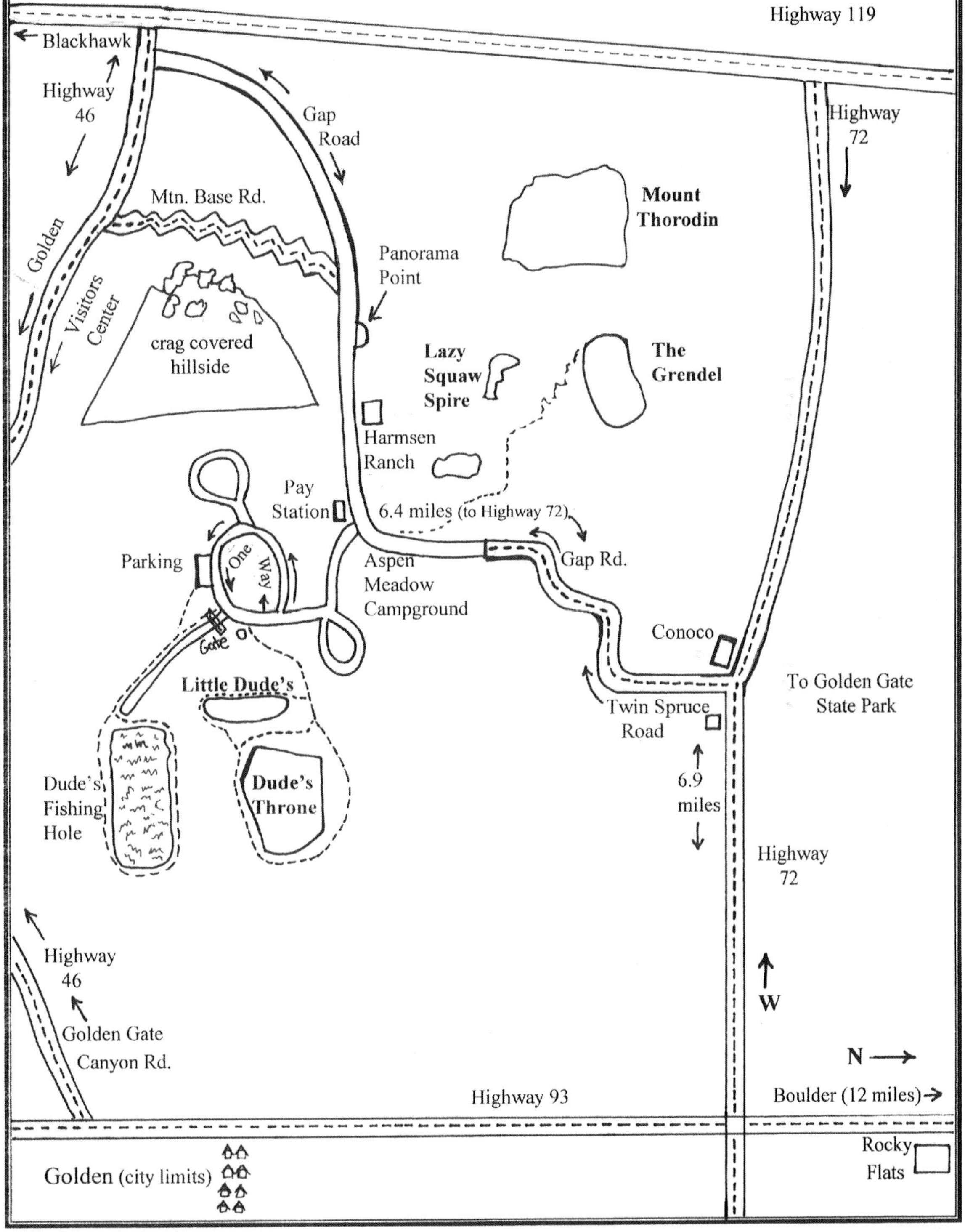

Kirk Miller at the 4th bolt of **GOLDEN GATE** (**** 5.11d/12a) on the west face. Photo: Vaino Kodas.

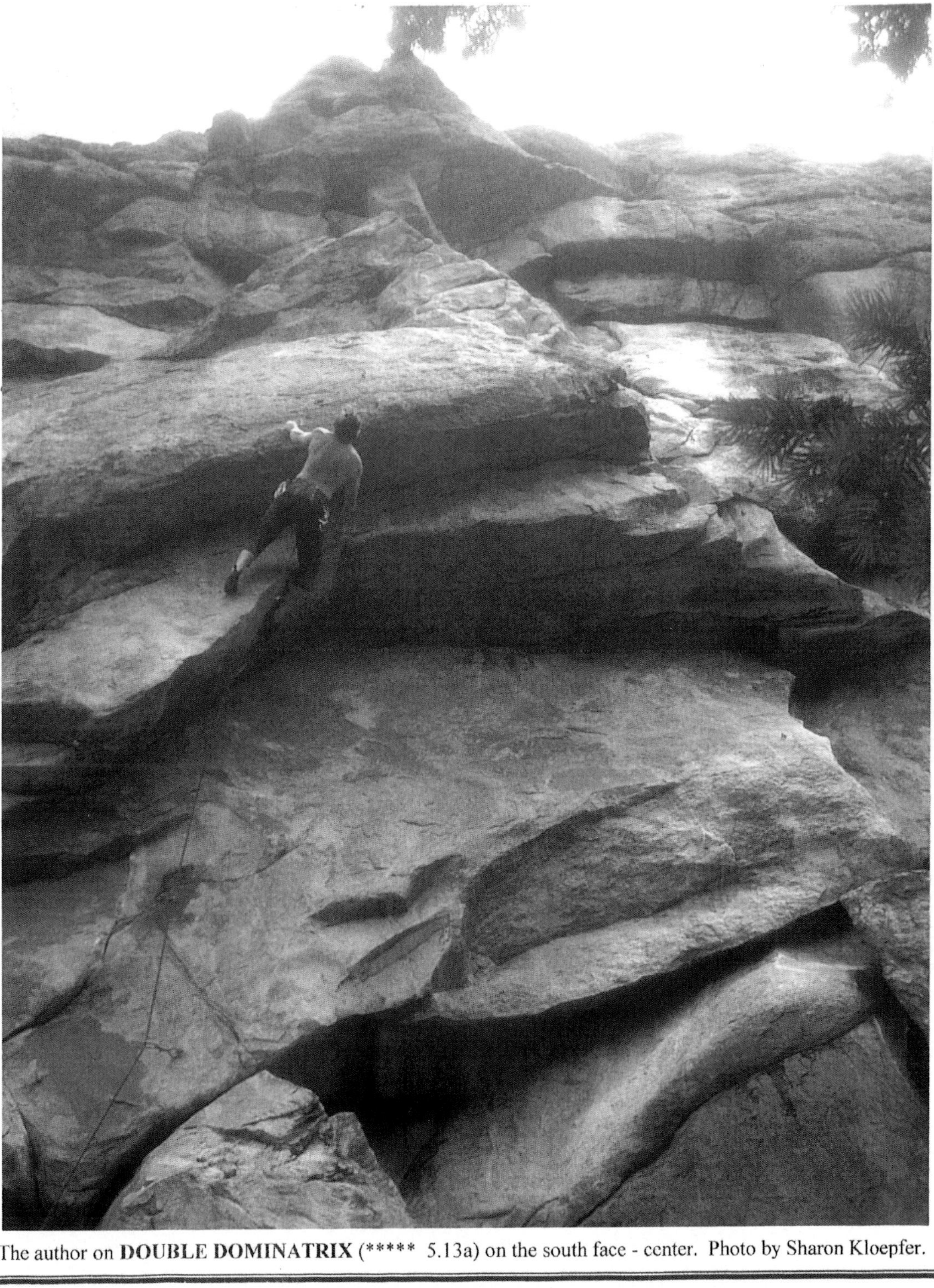

The author on **DOUBLE DOMINATRIX** (***** 5.13a) on the south face - center. Photo by Sharon Kloepfer.

GOLDEN GATE STATE PARK * DUDE'S THRONE * NORTH FACE * (The Throne Room)

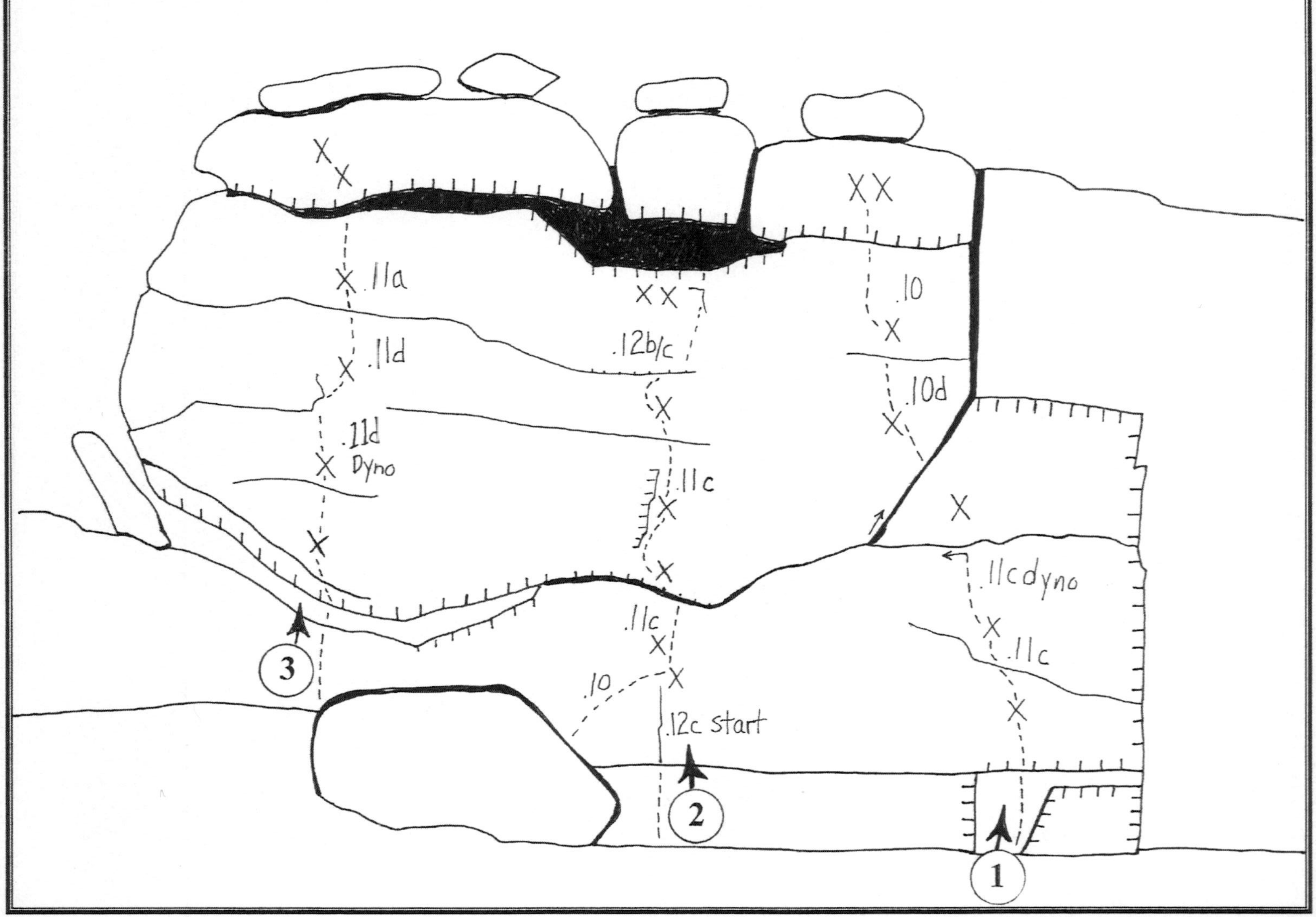

GOLDEN GATE STATE PARK * DUDE'S THRONE * NORTH FACE * (The Throne Room)

This overhung 35 foot high north-facing wall has three sustained routes on excellent rock with a varnished patina surface. The routes have intricate moves with a variety of holds. In the Spring and Summer, this face gets morning sun (since it faces northeast) and shade for the rest of the day.

1. **GREEN CHILE.** *** 5.11c 5 bolts / 2 bolt anchor. This climb ascends the right side of the face. Start at a small roof with an undercling. Reach a sloping horizontal break. The crux follows the break left & up, past the 2nd bolt, to a dyno for a bucket. Move left into a right-angling thin crack. Climb the crack for 6 feet. Move up & left to finish on the overhung face with good holds.
First ascent by Mark Rolofson & Kirk Miller on June 9, 2003.

2. **RED HOT CHILI PEPPER.** **** 5.12b/c 5 bolts / 2 Fixe rings. A difficult 5.12 boulder problem start is easily avoided by stepping off the boulder on the left and climbing up and right (.11) to a horizontal undercling jam crack. Ascend a short right-facing corner that quickly fades out. A powerful, intricate (.12b/c) crux using horizontal breaks leads past the last bolt to a jug right of anchor.
First ascent: Mark Rolofson, Vaino Kodas & Kirk Miller on June 14, 2003. First ascent with direct start: John Flunker on June 27, 2003.

2A. **RED CHILE.** **? 5.11b This is a link up that starts on **Red Hot Chile Pepper** and finishes on **Green Chile**. Climb up and clip the 4th bolt on **Red Hot Chile Pepper**. Move back down to the horizontal undercling crack, just below the 3rd bolt. Traverse right along the crack to join the last 2 bolts of **Green Chile**. First ascent: Ken Trout & Jim Garber in June 28, 2003.

3. **CHILI POWER.** ** 5.11d/12a 4 bolts / 2 bolt anchor. A powerful start pulls up on incut crimps for a dyno to a jug. Tricky moves continue upward past several horizontal breaks, as the difficulty gradually eases off. First ascent by Mark Rolofson on July 12, 2003.

GOLDEN GATE STATE PARK * DUDE'S THRONE * WEST FACE

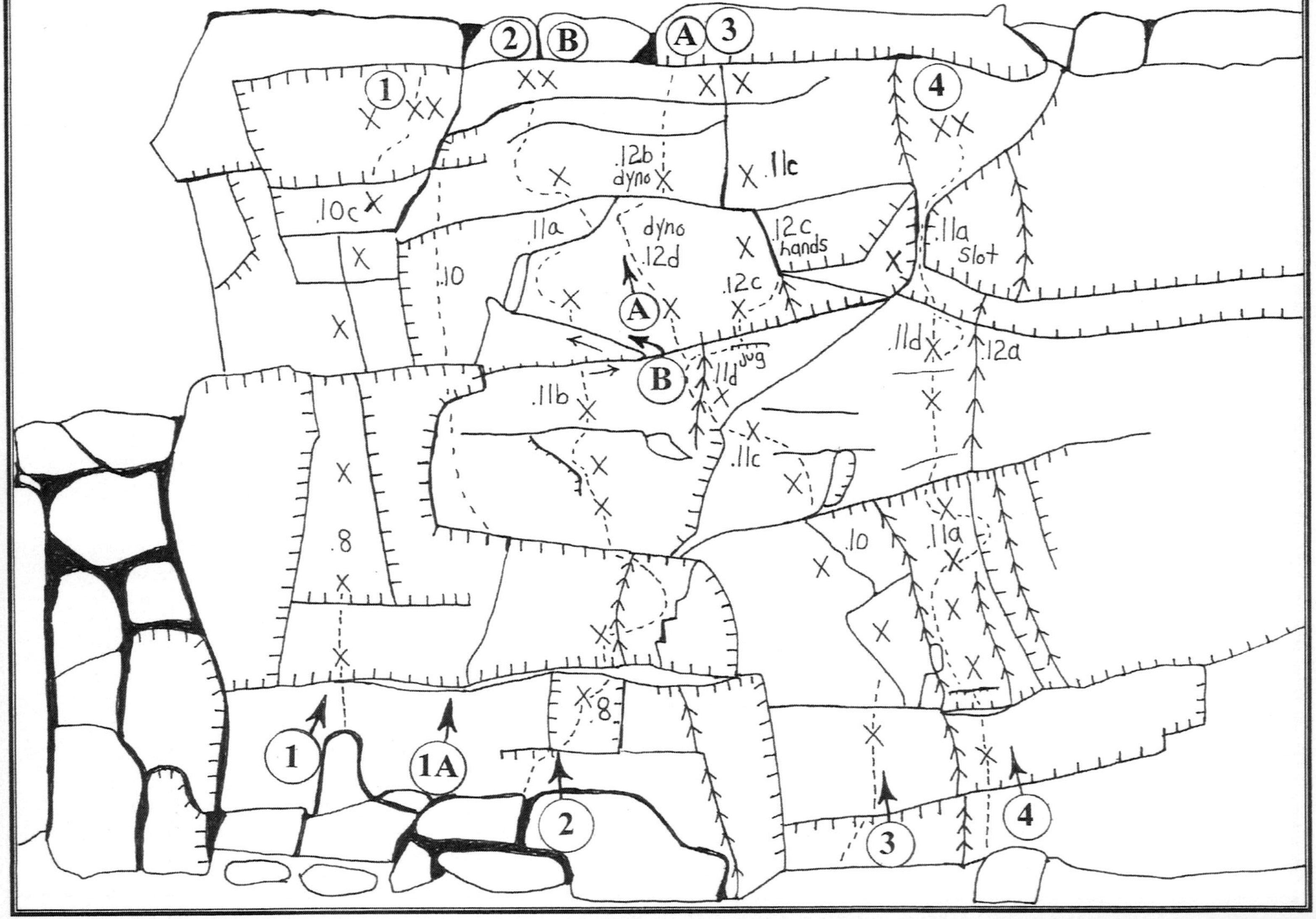

GOLDEN GATE STATE PARK * DUDE'S THRONE * WEST FACE

This overhanging (100-110 degree angle) west-facing wall is great for morning shade until 1 to 2 p.m. in the Summer. It can be very windy on this face. By late Fall, this face sees only late day sun, since it faces northwest.

1. **JOLLY RANCHER.** ** 5.10c 6 bolts / 3 bolt anchor. An easy start leads to a ledge. Start with a vertical crack, then use a horizontal crack & face holds to a reach small overhang. The crux moves up & right over the overhang to good holds above it. A tricky stand up over the lip finishes the climb. First ascent by Vaino Kodas, Mary Zuvela, Mark Rolofson & Kirk Miller on August 2, 2003

1A. **JOLLY SQUEEZE PARTY.** * 5.10 Top Rope. This juggy line is between **Jolly Rancher** & **Uplift Mofo Party Plan**. It is easily top-roped from the anchor of **Jolly Rancher**.

2. **UPLIFT MOFO PARTY PLAN.** **** 5.11b/c 7 bolts / 2 Fixe rings. Moderate climbing, starting along a crack, leads past the first 2 bolts & up low-angle rock to reach a small overhang. Pull past the overhang and ascend a pumpy overhung face via great jugs. Routefinding is key. A great pump! First ascent by Mark Rolofson, John Flunker & Kirk Miller on June 27, 2003.

3. **MAJOR DUDE.** ***** 5.12c/d 9 bolts / 2 Fixe rings. Ascend the steep face (5.9) just right of a right-facing corner to reach a stance at the base of the overhung face. Move up & left to 6th bolt Crank over a bulge & move up right to a jug or shelf below the lip of a small roof. Clip the 7th bolt above the lip & execute a crux sequence using a pinch on a short arete to reach brutal hand jams. Pull over the roof on a flared hand jam to reach a good jug on the right. Finish up overhung face moves.
First ascent by John Flunker & Mark Rolofson on July 19, 2003.

A. **PARTY TRICK.** *** 5.12d 8 bolts / 2 Fixe rings. Climb **Major Dude** past 6 bolts to just below the crux. Move left and clip a bolt in a black streak. Using small crimpers, dyno up & left to a jug. This crux would be much harder if climbed directly. Move back right and then up jugs to the last bolt. A wild dyno or reach gains a sharp incut jug. Finish on jugs to the anchor on **Major Dude.**
F.A.: Mark Rolofson in August 2003. F.F.A.: Vaino Kodas on June 5, 2004.

B. **MAJOR PARTY PLAN.** ***** 5.11d 9-10 bolts / 2 bolt anchor. This route links **Major Dude** to **Uplift Mofo Party Plan** for a great pumping jug haul. Climb **Major Dude** past 6 bolts to just below the crux. Move left and clip the crux bolt on **Party Trick**, in the black streak. If this bolt is hard to clip & you feel run-out, it is possible to clip the 7th bolt on **Major Dude** with a long quickdraw or sling before moving left. Traverse left along a horizontal crack to join **Uplift Mofo Party Plan** at the 5th bolt, which is climbed to its anchor.
First ascent by Mark Rolofson on July 17, 2003.

4. **GOLDEN GATE.** **** 5.11d/12a 8 bolts / 2 bolt anchor. This striking route ascends the left (west) side of the prow. Start just right of **Major Dude** on an arete. Move up and right on bulging face using a thin crack & face holds, past the 3rd & 4th bolts. Then, climb up the prow (5.11a/b) to gain a sloping ledge. Take a good rest on the ledge, because the crux is powerful. Climb the overhung face using several horizontal breaks. Use thin holds on the arete or make a big dyno, gain a good horizontal crack below a small roof. Reach over the roof to a blind jug. Finish with a fight through a chimney slot. Gain a good ledge & the anchor.
First ascent by Vaino Kodas, Mark Rolofson & Kirk Miller on July 13, 2003.

GOLDEN GATE * DUDE'S THRONE * SOUTH FACE * LEFT SIDE

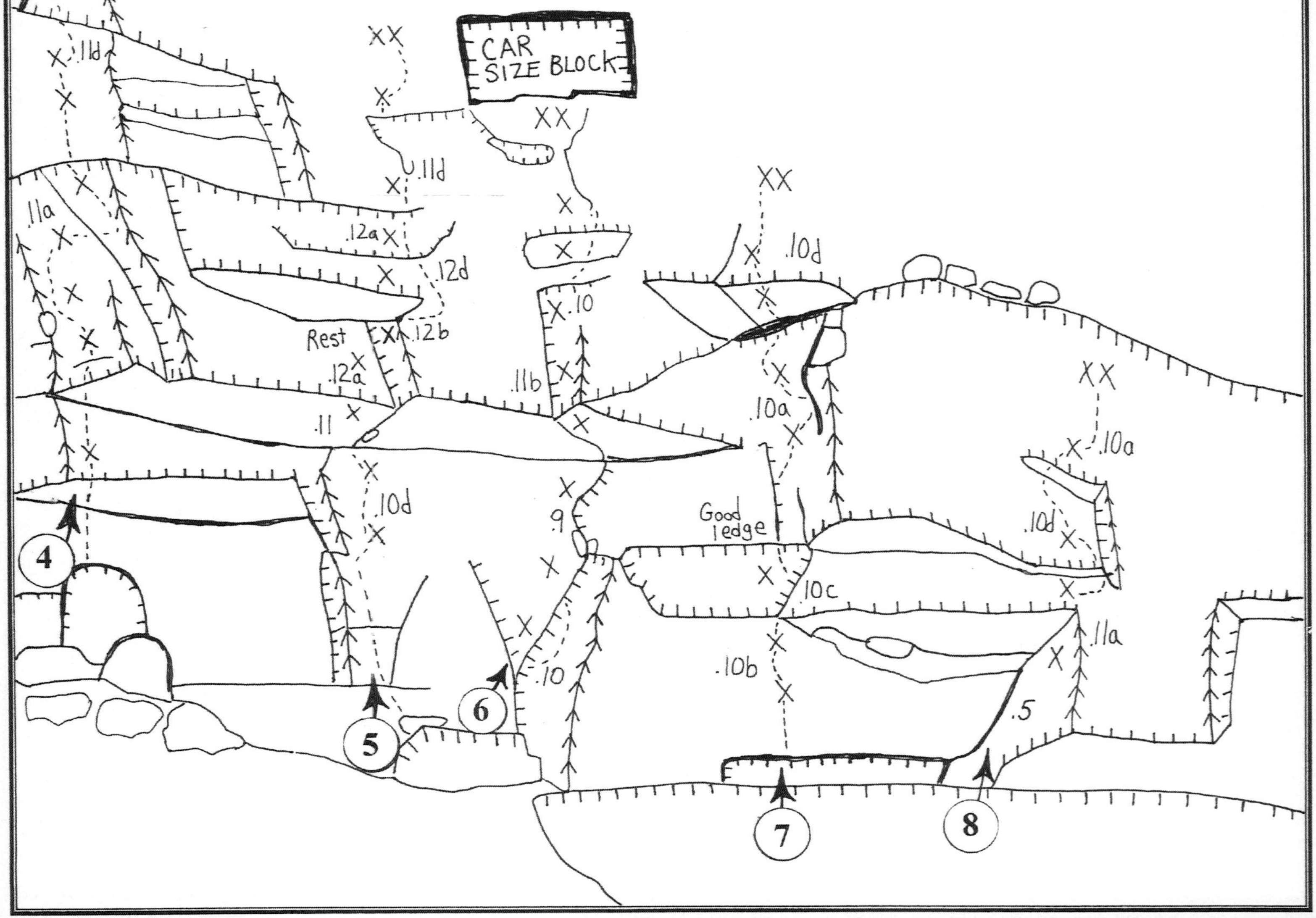

GOLDEN GATE * DUDE'S THRONE * SOUTH FACE * LEFT SIDE

4. **GOLDEN GATE.** **** 5.11d/12a 8 bolts / 2 bolt anchor. This route is located on the right end of the west face. See the previous pages for a complete topo drawing, a detailed route description & first ascent information.

5. **BRASS MONKEY.** **** 5.12d 9 bolts / 2 Fixe rings. Start 15 feet right of **Golden Gate.** Climb a vertical face up the right side of a short arete. Step left to undercling holds in a roof. Clip 3rd bolt & reach over the roof to a fingerlock in a small left-facing dihedral. Pull over the roof, past 4th bolt, (.12a) to gain a foothold rest at 5th bolt, underneath another small roof. Reach over the roof & right to clip 6th bolt. The crux traverses right a few moves, then powers up using poor crimpers to dyno for an undercling. A strange move off the undercling reaches a sloping shelf. At 8th bolt, the last strenuous moves lead to jugs & easier terrain.
Equipped by Kirk Miller & Mark Rolofson in May 2004. F.F.A.: Mark Rolofson on October 17, 2004.

6. **DUDE'S DIHEDRAL** **** 5.11b 8 bolts / 2 bolt anchor. Start 12 feet right of **Brass Monkey** from a block. This route climbs the obvious left-facing dihedral. Vertical moves lead to 1st bolt where slab moves lead up & right along the crackless dihedral, past 2nd bolt. A crack appears before 3rd bolt & disappears at the roof. Clip 4th bolt & find an undercling hold in the roof. Reach above the roof & into the dihedral to a fingerlock. The crux steps over the roof & liebacks up the corner, past 5th bolt, to better crack holds. Reach small shelf with jugs, below 7th bolt. Step right & pull onto the shelf. Pull over a small roof & follow good holds to the anchor.
First ascent by Mark Rolofson & Jimmy Menendez on July 10, 2004.

7. **MIGHTY APHRODITE.** **** 5.10c/d 7 bolts / 2 bolt anchor. Start from the left side of the ledge, at the base of wall. Step up on a small shelf & clip 1st bolt. Insecure slab moves lead to a tiny roof above 2nd bolt. Reach past 3rd bolt to a ledge. Lieback a short crack to stand up on the ledge. Ascend a bulging face with good holds to a tiny shelf underneath a roof. Clip 6th bolt in the roof. Execute a strange crux to reach hidden holds above the roof. An awkward step over the roof, past last bolt, ends at good holds & the anchor. An easier finish avoids the crux roof by moving right around it. First ascent: Mark Rolofson, Vaino Kodas & Dave Turner on October 9, 2004.

8. **SHORT DUDE.** *** 5.11a 4 bolts / 2 mussy hooks. Start from the middle of the ledge, at the base of wall. An easy flake crack leads up & right to 1st bolt. Move up a short left-facing dihedral to underneath the right side of a roof. The crux, past the 2nd bolt, moves right around the roof to the right side of the arete. Continue up overhung rock on good holds.
First ascent by Vaino Kodas & Mark Rolofson on October 8, 2004.

GOLDEN GATE * DUDE'S THRONE * WEST FACE & SOUTH FACE

WEST FACE

2. **UPLIFT MOFO PARTY PLAN.** **** 5.11b/c
3. **MAJOR DUDE.** ***** 5.12c/d
4. **GOLDEN GATE.** **** 5.11d/12a

SOUTH FACE - LEFT SIDE

5. **BRASS MONKEY.** **** 5.12d
6. **DUDE'S DIHEDRAL.** **** 5.11b
7. **MIGHTY APHRODITE.** **** 5.10c/d

Photos by Kirk Miller

SOUTH FACE - CENTER

9. **RAVEN'S BREW.** *** 5.11d
10. **HOWDY DOODY TIME!** ***** 5.11b
11. **OPEN SPACE COWBOY.** ***** 5.12a
12. **DOUBLE DOMINATRIX.** ***** 5.13a
13. **IMPEACHMENT DAY PARADE.** ***** 5.11d

RIGHT SIDE OF SOUTH FACE

14. **DUDE'S JAM CRACK.** ***** 5.11b
15. **BUSTER BROWN.** ***** 5.13a/b
19. **ANY DUDE'LL DO.** ** 5.10a/b PG-13
20. **JUGS OUT FOR THE LADS.** *** 5.9

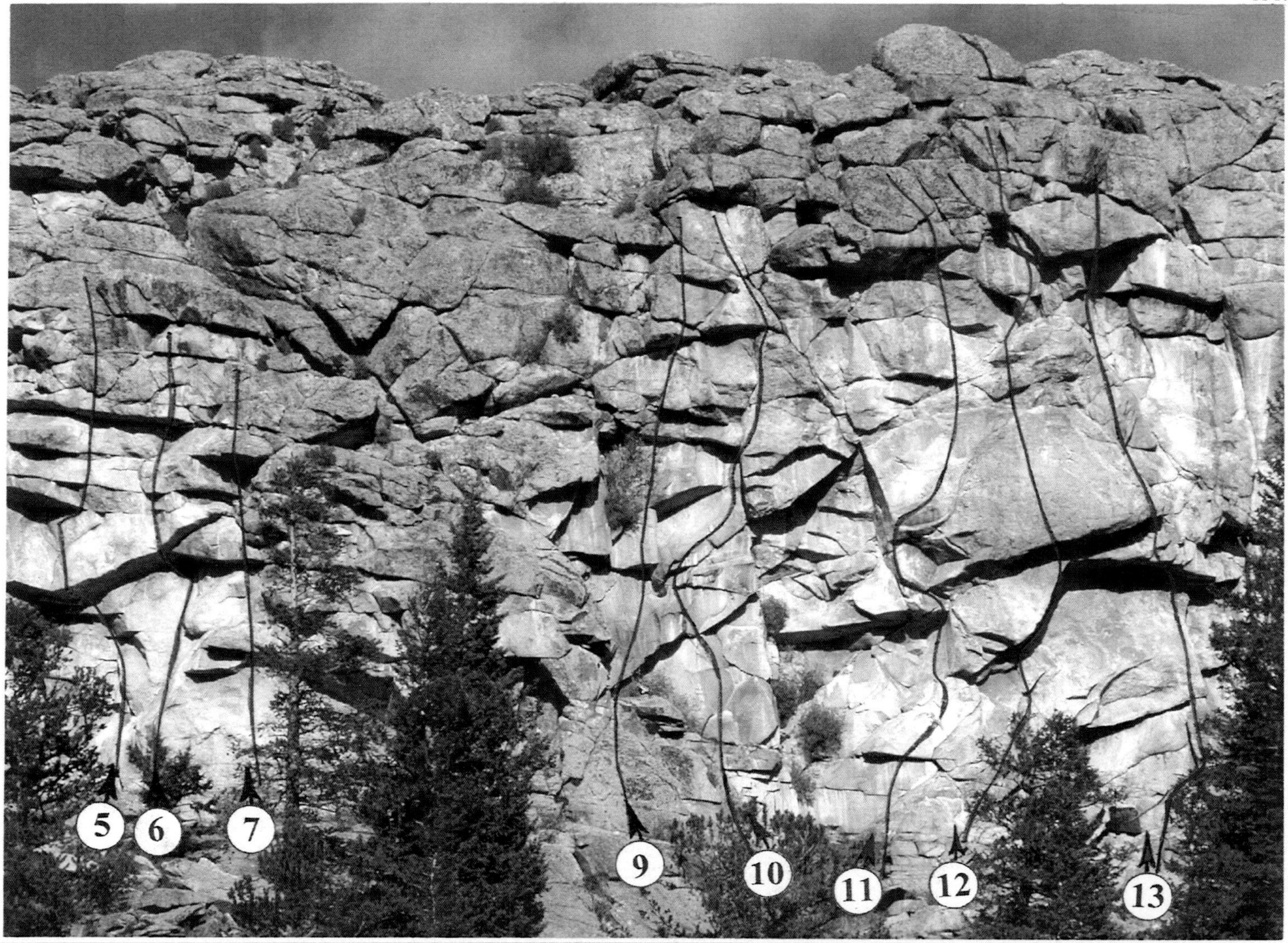
5
6
7
9
10
11
12
13

GOLDEN GATE * DUDE'S THRONE * SOUTH FACE - CENTER

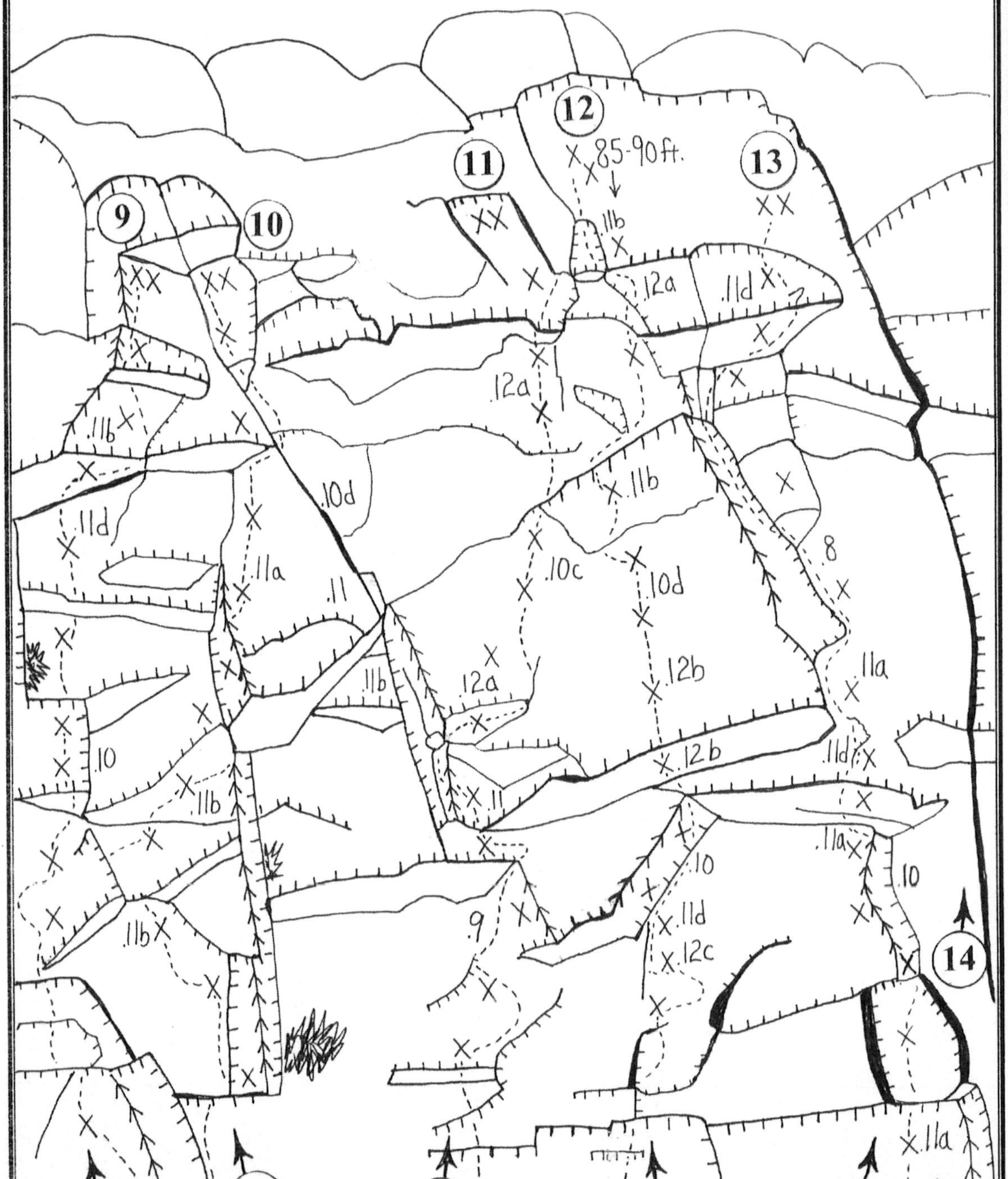

9. **RAVEN'S BREW.** *** 5.11d 10 bolts / 2 bolt anchor. Start on the right end of the ledge at the base of the wall. Climb a short arete to 1st bolt. Gain a ledge & then move up a larger ledge to the 2nd bolt. Climb slightly left up a tiny ramp corner & reach back right to good holds. At the 3rd bolt, lieback up an arete past 4th bolt. At 5th bolt, pull onto a small ledge. Step right & pull past a small roof to 7th bolt. The crux makes a long reach to a horizontal crack. Traverse right 5 ft. & move up a small left-facing corner. Finish up the arete on the left. F.A.: Kirk Miller & Mark Rolofson on August 7, 2004.

10. **HOWDY DOODY TIME!** ***** 5.11b 11 bolts / 2 Fixe rings. This climb ascends overhung red patina rock. Start with a right-facing ramp corner to reach 1st bolt & a good ledge below the 2nd bolt. Thin edges lead up short left-facing corner to below a sloping shelf. Move left & up, past 3rd bolt, to an undercling. Reach a pointed jug atop a short right-facing corner. Move up 4 ft. & then right past 5th bolt to reach an arete. Climb a few feet up the arete to a thin crack. The crack leads into a left-facing dihedral. The dihedral fades away. At 8th bolt, move right around the blunt arete & up the overhung face. At a small roof & 10th bolt, move right to gain a shelf. Move up the thin crack, then slightly left to finish up a face. Gain a sloping stance & the anchor. F.A.: Kirk Miller & Mark Rolofson on September 21, 2003.

11. **OPEN SPACE COWBOY.** ***** 5.12a 12 bolts / 2 bolt anchor. The first sport route on the crag. Wander up moderate climbing (some 5.9) along sloping shelves. Reach the first roof & clip 4th bolt. Strenuous 5.11 moves lead slightly right, then back left to a thin crack that leads up to a huge jug on the right wall of the left-facing corner. Move right, past 6th bolt, along an undercling in a roof (.11d/12a). Reach a thin crack & pull over the roof. Climb a steep slab (.10) to a tiny shelf below an overhung face. Ascend the overhung crux face (.12a) via a sequence of powerful moves to reach jugs over the lip of an overhang. A short crack leads to the anchor. F.A.: Mark Rolofson, & Kirk Miller on June 8, 2003.

11A. **MISSING LINK** *** 5.11d 7 bolts, plus #.4 Aliens - 3.5 Friend, small to medium stoppers / 2 Fixe rings. Climb overhung 5.11 moves past the first 5 bolts of **Open Space Cowboy**, to a huge jug. Here **Open Space Cowboy**, goes right to its 6th bolt and **Missing Link** goes left up the left-facing dihedral (with stoppers & Aliens). Climb the dihedral to a small roof at its top. Find a hold above the roof along a thin crack. Climb a left-leaning hand & finger crack to finish with the last two bolts of **Howdy Dowdy Time!** First ascent by Dave Turner & Mark Rolofson on November 9, 2003.

12. **DOUBLE DOMINATRIX** ***** 5.13a 12 bolts / 2 bolt anchor. This climb takes a direct line up the center of the face. Scramble up ledges to 1st bolt. Move up right to a foothold stance & 2nd bolt. Lieback up a vertical edge (.12c) to reach holds, past 3rd bolt, at the base of a right-leaning dihedral. Enter the dihedral (.11c) & find good lieback holds & a stem rest. Climb the dihedral to its end below the two-tiered roof. Clip 6th bolt in the upper roof. Execute a wild sequence (.12c) through two roofs to jugs above the lip. At 7th bolt, reach small crimpers & high step over the lip of the roof (.12b). Relax once standing on the jugs, at 8th bolt. Climb a steep slab to a small bulge. Pull the bulge (.11) via small holds to a sloping ledge. Move up right on this good rest ledge to reach 11th bolt. Power up & dyno left (.12a) to a good hold. Pull past a final bulge onto a protruding nose. Reach jugs & anchor.
First ascent: Mark Rolofson on May 23, 2004.

13. **IMPEACHMENT DAY PARADE.** ***** 5.11d 13 bolts / 2 Fixe rings. This long pitch passes two roofs. Start just left of a bush & climb a short face past 1st bolt to gain a ledge. Climb up a huge wedged, detached flake past 2nd bolt to a small ledge. Climb a small right-facing corner past 4th & 5th bolt to reach a 5 foot roof. Undercling left under the roof a few feet. Pull over the roof (.11d) to a jug. Follow tenuous moves above 8th bolt to reach a huge jug. Easier climbing leads up to the final roof. Move right along a horizontal break underneath the final roof. Reach a horn at the lip & pull over the roof (.11d). Long quickdraws and slings are recommended on the 3rd, 5th, 10th & 11 bolt to reduce rope drag. First ascent by Mark Rolofson, Kirk Miller & Stacy Carrera on October 12, 2003.

14. **DUDE'S JAM CRACK.** **** 5.11b See the following pages for topo drawing and a detailed route description.

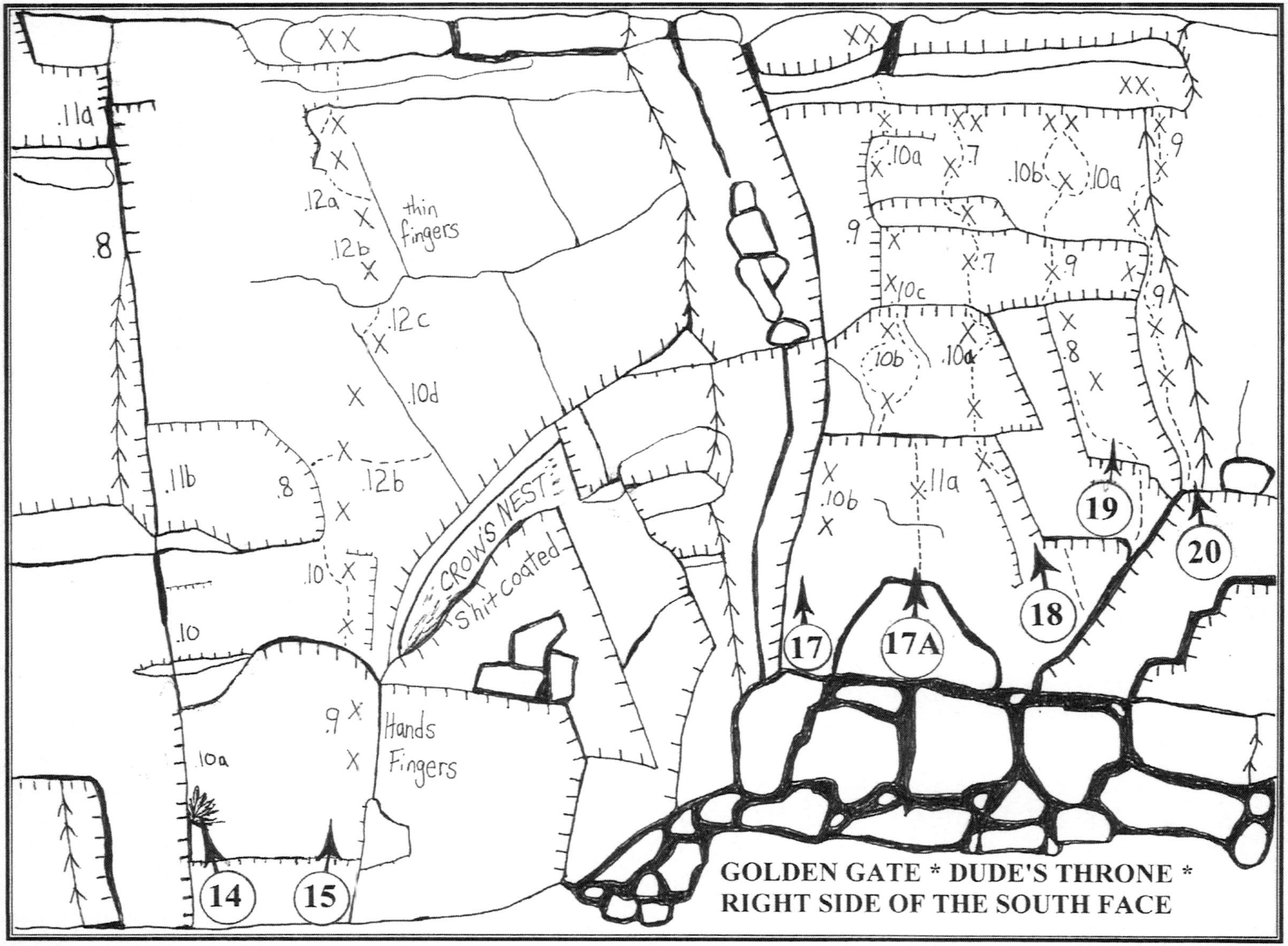

GOLDEN GATE * DUDE'S THRONE *
RIGHT SIDE OF THE SOUTH FACE

GOLDEN GATE * DUDE'S THRONE * RIGHT SIDE OF THE SOUTH FACE

14. **DUDE'S JAM CRACK.** **** 5.11b #3-6 micro stoppers or RPs, #6-10 stoppers, #.4 - .75 Aliens or small cams (one each), #1 Friend or #.5 Camalot (two-three), #1.5-2.5 Friends or #.75-1 Camalots (one-two useful), #3.5-4 Friends or #3-3.5 Camalots (one each) / 2 Fixe rings. Ascend the beautiful crack system, that switches from a right-facing to a left-facing corner. Begin in a small right-facing corner with a bush. The first hard section reaches over a tiny overlap past a thin section to hand jams. Shake out from jugs under a tiny roof. The crux is getting over the roof with thin jams & face holds. Gain a small shelf. Continue with ease along a thin crack to a second small roof. The final crux liebacks over the roof to a shelf. Move up & left to the anchor for **Impeachment Day Parade** or continue to the top. F.A.: Unknown.

15. **BUSTER BROWN.** ***** 5.13a/b 12 bolts / 2 bolt anchor. Climb a 5.9 finger & hand crack, past the first 2 bolts, to a good ledge atop a pillar. Move left & up to a lieback flake. Lieback the flake to where it traverses left. Traverse right (.12) above the lip of a roof, on small holds. Gain a left-angling dyke. The dyke fades out & the crux move uses to a tiny edge to reach an undercling. From the undercling, reach a finger crack, that is climbed for several hard moves to where it fades away. Move left & up on small holds to reach a large flake. Lieback up the flake and finish up jugs. First ascent: Mark Rolofson, belayed by Dianne Dallin on June 26, 2005.

WARM UP WALL * These 4 climbs ascend a 50 ft. vertical face on the right side on the south face.

17. **IN HARMSEN'S WAY.** *** 5.10c 8 bolts / 2 Fixe rings. Climb the hand & fist crack up a right-facing dihedral, past the first 2 bolts, to a horizontal break or tiny shelf. Traverse right on the shelf to the 3rd bolt. Stand up on the shelf using holds on the bulging face. A crux past the 4th bolt gains a sloping ledge. Gain another sloping ledge above the 6th bolt. Climb a tiny right-facing corner to a bulge at the last bolt. Pull past the bulge and onto a big ledge. First ascent by Kirk Miller on October 11, 2003.

17A. **IN DUDE'S WAY** *** 5.10d/11a 7 bolts / 2 bolt anchor. This is a one bolt direct start to **In Harmsen's Way**. Start off the top of a small boulder. Using a good left hand sidepull & tiny footholds, ascend the face to reach the horizontal break & 3rd bolt on **In Harmsen's Way**. First ascent: Mark Rolofson & Dave Turner on November 9, 2003.

18. **DUDE'S 5.9** *** 5.9+/10a 6 bolts / 2 Fixe rings. Start with moderate moves to a shelf and the 2nd bolt. Balance up on the shelf to reach a jug on a right-angling ramp corner & 3rd bolt. The crux pulls up the bulging face & onto the ramp to gain a small ledge. Wander up jugs to the anchor. First ascent: Kirk Miller, Mark Rolofson, Vaino Kodas & Mary Zuvela on June 14, 2003.

19. **ANY DUDE'LL DO.** ** 5.10a/b PG-13 4 bolts / 2 bolt anchor. A medium cam is optional above 1st bolt. Wander up ledges to the 1st bolt. Climb a short right-facing corner to the 2nd bolt & a tiny roof. Wander up the vertical face with good holds to the last bolt. A tricky crux can be climbed either just left of the last bolt, using a rounded sidepull for the left hand (.10b) or just right of the last bolt, on thin holds (.10a). Finish up jugs. First ascent by Kirk Miller and Lindie Brink in June 30, 2003.

20. **JUGS OUT FOR THE LADS.** *** 5.9 6 bolts / 2 bolt anchor. This route ascends the southeast arete of the crag. Belay high on a ledge on the right (east) side of the arete. Start with a small dihedral that fades away. Vertical face climbing with juggy holds leads up the arete staying mainly on the right side. First ascent by Mark Rolofson & Kirk Miller on June 23, 2003.

EAST FACE * On the right end of the crag there is a 40 ft. overhung east face, with only one crack climb. This face and its one route are not shown on the topo drawing.

21. **BAT SHIT CRACK.** *? 5.10 Bring nuts & cams. Climb up to & then over a small roof with some bat shit in the crack. Continue the crack to the top. It is possible to angle right up a diagonal crack for a harder finish. F.A.: Unknown.

GOLDEN GATE STATE PARK * LITTLE DUDE'S THRONE

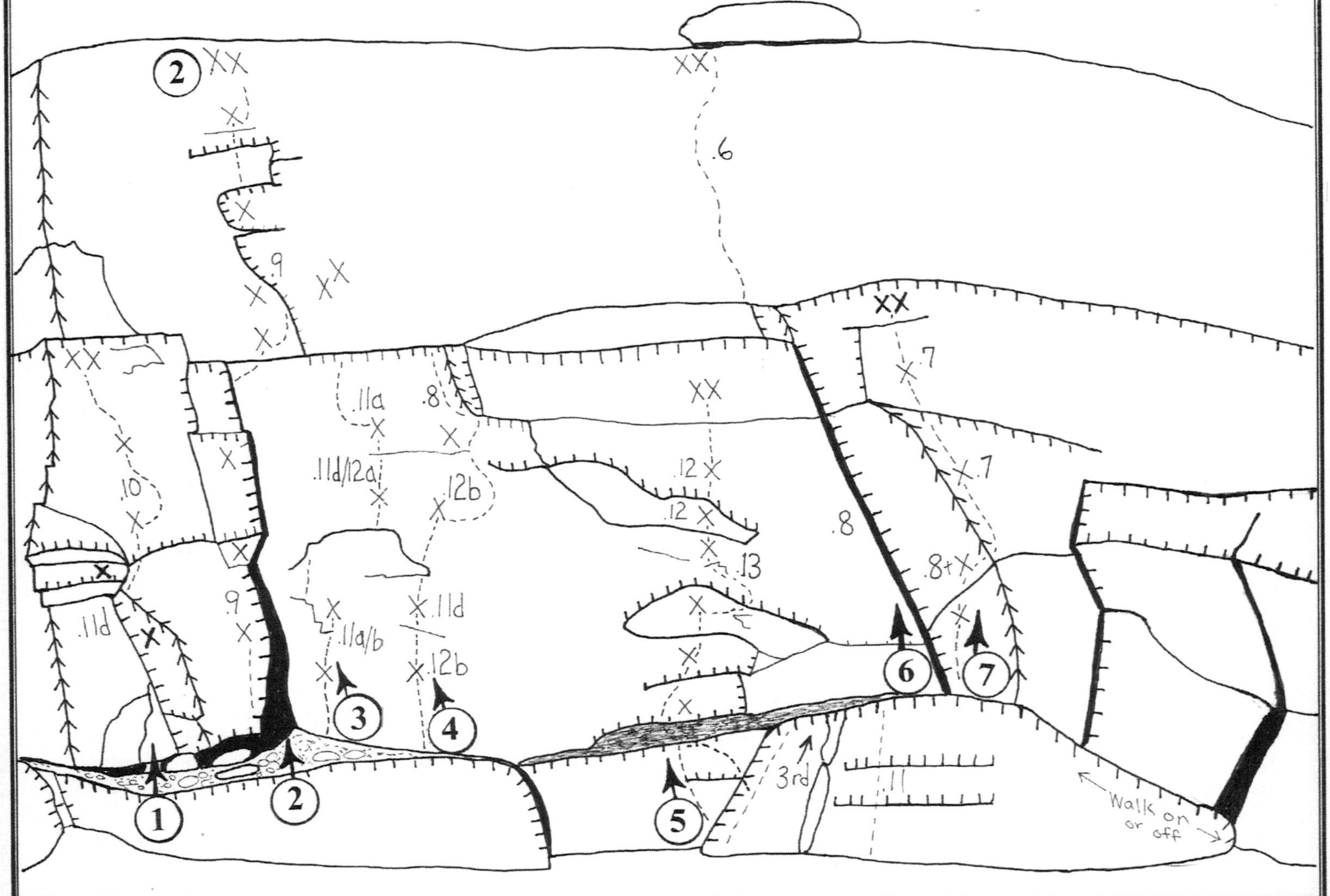

GOLDEN GATE STATE PARK * LITTLE DUDE'S THRONE

Little Dude's Throne is located below the west face of **Dude's Throne**. This smaller crag is 65 ft. high up its tallest section. It is hidden from view by the trees. The climbs are 30 to 50 feet long. Most of the routes ascend overhung faces on excellent rock with a varnished patina surface.

To Approach: Follow the trail to **Dude's Throne** almost to its end before reaching the talus below the west face. Walk downhill (south). After 100 to 150 feet, a small cliff starts to appear. Follow it downhill (right) along its base for another 100 feet. The path will turn into a ledge that leads to the leftmost route **Strange Brew**. Scramble down a short gully to the ground and walk right (east) to the base of **Big Lebowsky**. It is also possible to approach from the east to cliff's right side. Start from the middle of the south face of **Dude's Throne**. Below the ledge at the base of **Mighty Aphrodite**, **Short Dude** and **Raven's Brew** is a 15 to 20 feet high face. Walk downhill, from this short wall, through the talus and boulders for 300 feet. Angle west to the right side of **Little Dude's Throne**.

1. **STRANGE BREW.** ** 5.11d 4 bolts / 2 bolt anchor. Ascend a short left-facing corner to a small roof, via a strange sequence of powerful moves. Move right to pass the roof and finish up a vertical face. F.A.: Mark Rolofson & Ernie Moschovitz on August 24, 2003.

2. **MOONSHINE.** *** 5.9 7 bolts / 2 bolt anchor. Climb the large dihedral, that begins as a chimney, via face holds, stemming & liebacking. The start may be harder for shorter climbers than the grade indicates. The dihedral narrows to wide hand jams & then reaches a small ledge. Move right on the face along a horizontal break to reach to left-leaning crack. Follow this leaning crack to a ledge. Ascend a short vertical face to the top. F.A.: Mark Rolofson and Kirk Miller on August 16, 2003.

3. **HAMSTER MONKEY.** ** 5.11d 4 bolts / 2 bolt anchor. This climb ascends an overhung face with perfect rock via mostly nice incut holds and jugs. The start has good handholds and poor feet. Gain the top of a large, jug flake and traverse right for a few feet across it. The crux, past the 3rd bolt, involves a dyno to a sloping dish, if you're tall enough. Shorter climbers may need to use small, poor crimps & a heel hook. First ascent by Mark Rolofson and Ken Trout on July 26, 2003.

4. **HAMSTER KUNG FU.** ** 5.12b/c 4 bolts / 2 bolt anchor. This climb ascends an overhung face with perfect rock via mostly positive crimpers. A powerful, dynamic start past the first 2 bolts gains a jug on the right side of the large flake. Clip 3rd bolt off the jug and execute a finger wrenching traverse right on small positive crimpers. Reach good holds & finish up easier climbing past the 4th bolt.
First ascent by Vaino Kodas and Mark Rolofson on July 31, 2003.

4A. **KUNG FU MONKEY.** *** 5.12b 4 bolts / 2 bolt anchor. This direct line links up the start of **Hamster Kung Fu** (.12b) to the crux finish of **Hamster Monkey** (.11d). This route is short, but sustained and worth the effort! First ascent by Ken Trout on July 26, 2003.

5. **BIG LEBOWSKY.** **** 5.13 Project 6 bolts / 2 Fixe rings. This climb ascends a two-tiered overhang via small holds. Begin from the ground below the large ledge where **Hamster Kung Fu** starts. Climb 10 feet up a ramp corner & hand traverse left on a shelf, past 1st bolt. Gain a ledge & 2nd bolt. Move right under the overhang off a jug. Small holds lead over the overhang's lip to bigger edges below a second roof. Powerful moves lead to its lip. Finish up a short slab. F.A.: (5.12d A0) Mark Rolofson - Spring 2004.

6. **EASY DUDE.** * 5.8 Some small & medium nuts & cams, several large pieces to #4 Friend or #3.5 Camalot / 2 Fixe rings. This climb begins from a large ledge 12 feet up. Approach from its left side by scrambling up right or from its right side by walking back left. Climb a wide crack up a left-facing corner for 40 feet to a large ledge. Continue wandering up an easy face to the top. F.A.: Unknown.

7. **HUMMINGBIRD RODEO.** * 5.8+/5.9- 4 bolts / 2 bolt anchor. Start just right of **Easy Dude** from the same large ledge. A strenuous start climbs a right-angling flake crack, up gently overhung rock, to gain an easy slab on the right side of the arete. Climb the slab to the last bolt. Vertical moves lead past the last bolt to the anchor. First ascent by Kirk Miller and Mark Rolofson on April 9, 2005.

Stacy Carrera leading **UPLIFT MOFO PARTY PLAN** (**** 5.11b/c) on the west face of Dude's Throne. Photo: Vaino Kodas.

Mary Riedmiller on the first roof of **IMPEACHMENT DAY PARADE** (***** 5.11d) on the south face - center.

GOLDEN GATE * THE GRENDEL * SOUTH FACE (or Right Side)

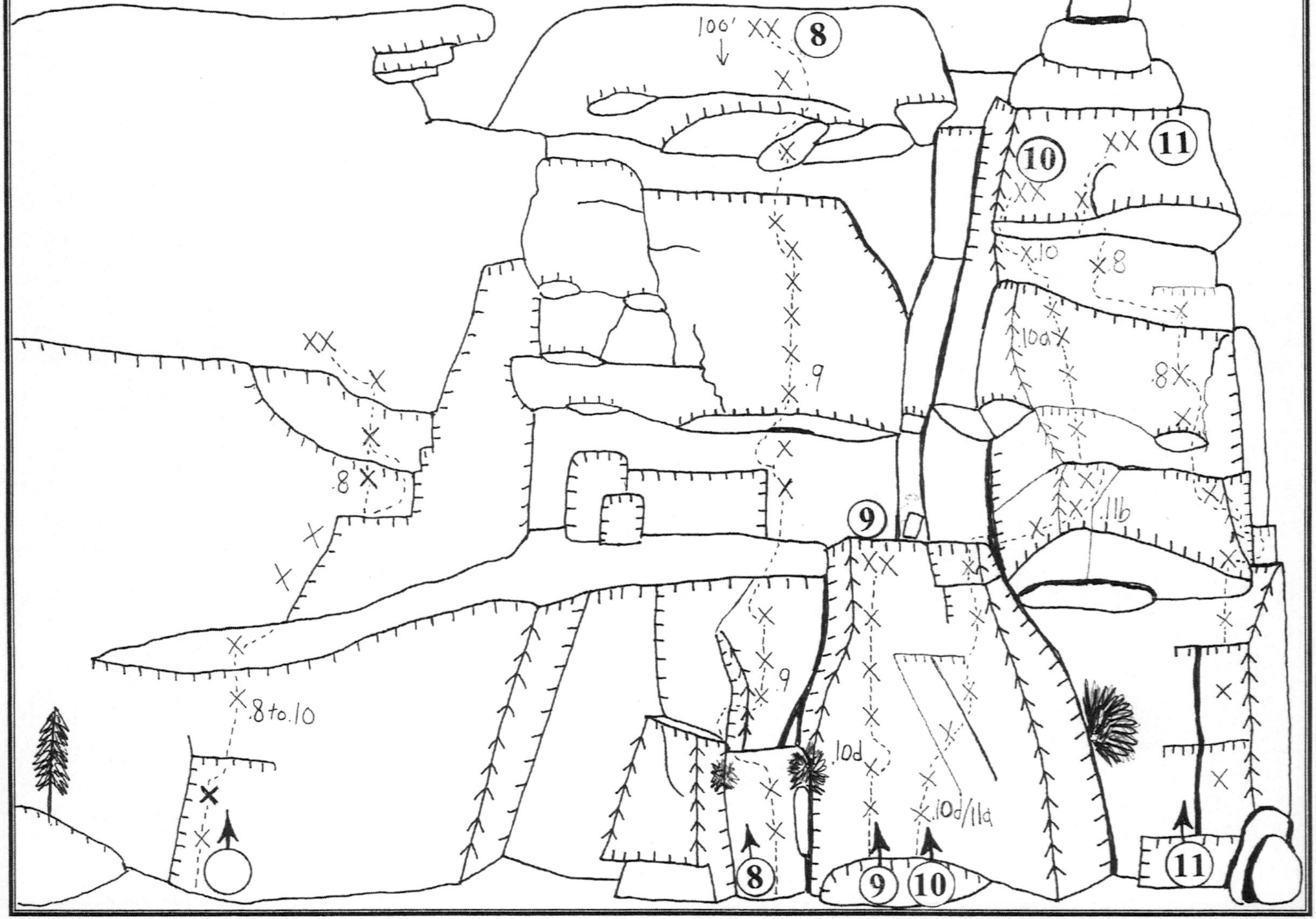

GOLDEN GATE * THE GRENDEL * INTRODUCTION AND THE APPROACH

The Grendel is a 100-140 ft. tall south-facing crag that is easily seen from Aspen Meadow Campground & Dude's Throne by looking northwest. It sits high up on a pine tree covered hillside above 9,500 feet elevation. This crag offers beautiful stone in a secluded location away from the crowds. In spite of its sunny south face, this cliff can be quite cold due to wind that can blast the hillside. For Summer, mornings are recommended to climb in the shade. By afternoon, the sun can make this crag unpleasantly hot, unless there are clouds or wind. The best months for climbing here are May, September and October (if it doesn't snow much). By November, the weather is less predictable even though on warm, calm days, climbing here may be possible. Climbing during the Winter months is too cold with chilling winds and too much snow on the approach.

The Approach takes 45 to 60 minutes. Even though the approach begins from Golden Gate State Park the cliff is located on National Forest land. Park after the entrance to Aspen Meadow Campground. Walk back west to Gap Road. Take a right and walk north along Gap Road for 100 feet to beneath the powerlines. Take a left and walk into the trees. After a short distance head slightly right (northwest) toward the crag. Look for cairns. Gain an old roadbed that the trail follows for most of the approach. This roadbed begins on flat ground and gradually steepens as it climbs the hill. After 20-25 minutes, the roadbed comes to a flat area. The **Lazy Squaw Spire** is 400-500 yards straight ahead. Follow cairns that lead off to the right. After crossing the flat area, switch-back uphill for 15 to 20 minutes to the left side of the southwest face of **The Grendel** below **Beo Wulf** & **Dane Land** (see following pages). Walk right along the base to the start of the routes. See the map of the area on page 121 for more information.

THE GRENDEL * SOUTH FACE (or Right Side)

7. **EXIT STAGE RIGHT.** * 5.8 to 5.10 (height dependent) 9 bolts / 2 bolt anchor. Begin 30 feet right of **Academic Freedom** (see following pages) and just right of a short low-angle slab at the base of the crag. Ascend a moderate face past 2 bolts to a ledge. Clip 3rd bolt & ascend a short vertical face to a large sloping ledge. This section is much harder for a shorter person & 3rd bolt may be difficult to reach. Gain the ledge & step right to an easy left-facing corner that angles up right. Follow the corner to another ledge & 7th bolt. Pull onto a sloping shelf & traverse left to finish. Long reaches off ledges to clip bolts make this an undesirable route for a short person. F.A.: Kirk Miller & Lindie Brink in Fall 2006.

8. **MOTHER GRENDEL.** **** 5.9 15 bolts / 2 bolt anchor. A 60 meter rope is just barely long enough to descend. A must do for the grade. Bring some long slings to reduce rope drag. Start with a narrow face between two bushy corners. Climb up the face past 2nd bolt & move left onto a ledge. Step right & climb a short vertical arete, past 3rd bolt, to a steep slab that ends on huge sloping ledge. Clip 6th bolt & ascend a steep face along a short right-facing corner. Clip 7th bolt with a long sling & clip out of 6th bolt to eliminate bad rope drag. Gain a small ledge on the left. The crux pulls over a small overlap, past 8th bolt, onto a steep face. Continue up this beautiful, long face with nice holds to ledge & 14th bolt below a small roof. Pull over the roof on the right. Move up & left to the anchor. F.A.: Sharon Kloepfer, Mark Rolofson & Kirk Miller on June 23, 2006.

9. **LEITNER ROUTE.** ** 5.10c/d 5 bolts / 2 Fixe rings. The crag's shortest route and ends 60 feet below the top. It was the first sport route on the crag. Ascend a steep face with an insecure crux past 2nd bolt. Continue with greater ease to the anchor. F.A.: Rick Leitner - Fall 2003.

10. **STRONG ARM TACTICS.** *** 5.11b 14 bolts / 2 rings. Begin just right of the **Leitner Route**. Ascend a steep slab on small holds, past the 1st bolt. Continue up the slab past left-leaning seams. Angle right onto the arete & 5th bolt. Gain a ledge above 6th bolt. Lean right across a gap to a face above a roof. At 8th bolt, stretch right around a prow to jugs over the lip. Swing out right with feet dangling & power over the roof. Climb a steep face to a ledge & last bolt. Move left to the arete & reach over an overlap to the anchor. F.A.: Mark Rolofson & Kirk Miller in July 5, 2010.

11. **THE MONSTER MASH.** ** 5.8 10 bolts / 2 bolt anchor. This moderate climb ascends the right side of the south face. Climb up to a ledge & 1st bolt. Follow an easy wide crack to a ledge. Pull over a small overlap on the right, past 4th bolt. Wander up to a ledge & 6th bolt. Climb a steep face past 2 bolts to a long, narrow ledge. Traverse left 10 ft. & reach 9th bolt. A short vertical face leads to a roof. Move left on a horizontal crack to where the roof gets smaller. Pull over the roof on jugs. Move right to the anchor. F.A.: Kirk Miller & Mark Rolofson on July 5, 2010.

GOLDEN GATE * THE GRENDEL * SOUTHWEST FACE

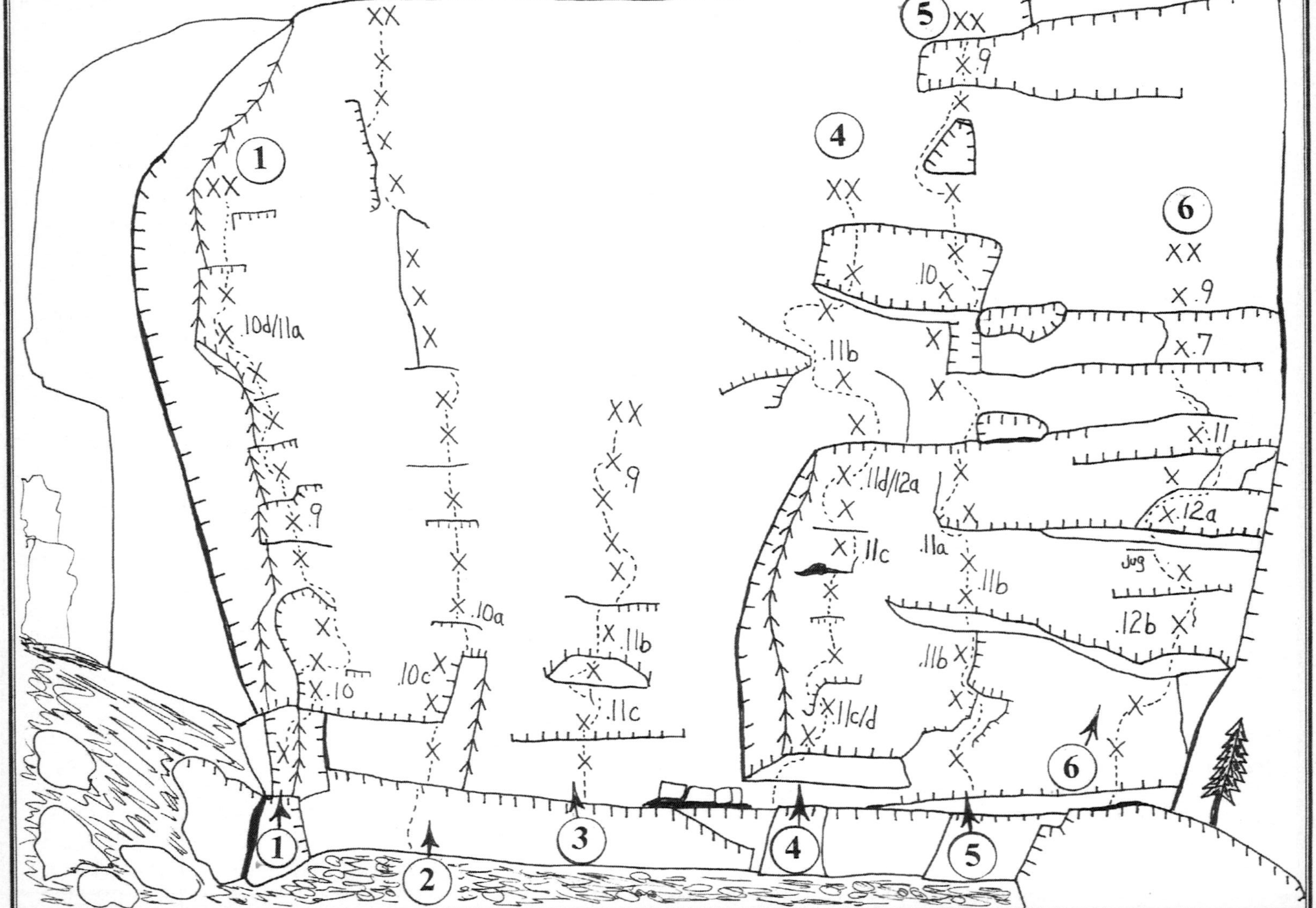

GOLDEN GATE * THE GRENDEL * SOUTHWEST FACE

1. **BEO WULF.** ** 5.10d/11a 11 bolts / 2 bolt anchor. This route ascends the prow on the left side of the southwest face. Clip the 1st bolt & climb an easy left-facing corner to a horizontal break. Clip 2nd bolt & step right on the face. Pull over a small bulge using a crack on the left in a tiny left-facing corner. Move up a few feet & then right past 3rd bolt to a stance. Follow easy terrain up to a ledge & step left to 5th bolt. Climb a short vertical face to another ledge. Continue up the face moving onto a blunt prow to gain another stance. At 8th bolt, move up & left to a small roof. The crux pulls over the roof at 9th bolt. Finish up easier terrain. F.A.: Kirk Miller & Mark Rolofson on Sept. 15, 2007.

2. **DANE LAND.** ***** 5.10c 16 bolts / 2 bolt anchor. A 70 meter rope is useful. If you have a 60 meter rope, start from the ledge below the 1st bolt & tie a knot in the end of the rope. Scramble 12 ft. up to a ledge & clip the 1st bolt. Reach over a tiny roof & ascend a small overhung corner, past the 2nd & 3rd bolt. At the top of the corner, gain a shelf. Continue up a steep face between a series of small shelves. Move left & follow cracks. Finish up a moderate face to the top of the wall. F.A.: Kirk Miller & Lindie Brink in July 2007.

3 **PEBBLE IN THE SKY.** *** 5.11c/d 8 bolts / 2 bolt anchor. Scramble up to a ledge below two tiers of small roofs & clip 1st bolt. The first crux, past 2nd bolt, is climbing over the first small roof to reach holds below the second roof. Clip 3rd bolt in this roof. The second crux pulls over the second roof, past 4th bolt, & moves right to a small ledge. Wander up 5.9 climbing, moving left & up, then back right & up to the anchor. First ascent by Kirk Miller in August 2007.

4. **FREEDOM FIGHTER.** **** 5.11d/12a 11 bolts / 2 Fixe rings. Start 10 feet above the ground from a ledge below a roof. Clip the 1st bolt in the roof. Maneuver right & up to holds just over the lip. Sidepull moves lead past the 2nd bolt. Gain a tiny stance & the 4th bolt. Move up & right, past a large horizontal crack, to a thin horizontal seam. Traverse left on the seam & climb up the face to 7th bolt. The crux moves up & right, on small edges to gain a small ledge. Step to the left end of the ledge. Climb up & left, past the 9th bolt, to a stance. Move back right to a small roof. Pull over the roof & follow jugs to a small ledge & the anchor. F.A.: Mark Rolofson & Kirk Miller on June 18, 2006.

5. **PIERCED LIP LOCK.** **** 5.11b 14 bolts / 2 bolt anchor. Easy moves lead to the ledge system & the 1st bolt. The difficulties begin at the 2nd bolt. Move slightly right up a steep ramp to a small roof. Move left around the roof & up a short left-facing corner to below a small roof. Reach a jug, with a small hole through it, on the lip of the roof & clip 4th bolt. This jug is the "pierced lip" the route is named after. Pull over the roof & follow small edges up & left to a good flake. Lieback up the flake for a few moves. Gain a ledge with a large block on its right side & clip 8th bolt. Move up into a short left-facing corner to a small roof. Move right around the roof to a stance on a small ledge. Reach another ledge & 12th bolt. Climb up a large block to its top. Pull over a tiny roof, past the last bolt to gain a good ledge & the anchor.
First ascent: Kirk Miller & Mark Rolofson on June 4, 2006.

6. **ACADEMIC FREEDOM.** **** 5.12b 9 bolts / 2 Fixe rings. Currently the hardest route on the crag. This route ascends a series of small roofs or overlaps. Begin atop a large boulder that sits against the base of the wall forming a large ledge. Ascend a slab right of an easy crack. At 2nd bolt, step right into the crack & move up to a small roof. Clip 3rd bolt above it & execute the technical crux to gain an undercling crack under the second overlap. Move left past 4th bolt & reach a jug. Clip 5th bolt at the lip of a third roof. The second crux angles right on a sloping diagonal holds to tiny shelf under a final bulge. Pull over the bulge & follow shelves up left on a steep slab. Gain a small ledge at 8th bolt & then another ledge to reach the anchor. First ascent by Mark Rolofson belayed by Kirk Miller on November 3, 2007.

KEY FOR TOPOS

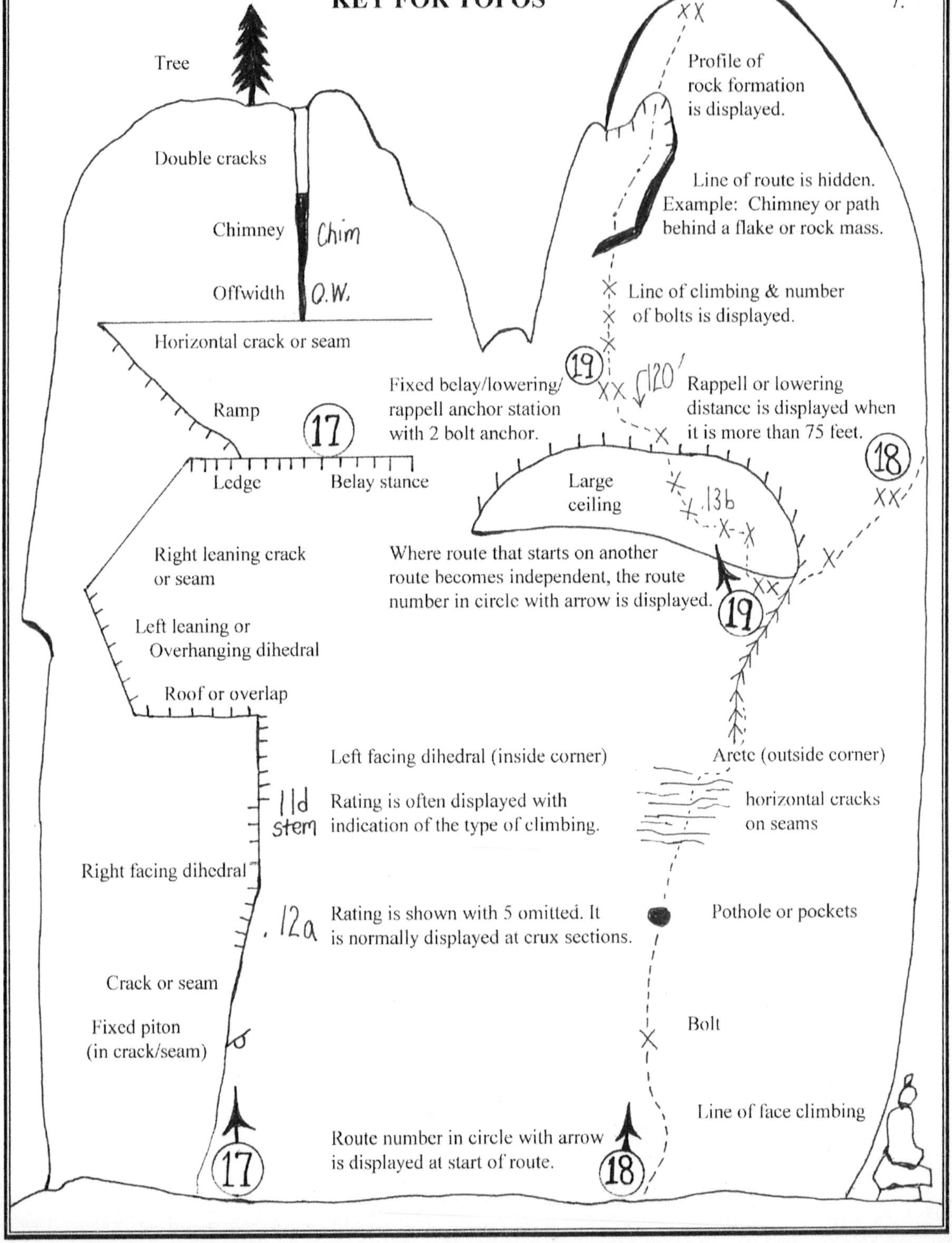
Tree
Double cracks
Chimney
Chim
Offwidth
O.W.
Horizontal crack or seam
Ramp
17
Ledge
Belay stance
Right leaning crack or seam
Left leaning or Overhanging dihedral
Roof or overlap
Left facing dihedral (inside corner)
11d stem
Rating is often displayed with indication of the type of climbing.
Right facing dihedral
.12a
Rating is shown with 5 omitted. It is normally displayed at crux sections.
Crack or seam
Fixed piton (in crack/seam)
17
Route number in circle with arrow is displayed at start of route.
18
Profile of rock formation is displayed.
Line of route is hidden. Example: Chimney or path behind a flake or rock mass.
Line of climbing & number of bolts is displayed.
19
Fixed belay/lowering/ rappell anchor station with 2 bolt anchor.
120'
Rappell or lowering distance is displayed when it is more than 75 feet.
18
Large ceiling
.13b
Where route that starts on another route becomes independent, the route number in circle with arrow is displayed.
19
Arete (outside corner)
horizontal cracks on seams
Pothole or pockets
Bolt
Line of face climbing